LEADERSHIP OF PUBLIC BUREAUCRACIES

 Advances
in Public
Administration

Sponsored by
the **Public Administration Theory Network**
and **Lewis and Clark College**

Advances in Public Administration is a series of books designed both to encourage and to contribute to the vital processes of rethinking public administration and reconceptualizing various aspects of the field in an insightful manner that goes well beyond traditional approaches.

LARRY D. TERRY

LEADERSHIP OF PUBLIC BUREAUCRACIES

The Administrator
as Conservator

 Advances in Public Administration

Foreword by Douglas F. Morgan, *Lewis and Clark College*

Sponsored by the **Public Administration Theory Network**
and supported by **Lewis and Clark College**

UPA LIBRARY

SAGE Publications
International Educational and Professional Publisher
Thousand Oaks   London   New Delhi

For information address:

SAGE Publications, Inc.
2455 Teller Road
Thousand Oaks, California 91320

SAGE Publications Ltd.
6 Bonhill Street
London EC2A 4PU
United Kingdom

SAGE Publications India Pvt. Ltd.
M-32 Market
Greater Kailash I
New Delhi 110 048 India

Printed in the United States of America

Library of Congress Cataloging-in-Publication Data

Terry, Larry D.
    Leadership of public bureaucracies: the administrator as
conservator / Larry D. Terry.
        p.   cm.—(Advances in public administration)
    Includes bibliographical references (p. 185-195) and index.
    ISBN 0-8039-7146-X.—ISBN 0-8039-7147-8 (pbk.)
    1. Leadership.   2. Bureaucracy.   3. Public administration.
I. Title. II. Series.
JF1525.L4T47   1995
350.003'23—dc20   95-11385

This book is printed on acid-free paper.

95   96   97   98   99   10   9   8   7   6   5   4   3   2   1

Sage Production Editor: Diana E. Axelsen
Sage Typesetter: Andrea D. Swanson

DEDICATED TO

Charles T. Goodsell and Gary L. Wamsley

Contents

Foreword

◆ THE RELATIONSHIP between leadership and democracy is much like our metaphorical dances with wolves. Each dance is spiritually mysterious; short, but episodic; and, above all, always filled with uncertainty and danger. However, unlike Native American dances with wolves, our metaphorical dance represents tension and conflict, rather than harmony and peace. If *democratic* leadership is a conflict-laden notion, perhaps even something of an oxymoron, how much more so is *bureaucratic* leadership. In fact, bureaucratic leadership has been characterized by one observer as a history of sheep in wolves' clothing (Karl, 1987). Neither leadership in general nor bureaucratic leadership in particular fits easily with our American system of constitutional governance. Both are seen as somehow antidemocratic—a fundamental violation of the principle of accountability, of being "on tap, not on top."

In this book, Larry Terry seeks to legitimate the exercise of bureaucratic leadership. He accomplishes this task by drawing on three bodies of research and writing that have not traditionally been joined: the legal, the managerial, and the sociological. The

legal body of research and writing locates the legitimacy of bureaucratic authority in our rule-of-law system of constitutional governance. The managerial body of research and writing emphasizes the
efficient and effective functioning of organizational systems as the
basis for legitimating the exercise of administrative discretion. Finally, the sociological body of research and writing sees legitimacy
as an evolutionary and socially constructed process that occurs
interactively with other social entities over an extended period of
time. Terry argues that bureaucratic leadership requires a careful
cultivation of each of these three different sources of legitimacy.

The American legal framework is for Terry's bureaucratic leadership what the Constitution was for Lincoln's Declaration of Independence: a frame of silver encompassing a picture of gold. Leadership, like the Declaration of Independence, evokes images of taking
risks and moving from the known to the unknown. On the other hand,
the Constitution also evokes somewhat contrary images of staying on
course, erring on the side of caution, and resolving doubt about what
to do by choosing the known over the unknown. For Terry, bureaucratic leadership in the first instance requires adherence to the both
the spirit and the letter of the law, grounding all that one does as an
agency within this universe of discourse. Terry argues that this skill
is critical to conserving a successful agency mission in the face of
ambiguity, uncertainty, and protracted political conflict.

In contrast to the legal tradition, the managerial body of research and writing locates the legitimacy of bureaucratic authority
in the efficiency and effectiveness of public organizations and
managerial systems. Drawing from the managerial tradition, Terry
argues that bureaucratic leadership requires careful attention to
the conventional instruments of managerial control, such as executive recruitment, training, constituency support and cultivation, organizational design, and policy development and implementation. Although his categories of analysis differ from those
found in more conventional management-oriented texts, the instruments of organizational control necessary for the successful
exercise of leadership are all given their just due.

The challenge of legitimating bureaucratic leadership does not
end with managerial and legal success. Both sources of legitimating authority get translated into administrative practice through
the medium of public organizations that have long-standing exis-

tence as social entities. Terry draws heavily on Philip Selznick to remind us that public bureaucracies acquire much of their presumptive moral authority through the incremental social process of developing unifying values that meet the needs and expectations of the community. Thus, in addition to being successful on the managerial and legal fronts, bureaucratic leadership requires cultivating and guarding what Terry (drawing from Selznick) calls institutional integrity. Like personal integrity, institutional integrity cannot be understood by reducing it to a simple summary list of interests or of moral principles and values. Integrity cannot be discovered by looking at mission statements, strategic plans, and organizational structures or practices. Although it includes all of these things, it is not reducible to any one of them or, for that matter, to any single combination. Integrity is what gives both organizations and individuals their distinctive unifying "life course."

According to Terry, bureaucratic leaders must pass the legitimacy tests in all three areas—legal, managerial, and institutional—before they can properly be regarded as legitimate stewards of the public trust. Only when each of these three sources of bureaucratic authority is properly cultivated is a career administrator exercising leadership or what the author calls *administrative conservatorship.*

To some, administrative conservatorship may conjure up images of leaders of public bureaucracies who are excessively predisposed to protect the status quo. Others, however, may take offense at the wide latitude Terry gives administrators to alter institutional structures and practices in order to preserve the integrity of the organization in the face of significant external changes. This latitude is discussed in Chapter 2 under the topic of initiating leadership. In short, Terry's notion of administrative conservatorship embodies a complex mixture of legal, managerial, and institutional sources of legitimating authority, a mixture too complex to be accurately captured by formulaic summaries that describe it as either too static or too centralized.

Terry's effort to reconcile bureaucratic leadership with democratic governance is not an easy undertaking. It is made even more difficult by widespread ideological dissensus about the proper role of our institutions of governance and by a pervasive social anomie that deprives public agents of the assistance of mediating social structures in carrying out their work. The traditional institutions of the family, schools, churches, and social and political associations are either in widespread disarray or have balkanized into warring camps. But these challenges make Terry's book that much more timely, especially as we attempt to better address the following three questions central to current activities at the bureaucratic level. First, what role can and should bureaucratic leadership play in redefining the role of state and local governmental entities within our system of federalism? Second, what role can and should bureaucratic leadership play in redefining the service delivery relationship between governmental organizations and entities in the nonprofit sector? Finally, what role should administrators play in deciding what can and should be entirely privatized?

Although it does not offer a final answer to these critical questions, Terry's book gives career administrators the necessary grounding to participate proactively in the discussion by providing them with legitimating authority in two critical domains of democratic governance. First, at the level of democratic process, bureaucratic life embodies practices that in the past have been central to our system of democratic governance. Whether it be the practices of affirmative action or the equitable and fair treatment of clients and employees, no amount of reordering, privatization, or contracting out will cause these concerns to disappear. Second, at the substantive policy level, bureaucratic life embodies weighty purposes and goals of our democratic order. These too will not disappear in the current process of taking stock. On both procedural and substantive grounds, Terry's notion of administrative conservatorship makes bureaucratic participation in this debate not only a right but a democratic duty. His ultimate goal is to transform bureaucratic leadership into the kind of dance with wolves that begins to look more like the Native American dance of peace and harmony than a continued history of sheep in wolves' clothing.

Douglas F. Morgan
Lewis and Clark College

Reference

Karl, B. (1987, January). The American bureaucrat: A history of sheep in wolves' clothing. *Public Administration Review, 47*, 26-34.

Series Editor's Introduction

◈ THE RATIONALE for this series lies in the ongoing need to reexamine and enrich thinking in the field of public administration. It can be argued that few fields need efforts of this sort more urgently. Twenty years ago, Vincent Ostrom declared that an "intellectual crisis" existed in public administration. Significantly, that crisis has continued unabated into the 1990s. Meanwhile, the public's faith in the administrative state has declined precipitously, and, in the words of Herbert Kaufman, bureaucrat bashing has become "pandemic."

Intellectually, this crisis lies in the discrepancy between the field's 19th-century roots and the postmodern realities we must face at the turn of the 20th century. Despite 20 years of intellectual foment by academics, most practitioners still adhere to a model of public administration shaped in a world that no longer exists. The Progressive era that gave birth to modern American public administration was an age that believed in universal technical/rational solutions to political, social, and even moral problems. It was a time in which strong Western nation-states and their empires were commonly viewed as the anointed agents of progress and civilization. Most of all, it was a period in which government was beginning to be seen as part of the answer, rather than part of the problem.

Virtually none of these views holds in the contemporary world, yet public administration and its literature have been indelibly marked by these roots. As a result, it remains grounded in the classic model of the centralized nation-state at a time when a global economy is a reality, Western empires disintegrate, and a new feudalism based upon warring ethnic and racial communities seems emergent. Its literature still takes a largely technical/rational view of the world, though the practice of public administration increasingly requires decidedly *nontechnical* ethical and political decisions. Even more troubling, although a thorough reevaluation of first principles and assumptions is in order, the literature, like the field itself, too often retreats into bureaucratic defensiveness or formulaic "solutions" to problems.

It can be argued, then, that public administration badly needs new literature that reexamines its basic premises. There is little question that the materials for this reexamination are present. Certainly they exist in disciplines such as history, philosophy, the humanities, and the social sciences. They range backward and forward in time. Some present a vision of existence in a disordered, fragmented, but exciting postmodern world. Some reach backward to apply traditional philosophic thought to current issues. Others suggest radically new ways to view human thought and action. Still others depict an environmentally centered world in which people are no longer masters but stewards of the world in which they live.

Because public administration often is referred to as an inter-disciplinary study, it seems reasonable to expect it to break out of its traditional paradigm and use this body of knowledge to advantage. Two factors seem to prevent this, however. First, to the degree public administration has drawn on other disciplines, it has chosen to rely upon those that fit most easily into its universalistic and rational tradition. Thus, modern economics, analytic philosophy, systems analysis, and behavioral science all have had far more impact on the field than history, contemporary social philosophy, humanities, or qualitative social science research.

Second, to the degree that scholars have developed alternative conceptual rather than technical approaches to public administration, they are more frequently the subject of debate among academics than grist for the professional mill. Academic movements in public administration calling attention to constitutional history, critical theory, Jungian psychology, and postmodern thought have had surprisingly little impact outside scholarly journals. The reasons for this are severalfold. Until recently, the intellectual crisis in the field has not been clearly tied to what might be called the operational crisis in public administration. The traditional paradigms of public administration might be questioned intellectually, but at the level of practice, the general philosophy was "If it's not broken, don't fix it."

In addition, it can be extremely difficult to relate philosophic and social theory to practice in a manner that is readily accessible to students and practitioners. It is inherently difficult to frame much of this thought clearly and cogently enough to speak to individuals who have little background in fields such as history or philosophy. It is even more of a challenge to show how such theories relate to practice in concrete ways, and, conversely, to criticize the applicability of these theories in terms of the experience gained from using them in practice. Yet, unless these two tasks can be accomplished, a firm linkage between theory and practice rarely is achieved.

However, it can be argued that public administration has reached the point at which this situation is ripe for change. In this country, political gridlock, fiscal deficit, administrative scandal, and the sheer inability of government to deal with human needs ranging from health care to disaster relief have caused people to question the viability of the American administrative state as never before. In short, it is harder and harder for thoughtful practitioners and students to dismiss the crisis in public administration as merely "intellectual."

Advances in Public Administration is an occasional, open-ended series designed both to encourage and to contribute to the vital process of rethinking public administration in the light of the issues just discussed. To this end, the editorial board has sought works that meet the following set of criteria as far as possible. Each volume will seek to reconceptualize some aspects of the field in an insightful manner that goes well beyond traditional approaches to the subject. Specific goals will be to accomplish the following:

- Stimulate students and practitioners to reflect critically on the practice of public administration
- Utilize cutting-edge conceptual materials drawn from a variety of disciplines, especially those that have had less impact on the study and practice of public administration
- Apply theory to practice and conversely use practice to evaluate theory
- Set forth complex theoretical concepts in an understandable manner without unduly sacrificing their meaning or content
- Provide adequate background material for those readers unfamiliar with the disciplines upon which the work draws
- Be of potential use as classroom material in graduate and/or upper division courses in public administration

The series will consist of monographs, texts, closely edited collections and an occasional reissue of a valuable out of print work. Although the works will vary in topic, they will be unified by the editorial selection criteria just outlined.

As Coordinating Editor of **Advances in Public Administration,** I wish to take this opportunity to thank the members of the series Editorial Board, the Public Administration Theory Network, and Lewis and Clark College for their generous sponsorship of this project. Finally, I would be extremely remiss if I did not recognize the efforts of my Associate Editors Camilla Stivers and Guy Adams and those of Carrie Mullen of Sage Publications and my colleague Dr. Douglas Morgan for the unfailing support and encouragement they have given me in launching the series.

Henry D. Kass
Coordinating Editor
Lake Oswego, Oregon

Preface

◆ TWENTY YEARS before the "excellence in leadership" movement stormed America, a collection of writings under the
auspices of the Academy of Arts and Sciences was published as
Excellence and Leadership in a Democracy (Graubard & Holton,
1962). These writings by prominent scholars from many disciplines addressed topics ranging from "Excellence and Leadership
in President and Congress" to "The Psychodynamic Aspects of
Leadership." In his chapter on administrative leadership, Don K.
Price (1962), dean of the former Harvard Graduate School of Public
Administration, argued that we as a nation must accept that
excellence in "high administrative positions" is essential if our
government is to meet the challenges of an increasingly complex
society. Price suggested that government must enlarge its share of
the nation's best administrators because "a great empire and little
minds go ill together" (p. 172).

After arguing persuasively for excellence in high-level administrative positions, Price (1962) concluded by stating that "we do
not really want administrative leadership: we want political leadership which requires a strong administrative underpinning" (p. 184).

The professional administrator "must try to reconcile our technology with our democratic values. . . . The purpose of his profession is to carry, with a high degree of concentrated responsibility, the moral burden that in a free society must be shared by all citizens" (p. 184).

Price's (1962) comments reflect many Americans' ambivalence about the idea of administrative leadership. On one hand, we demand excellence from high-level administrative officials. We expect them (as we should) to be responsive to elected and appointed political elites, the courts, interest groups, and the citizenry. We expect administrative officials to "bridge the great gap between the way the scientists think and work and that of the politician" (p. 184). We expect them to assume a significant share of moral responsibility for preserving the values of the American political regime. On the other hand, we expect ranking administrative officials wholeheartedly to accept and fulfill their complex responsibilities *without* exercising broad discretionary power and authority. We expect them to accept the notion that they do not have a legitimate role in governance. We expect administrative officials to pretend that what we ask of them requires anything but leadership.

The ambivalence expressed by Price and others toward administrative leadership is understandable, especially in view of the American founders' concern about the arbitrary use of political power. The founders worried that the exercise of substantial discretion by government officials would lead to arbitrariness and, in turn, the inevitable decline of individual freedom. The expansion of the administrative state since the New Deal has prompted many observers to renew the founders' concern. Prominent scholars, most notably Theodore Lowi (1979) and David Schoenbrod (1993), have warned that the increased delegation of broad discretionary power from the legislature to administrative agencies is a threat to democracy. Lowi (1993b), in particular, argues that the delegation of broad discretionary power (and the exercise of such power by nonelected administrative officials) "deranges virtually all constitutional relationships and prevents attainment of the constitutional goals of limitation on power, substantive calculability, and procedural calculability" (p. 150).[1]

Although the concerns of Lowi and his colleagues deserve careful consideration, I do not share their concerns for several reasons. First, the delegation of broad discretionary powers to administrative agencies and career civil servants is not some type of aberration. Even Lowi (1993b) concedes this point when he states that "delegation of power is an inevitable and necessary practice in any government. No theory of representative government is complete without it" (p. 149). Second, career civil servants in general and high-ranking administrative officials in particular must exercise broad discretionary power to fulfill their agencies' legally mandated responsibilities. I doubt that anyone would take the Internal Revenue Service, the Virginia Department of Child Support Enforcement, or the Cleveland Department of Housing and Building Inspections seriously if they did not have broad discretionary powers to enforce their respective laws. Third, the delegation of broad discretionary power to administrative officials is essential if they are to pursue and protect the public interest. The National Park Service needs broad discretionary power to preserve the beautiful national parks for future generations. The Federal Aviation Administration needs broad discretionary power to regulate air traffic in the interest of safety.

The fact that administrative officials are delegated and exercise broad discretionary power reserves them a seat at the table of governance. Governance requires statesmanship, and statesmanship requires leadership. Because administrative officials are active participants in governance, I must conclude that they are engaged in the art and practice of leadership. Thus, contrary to what Price asserts, Americans do want administrative leadership. In fact, *we need administrative leadership* if the United States is effectively to address the challenges of the 21st century.

This book is about administrative or bureaucratic leadership. Although career civil servants provide leadership at all levels within public bureaucracies, I am especially interested in institutional or executive-level leadership.[2] In the following pages, I offer a normative theory of bureaucratic leadership that gives administrative executives an active and legitimate leadership role in governance. I characterize administrative executives as *conservators* because they are entrusted with the responsibility of preserving the integrity of public bureaucracies and, in turn, the values and traditions of the American constitutional regime. Administrative executives are actively engaged in a special type of leadership I call *administrative conservatorship,* which is, to use George Will's (1983) term, a form of "conservative soulcraft" (p. 156).[3]

I argue that public bureaucracies are national treasures because it is through these institutions that the authoritative allocation of resources is made to sustain the Republic's cohesion and moral balance. The need to protect the integrity of these valuable institutions has never been greater. In recent years, public bureaucracies have become a laboratory for politicians, "policy wonks," and academicians determined to test their abstractly conceived innovations under the guise of improving government performance. There is certainly room for improving the performance of public bureaucracies, but these improvements must be made with care and must be guided by the accumulated knowledge, experience, and traditions of the political community.

In Chapter 1, I argue that the subject of bureaucratic leadership has not received the scholarly attention it deserves. I attribute this neglect to America's deeply rooted fear of bureaucratic power, the myopia created by Progressive Era reforms and scientific management, and the scholarly quest to reconcile bureaucracy with democracy. I also establish a normative foundation for my theory and introduce the concept of administrative conservatorship.

Chapter 2 presents a model of administrative conservatorship. I discuss the idea of preserving institutional integrity and how it relates to the theory of administrative conservatorship. Next, I outline a continuum of leadership roles performed by administrative conservators as well as their three primary functions: conserving mission, conserving values, and conserving support.

In Chapters 3, 4, and 5, I offer prescriptions for maintaining the integrity of public bureaucracies. Rather than offering innovative strategies, I draw instead on the experience, knowledge, and intellectual tradition of scholars and practitioners who have preceded me. My prescriptions are based on an organization of the existing literature as well as on my own documentary research and interviews with administrative executives.

Chapter 3 focuses on conserving mission. The mission of public bureaucracies is defined by legislative mandates and other legally binding acts. I argue that the concept of authority is central to the notion of conserving mission. I suggest that the administrative conservator is entrusted with the responsibility of preserving and nurturing authority embodied in legal mandates that determine the mission of public bureaucracies. Strategies for conserving mission focus on preserving the executive and nonexecutive authority granted to public bureaucracies.

Conserving values is the topic of Chapter 4. Contrary to the views of many organization and leadership theorists, I argue that preserving the core values of public bureaucracies is a task that exceeds the capacity of any one individual. The administrative conservator needs assistance, especially from the agency's executive cadre. Consequently, my prescriptions for conserving values concentrate on building and maintaining a viable executive cadre.

In Chapter 5, I offer strategies for conserving support, both external and internal. The preservation of external support is discussed within the context of maintaining a favorable public image and sustaining strength with salient publics. To preserve internal support, special attention is devoted to building and maintaining commitment among internal interest groups.

Chapter 6 presents an overview of my theory. I use this opportunity to discuss the potential dark side of administrative conservatorship. I illustrate how the prescriptions outlined in Chapters 3, 4, and 5 can be distorted and abused by those who hide behind the shield of administrative conservatorship. Nevertheless, I conclude, more positively, that conscientious administrative executives are friends of the Republic and protectors of the American political regime.

The idea for this book germinated when I was a doctoral student at Virginia Polytechnic Institute and State University. During my first year of graduate studies, I took a course titled "Leadership and Complex Organizations." On the extensive reading list, two books made a particular impression on me: Eugene Lewis's (1980) *Public Entrepreneurship* and Philip Selznick's (1957) *Leadership in Administration*. Lewis's account of the organizational lives of J. Edgar Hoover, Hyman Rickover, and Robert Moses enlivened classroom discussions. All the students were fascinated by the characters and the stories behind their rise to power and eventual fall. Selznick's book also generated excitement. What he had to say made sense to me, partly because I had recently resigned from an administrative position with a state agency to return to graduate school. Selznick spoke to my experiences; his theories and concepts also seemed to explain the actions of my former agency director, Frederick O. McDaniel, and other administrators whom I respected during my tenure in state government. Most of the administrators I knew or had observed from a distance, however, did not fit Lewis's profile of a public entrepreneur. These observations, coupled with the entrepreneurial craze that ushered in the 1980s, prompted me to question the long-term value, relevance, and applicability of the entrepreneurial model to public administration. Although I appreciated the importance of building institutions (Lewis's entrepreneurs were masters at this task), I concluded that Selznick was right; institutional leaders must also *maintain* institutions through time. During the early 1980s, the maintenance of public bureaucracies (or any organization, for that matter) was not something leadership scholars spent much time writing about. This lack of interest in maintaining institutions led me to write a dissertation on administrative conservatorship. Many of the core ideas and some of the material from my dissertation are included in this book.

I would like to express my gratitude to the people whose support, encouragement, and critical comments were essential to the completion of this book. First, I thank the faculty of the Center for Public Administration and Policy at Virginia Tech for providing an intellectually stimulating and supportive environment for pursuing ideas. I also thank several scholars who took time from their busy schedules to read the manuscript in its various stages over the years. Some tried to show me the error of my ways, whereas others tried to prepare me for the inevitable attacks by critics taking issue with my classical or Burkean conservative position. I am indebted to Herbert Kaufman, Lawrence F. Keller, Laurence J. O'Toole, Anne-Marie Rizzo, John A. Rohr, Philip Selznick, Michael Spicer, James Stever, Camilla Stivers, and Dwight Waldo.

I owe Henry D. Kass (series coordinator), Douglas Morgan (editor for this volume), and Carrie Mullen, the public administration editor at Sage Publications, a special thanks for quickly bringing this book to press. The professional manner in which they performed their responsibilities provides a standard and example for others in the publishing industry. I am honored that they included my book as part of this series.

Jennifer Alexander (my "better half") and "the gang" (my children) have been a source of strength. They have tolerated my preoccupation with the manuscript for more years than any of us would like to remember. Their love, patience, and understanding made it much easier for me to complete this project.

I have dedicated this book to Charles T. Goodsell and Gary L. Wamsley, two scholars who have profoundly influenced my intellectual growth and development. Charles has been a source of inspiration. It was in his living room one evening in Blacksburg, Virginia, that the term *administrative conservatorship* was coined. Charles's creativity, high standards, and demand for intellectual quality have provided me with a lifelong example of what constitutes a *true* scholar. His kindness and willingness to give advice and counsel to students as well as peers are qualities I admire a great deal.

Gary founded the Center for Public Administration and Policy at Virginia Tech. Largely because of Gary's leadership, it has gained an international reputation as a place where questions of governance are taken seriously. Gary has helped me understand the value of building as well as maintaining an institution—he has been successful at both. He is a creative theoretician who understands and appreciates the relationship between theory and practice. Gary is a friend and mentor whose low-keyed demeanor, sense of humor, and most important of all, *love of tradition*, are truly special.

To Charles and Gary I say, thanks. I love you both.

Larry D. Terry
Maxine Goodman Levin College of Urban Affairs,
Cleveland State University, Ohio

Notes

1. A version of Lowi's chapter was first published in the *American University Law Review* (Lowi, 1987).

2. Douglas Morgan brought to my attention that managers and operators, to use James Q. Wilson's (1989) classifications, also provide leadership in preserving the integrity of public bureaucracies. I think he is correct. Public administration theorists should devote more attention to leadership at these levels.

3. Will (1983) argues that "statecraft" is "soulcraft." According to Will, conservative soulcraft "pertains to the conservation of values and arrangements that are not subjects of day-to-day debate" (p. 156).

Bureaucratic Leadership in
a Democratic Republic

AT CENTURY'S END, the United States is confronted with a host of complex problems that touch every segment of society. The nation's urban communities are in crisis as homelessness, crime, and severe poverty continue to take their toll. Once again, our public education system is under attack. The embarrassing discovery that millions of adults are illiterate has stoked the fires of education reformers who believe that massive changes are needed for America to compete successfully in a rapidly changing, increasingly interdependent world. The number of Americans who lack adequate health care because of prolonged unemployment or

AUTHOR'S NOTE: Some of the material in this chapter has been drawn from my article "Leadership in the Administrative State," *Administration & Society*, Vol. 21, No. 4 (1990), pp. 395-412, copyright © 1990 by Sage Publications, Inc.

underemployment has become a national disgrace as U.S. corporations continue to move manufacturing operations abroad. Although labor officials and the general public have expressed out-
rage over the loss of well-paying jobs and the displacement of
thousands of blue-collar and white-collar workers, they seem
virtually helpless in dissuading corporations from pursuing this
"competitive" cost-saving strategy.

The nature and scope of these and countless other problems
and the perception that public and private institutions are ineffective in solving them have sparked a renewed interest in leadership.
Americans from Wall Street to Main Street are expressing dissatisfaction with the performance of leaders in government, business,
and labor. In fact, it seems that the United States is in the midst of
a leadership reform movement. From all indications, this movement is gaining momentum and has turned into a referendum on
the quality of leadership in this country. A consensus is emerging
that more effective leadership is needed to rescue the United States
from the valleys of decline. There is a perception that if only
leaders were up to the challenges, our complex problems would
somehow disappear.

The Neglect of Bureaucratic Leadership

In all of this talk about more effective leadership, the topic of
bureaucratic leadership is conspicuously absent. By bureaucratic
leadership, I mean institutional leadership in the administration
of public bureaucracies within the executive branch of all levels
of government.[1] More specifically, bureaucratic leadership is an
active process that emanates from the executive branch and entails
the exercise of power, authority, and strategic discretion in pursuit
of the public interest.

The lack of scholarly interest in bureaucratic leadership seems
odd given the prominent role of public bureaucracies in our democratic society. Even scholars in the fields of public administration
and political science have focused little attention on leadership in
public bureaucracies until recently.[2] The question immediately
comes to mind: Why has there been so little scholarly interest in

the role and function of bureaucratic leaders? Jameson Doig and Erwin Hargrove (1987) offer several reasons. First, scholars (particularly political scientists) have emphasized the influence of interest groups in the public policy process. Second, a great deal of negative attention has been devoted to studying the consequences of "bureaucratic routine and institutional processes" (p. 2). Third, political scientists and others in their quest to understand leaders have not experienced much success in discovering "regularities in the messy data of political life" (p. 2). Fourth, influential scholars, most notably Herbert Kaufman (1981a), have perpetuated the belief that public bureaucracies are guided by powerful forces beyond the control of individual leaders. Career executives are viewed as making little difference in how their agencies perform.

Although Doig and Hargrove's (1987) explanations seem reasonable enough, other reasons merit serious consideration. The neglect of bureaucratic leadership may arise from a combination of related factors, including Americans' deeply rooted fear of bureaucracy, the myopia created by Progressive Era reforms and scientific management, and the unintended consequences of scholarly attempts to reconcile bureaucracy with democracy.

The Fear of Bureaucratic Power

The rise and expansion of public bureaucracies, especially at the national level, have generated a great deal of hostility toward public bureaucracies and career civil servants. Although such growth has been in response to a complex mixture of socioeconomic and political conditions, the expansion of public bureaucracies is nevertheless viewed by many as a threat to democracy. (See Crenson & Rourke, 1987; Nelson, 1982; Skowronek, 1982.) Public bureaucracies have been aggressively attacked by segments of the general public, the news media, the academic and business community, the judiciary, and the political establishment. These attacks have contributed to a legitimacy crisis for public bureaucracies. James O. Freedman (1978) goes straight to the heart of the matter when he says that "the growth of the administrative process has raised troubling questions concerning its implications for the character of American democracy, the nature of American justice and the quality of American life" (p. 260).

Although critics offer different arguments to substantiate their attacks, the fear of bureaucratic power is a common theme. Public bureaucracies are perceived as wielding too much power. Critics charge that career civil servants have accumulated vast amounts of power and thus are no longer responsive and accountable to elected political authorities. This so-called unaccountable power is regarded as incongruent with the values of the American democratic system.

The fear of governmental power is inextricably interwoven into the fabric of our society. As noted by Samuel P. Huntington (1981), the "opposition to power, and suspicion of government as the most dangerous embodiment of power are central themes in American political thought" (p. 33; quoted in Kellerman, 1984, p. 66; see also J. Q. Wilson, 1975). Critics of bureaucracy quickly point out that the enormous power exercised by bureaucrats in the so-called fourth branch of government is incompatible with the constitutional design envisioned by the founders. They suggest that the founders did not anticipate nor would they approve of a powerful, largely autonomous political institution controlled by nonelected and nonpolitically appointed public officials. The founders were deeply concerned, so the argument goes, about the possibility of substantial power residing in one person or political institution. This explains their rejection of the notion of the president as "leader" as well as their preoccupation with the need to check the exercise of political power.[3]

Kenneth J. Meier (1987), a leading critic of bureaucratic power, expresses many of the aforementioned concerns. According to Meier, the bureaucracy has been transformed into a "political institution" (p. 134). This transformation is the result of several factors, including the nature of American politics, which forced the legislative branch to share its policy-making powers with career public servants; the fragmentation of political power among governmental institutions; the task demands and organizational requirements of modern public policy; and the nature of the bureaucratic function that gives administrative officials considerable discretion in implementing public policy (see Meier, chap. 3).

Meier contends that because the bureaucracy is indeed a fourth branch of government, its enormous power should be controlled and checked similar to that of the other branches of government.

Meier is not alone in his fear of bureaucratic power. The ominous specter of a powerful, imperial bureaucracy controlled by a cadre of unaccountable technocrats has also heightened the concerns of many other Americans as well. The fear of bureaucracy has become so pervasive in recent years that Herbert Kaufman (1981b) describes the situation as a "raging pandemic" (p. 1). Antibureaucratic forces have responded to such fears by devising strategies to strip public bureaucracies of their power. These strategies include, among others, extensive politicization of bureaucracy; constant reorganization; extensive use of deregulation and budget, program, and personnel cuts to reduce the size of government; the exclusion of career executives from policy discussions and formal processes; and expansion of the size of both executive and legislative staffs to reduce the expertise gap between these branches of government and public bureaucracies. (See Farazmand, 1989; Lane & Wolf, 1990; F. E. Rourke, 1987.) These strategies are guided by the assumption that bureaucratic power can be curtailed by severely reducing and tightly controlling the discretion and authority of administrative officials.

Supporters of public bureaucracies contend that the aforementioned power-stripping strategies have caused serious long-term damage and have undermined the capacity of administrative institutions of government to serve the public good (e.g., Adams, 1984; Rosen, 1983, 1986; Wildavsky, 1988; Wolf, 1987). Supporters argue that such strategies not only have weakened public institutions but also have relegated the notion of bureaucratic leadership to a meaningless status. Critics respond that the concept of bureaucratic leadership is a contradiction in terms and thus deserves the dubious status of oxymoron. Why should anyone be concerned about bureaucratic leaders if there is no need for them? After all, the weakening of public bureaucracies is intended to limit the power, authority, and strategic discretion of career executives. Moreover, because the founders were reluctant to use the term *leader* when referring to the president, an elected political official, it stands to reason that the notion of bureaucratic leadership would have little intellectual currency.

The Progressive Legacy

In addition to the fear of bureaucratic power, the Progressive legacy has contributed significantly to the neglect of bureaucratic leadership. Laurence O'Toole (1984) argues that American public administration is deeply rooted in the reform tradition. "American public administration," writes O'Toole, "has retained an orthodoxy—an orthodoxy of reform—in its continuing series of attempts to reconcile the tensions which democracy and bureaucracy pose for each other" (p. 143). O'Toole and other scholars attribute the reformist character of public administration to the Progressive Era, that seemingly optimistic period that gave birth to the self-conscious public administration movement (see Karl, 1987; Stever, 1988).

The Progressive Era stands as a paradox when examined from the perspective of bureaucratic leadership. Although this era had a positive influence on the development of American public administration, it also created a myopic outlook on the development of bureaucratic leadership theory. Progressive Era political reforms, especially those designed to make administration of public bureaucracies more "efficient" and "businesslike," were largely antibureaucratic leadership in nature.

After the Civil War, the United States invested a substantial portion of its physical and intellectual resources in industrial and technological development. Although this investment yielded high returns in the form of material development, it was not without costs. In the eyes of many Progressive reformers, America's addiction to material development had a devastating effect on the nation's morality as well as on its natural resources.[4] This reckless pursuit of materialism was considered dangerous; it placed the country on the brink of moral bankruptcy. The Progressives believed that immediate action was needed to save America and that the state should assume a primary role in this rescue operation.

Although Progressives were extremely critical of what they perceived as the moral deterioration of American institutions, they were by no means revolutionaries. Many reformers had a great deal of respect for institutions, especially governmental institutions, and favored reforms that would produce orderly social change. Because the Progressive movement relied heavily on a positive conception of liberalism in which the state played a primary role in achieving social progress, it became painfully clear to many reformers that the movement's long-term success hinged on eliminating the political corruption that permeated every level of government. This realization prompted reformers to direct their energies to changing the political system.

Progressive political reform began at the municipal government level and spread rapidly to the state and national levels. Reformers sought sweeping changes in the processes by which political officials were selected as well as in the structure of government itself. The latter reforms are of special interest in this discussion because of their direct bearing on bureaucratic leadership.

Reformers intent on modifying the structure of government embraced efficiency as a normative criterion for judging the "goodness" of government. They believed that "good government," one free of graft and corruption, and "efficient government" were so closely linked that a distinction between the two was difficult to discern. It was generally presumed that a more efficient government would eliminate opportunities for dishonesty (see Karl, 1963, esp. chap. 1).

Progressive reformers were not always consistent in their use or application of the term *efficiency*. When political reformers spoke of efficiency, however, they usually meant commercial efficiency, or the output-input ratio of dollars. More specific, governmental efficiency meant providing public services with a minimum amount of waste, duplication, and expenditure of tax dollars. Political reformers were obsessed with the idea of commercial efficiency. This obsession was directly linked to their love for the business enterprise model, which should come as no surprise because many reformers were businesspersons. Businesspeople-reformers were fond of comparing government with a business corporation. At least as far back as 1868, the National Manufacturers' Association affirmed in a resolution that it was "indispensable that public affairs be conducted on business principles" (as quoted in Nelson, 1982, p. 120). Thus, reformers sought to apply the business enterprise model to government. In many respects, this logic made sense. It was difficult to argue with the unprecedented success that businesses experienced during the post-Civil War years. If business principles and practices enhanced efficiency and, in turn, the profitability of private enterprises, why couldn't they work in government? Businesspersons-reformers were convinced that government ought to be run as an efficient business enterprise. As Samuel P. Hays (1964) has shown, the business enterprise model became the guiding light of political reformers:

> The guide to alternative action lay in the model of the business enterprise. In describing new conditions which they wished to create, reformers drew on the analogy of the "efficient business enterprise," criticizing current practices with the argument that "no business could conduct its affairs that way and remain in business," and calling upon business practices as the guides to improvement. (p. 168)

The business enterprise model advocated by political reformers contained three basic elements. First, the model placed a heavy emphasis on the application of *scientific methods* as a means of achieving commercial efficiency. This deep abiding faith in science was a reflection of the times.

> Reformers . . . turned to science to accomplish their reconstructive task. . . . This new scientific spirit permeated every discipline related to the art of government. . . . Historians, economists, political scientists and lawyers all assumed that if they could successfully use neutral and objective scientific methods to ascertain the facts, their knowledge of the facts would guide them to proper solutions of the problems the nation faced. (Nelson, 1982, pp. 82-84)

Second, the model promoted the use of *experts* who possessed skills, knowledge, and technical training in the application of scientific methods. The idea of scientific experts was appealing to political reformers because of its widespread acceptance in private industry. Such acceptance was largely because of the success of Frederick W. Taylor's (1911) system of scientific management. Reformers adopted Taylor's argument that the scientific expert was the key to efficiency because the expert possessed technical know-how essential for the discovery and application of the scientific laws of work.

Third, the business enterprise model relied on the concept of a *strong executive* who exerted control over the enterprise by centralizing the decision-making process. Reformers assumed that a strong executive could provide direction to government activities and thus eliminate corruption, waste, and inefficiency (Haber, 1964, esp. chap. 6).

The Influence of Scientific Management

The Progressives' love affair with the business enterprise model obscured the vision of bureaucratic leadership. The business enterprise model contained strong antibureaucratic leadership biases. As mentioned earlier, the business enterprise model incorporated Taylor's philosophy of scientific management, which was inherently antiexecutive leadership in nature. Often overlooked is that Taylor distrusted management as much as he distrusted the workers. Taylor was explicit about his desire to perfect a factory that operated efficiently without guidance from top-level managers. This partially explains why Taylor's system vested power and authority in the planning department, that enclave of scientific experts who placed method over human abilities (Haber, 1964). It was not until 1919 when H. S. Person, president of the Taylor Society and dean of Dartmouth's Amos Tuck School of Administration and Finance, proposed a distinction between administration and management that Taylorites acknowledged the importance of executive leadership. In a clear separation of facts from values, Person asserted that the "moral, social, and political aspects of an enterprise" (quoted in Haber, 1964, p. 160) were the exclusive domain of administration and the responsibility of executives. Because of the functions associated with administration, Person conceded that people of special qualities were probably needed. In Person's conceptual scheme, management involved the use of scientific methods and therefore was the responsibility of scientific experts. In strict adherence to the scientific management doctrine, he argued that correct methods, not extraordinary talents of humans, were of utmost importance.

When political reformers transferred the business enterprise model to government, they modified aspects of Taylor's scientific management system to conform with Progressive ideology. They retained, however, the idea that scientific experts, the new proto-type of public administrators, were solely responsible for *facts* and not *values*. Moreover, reformers had warmly embraced the notion that correct methods were superior to the extraordinary talents of humans. These principles were often integrated into the design of executive training programs for administrative officials. Samuel Haber (1964) points out that the Bureau of Municipal Research's prestigious Training School for the Public Service was heavily influenced by scientific management:

> The Bureau proposed to aid the public servant and eventually replace him with a new and better type. A Training School for Public Service was established for training administrative executives and to "help make the public service a profession of equal standing with law and medicine." Bureau officials were quick to urge the use of principles of scientific management. Like Taylor, the Bureau directors argued that correct methods rather than extraordinary persons opened the way to lasting reform. In the Bureau's training school, the "literature on efficiency" became required reading and Saturday luncheon meetings were set up for discussion of it. (pp. 112-113)

By accepting the fact/value dichotomy as well as the primacy of correct methods over the special qualities of individuals, political reformers also disregarded leadership in the realm of administration. Bureaucratic leadership as envisioned here involves more than a preoccupation with facts, scientific assessment, and commercial efficiency, as Person and later organization theorists acknowledged. Bureaucratic leadership entails a broad understanding of organizational functions and social processes; it requires a keen awareness of the moral, social, and political aspects of the enterprise. In other words, bureaucratic leadership is concerned with values.

Political reformers also sought to put into practice the concept of a strong executive. In doing so, they further diminished the need and importance of bureaucratic leaders. When political reformers referred to a strong executive, they usually meant a strong *political* executive rather than a strong *administrative* executive. The strong political executive was regarded as one who possessed high moral standards as well as executive know-how and political savvy needed to direct the activities of governmental institutions (Haber, 1964).

Political reformers were blinded by the notion of a strong political executive; they could not see the need or value of bureaucratic leadership as conceptualized here. Leadership was a slippery phenomenon that could be seen and observed only outside the realm of administration. Political reforms, such as those recommended by Theodore Roosevelt's Keep Commission (1905-1909), the Taft Commission on Economy and Efficiency (1912), and later Franklin Roosevelt's Committee on Administrative Management (1937), reinforced this perception.

The Scholarly Quest for Reconciliation: Traditional Hierarchical Theory

Ironically, scholarly attempts to reconcile bureaucracy with democracy have deflected attention from the importance of bureaucratic leadership. Many writers in their quest to answer the nagging question regarding the legitimate role of bureaucracy in democratic government have offered prescriptions that deny public administrators an active administrative leadership role. This is especially true for scholars who embrace either the hierarchical or the pluralist interpretive framework for understanding public bureaucracies.[5]

Writers from the hierarchical perspective acknowledge that the value orientations of bureaucracy (efficiency) and democracy (responsiveness to the public will) are at odds.[6] This does not, however, lead to the foregone conclusion that bureaucracy cannot be squared with democracy. The conflict created by different value orientations can be resolved or at least minimized if the roles and responsibilities of bureaucracy can be clearly defined within the boundaries of the democratic system. Proponents of the hierarchical approach suggest that a complementary relationship can and should exist between bureaucracy and democracy. There are, however, strings attached. First, bureaucracy must occupy and remain in a subordinate position with respect to other democratic processes and institutions. Second, career civil servants who administer the bureaucracy must assume a subservient role and faithfully execute the commands of political superiors. Career executives must concern themselves with only the nuts and bolts of administration and leave the important questions of policy to elected political authorities. This perspective is best reflected in the classic works of Woodrow Wilson (1887/1978) and Frank Goodnow (1900), which have contributed significantly to the famed politics/administration dichotomy.

For nearly half a century, the Wilson-Goodnow line of demarcation between politics and administration has been criticized by prominent theorists, beginning with Leonard D. White (1939), followed by Dwight Waldo (1948) and Paul Appelby (1949). Critics of the politics/administration dichotomy contend that when viewed in a descriptive sense, the dichotomy fails to comport with the realities of the political system. Career executives are more than mere executors of public policies formulated by elected officials; they participate actively in both formulating and implementing public policy.

Although many scholars were preoccupied with discrediting the politics/administration dichotomy, the question of bureaucratic leadership received little serious attention. This oversight is unfortunate, because a careful reading of Wilson (1887/1978), in particular, suggests that he was not at all uncomfortable with an active administrative leadership role for public administrators. Although Wilson initially restricted this role to what in retrospect is a narrowly defined sphere of administration, he nevertheless saw administrators as active individuals who could and should use their ingenuity, power, and discretion in the "detailed and systematic execution of public law" (p. 11). Wilson observed that

> The broad plans of governmental action are not administrative; the detailed execution of such plans is administrative. . . . This is not quite the distinction between Will and answering Deed, because the administrator should and does have a will of his own in the choice of means for accomplishing his work. *He is and ought not be a mere passive instrument* [italics added]. The distinction is between general and special means. (p. 12)

Once the relationship between bureaucracy and democracy was defined in complementary, yet hierarchical terms, scholars shifted attention to ensuring that public bureaucracies remained in their rightful, subordinate position. Because the concept of subordination embodies the notion of control by higher authorities, scholars sought ways to regulate and constrain the activities of bureaucracy and, in turn, the behavior of career civil servants.

The issue of controlling bureaucracy emerged as a salient topic during the 1930s and 1940s and was frequently discussed within the context of bureaucratic responsiveness and accountability. It was generally assumed that public bureaucracies were "under control" if (a) they were responsive, that is, they strictly adhered to the dictates of political superiors and other democratic processes and institutions; and (b) they could answer for their actions if required to do so (Gruber, 1987; Romzek & Dubnick, 1987). To ensure bureaucratic responsiveness and accountability, the strategy of choice for many was the imposition of formal external controls in the form of laws, rules, detailed procedures, and regulations—in vernacular, red tape.

The emphasis on formal external controls fueled a debate concerning the nature and extent of such controls and their influence on the discretion of administrative officials.[7] Although scholars debated at great length the question of just how much discretionary power and authority these officials should have, the issue of bureaucratic leadership remained in the background. Presidential and congressional leadership occupied center stage, whereas providing direction and control over public bureaucracies became essential elements of the political leadership experience. Charles Hyneman (1950) expresses this point of view:

> If administrative officials and employees are expected to conduct themselves within limits that are acceptable to the American people as a whole, there must be authoritative ways of telling them what the American people want them to do. The authority on these matters, as I have already pointed out must be in the political branches of government—Congress and President. The direction and control which the political branches of government exercise over the administrative branch is what makes government in operation government according to the will of the people. (pp. 47-48)

The hierarchical approach provided, at least in theory, an attractive solution to the bureaucracy/democracy problem. Nevertheless, this approach had an adverse effect on the development of theory concerning bureaucratic leadership because of several reasons. First, most hierarchical theorists patently reject the notion of an active administrative leadership role for career executives. Consequently, career executives are denied the right to exercise power, authority, and strategic discretion in pursuit of the public interest. Second, the inherently mechanistic nature of traditional hierarchical theory reduces career executives to merely "instruments" or "tools" that could and should be used by elected and politically appointed elites to accomplish some externally defined end. The purely instrumental nature of this perspective leaves little room for the exercise of administrative leadership; career executives are restricted solely to the rational coordination of means. As a result, they are excluded from serious discussions regarding the determination of means as well as ends, an indispensable part of the leadership experience.

The Quest Continues: The Pluralist Alternative

The foundation of traditional hierarchical theory started to crack as scholars began to realize that formal external controls could not eliminate the discretion of administrative officials. Regardless of how cleverly crafted these formal controls were, administrative officials often found ways to retain and exercise a certain degree of discretion. Moreover, it became clear that administrators did not conform to the passive, instrumental role prescribed for them by many hierarchical theorists. Administrative officials were active participants in informal political activities designed to build and sustain support for their programs and policies. These revelations prompted scholars to continue searching for ways to legitimate the role of bureaucracy in the democratic system. Many turned to the pluralist model of politics as a viable alternative to the hierarchical approach (e.g., Dahl, 1956; Leiserson, 1942; Truman, 1951).

The pluralist model draws heavily on the Madisonian conception of democracy. It emphasizes the active participation of multiple interest groups in the political process as well as the dispersion and counterbalancing of governmental power. From the pluralist perspective, public bureaucracies are legitimate to the extent to which they (a) provide interest groups ample access and opportunities to participate in the political process and (b) function as a forum for interest group competition and bargaining, which produce policies in the public interest. When contrasted with the hierarchical approach, the pluralist model seems to provide a more palatable description of bureaucratic behavior within the American political system (J. P. Burke, 1986). Even so, the pluralist model is subject to the same criticism leveled against the hierarchical approach, although it includes public administrators' involvement. It denies public administrators an active administrative leadership role in the political process. Although pluralist scholars such as Robert Dahl (1956), David Truman (1951), and Avery Leiserson (1942) describe a meaningful role for public administrators as active mediators, they stopped considerably short of advocating the type of leadership role advanced here. Administrative officials are cast in a passive role of referees in an arena in which interest group competition and bargaining occurs. According to J. P. Burke (1986), the administrator "is not an active responsible agent making a positive contribution to policy formulation and implementation; rather, he is a blank slate upon which are written the demands of external groups and interests" (p. 19). Instead of exercising power, authority, and strategic discretion in pursuit of the public interest, the administrator's principal responsibility is to "register whatever compromise or accommodation results from the competition of relevant interests" (p. 19). Given this image of public administrators, it is not difficult to understand why the subject of bureaucratic leadership remained on the periphery of scholarly discussions.

Leadership in Administration

Despite the objections and concerns of many commentators, public bureaucracies will continue to occupy a dominant role in the American political system. As the American people place more and more demands on government, it is clearer with each passing day that democracy is dependent on bureaucracy. We can no longer afford to ignore the leadership role of administrative officials. The manner in which public bureaucracies are organized and administered has a profound effect on their capacity to serve the public good. As James Q. Wilson (1989) puts it, "organization matters" (p. 14).

It is time to put leadership back into the administration of public bureaucracies. This is not an easy task because of the long legacy described above. To succeed at this task, scholars need to develop a normative theory of bureaucratic leadership—a theory that is grounded in the American constitutional tradition and accords a certain legitimacy to the role of public bureaucracies and career civil servants in the democratic system of government. The purpose of this book is to offer such a theory. I begin this challenging task by developing a normative foundation that creates a legitimate role for public bureaucracies in the American political system. The works of John A. Rohr (1986), Brian J. Cook (1992), and Michael W. Spicer and myself (1993) are used for guidance. I briefly review each work and then summarize prescriptive elements that provide the foundational building blocks for developing a theory of bureaucratic leadership. Using these building blocks, I offer a theory of bureaucratic leadership that provides career executives with a legitimate role in the system of democratic governance.

The Constitutional Legitimacy of the Administrative State

In *To Run a Constitution: The Legitimacy of the Administrative State*, Rohr (1986) sets out to "legitimate the administrative state in terms of constitutional principles" (p. ix). Rohr builds his case by constructing a complex three-part argument. First, he attempts to illustrate that the administrative state is compatible with the constitutional design envisioned by the founders. Characteristic of Rohr's style of presentation, this argument has a tripartite structure. He begins by asserting that the separation-of-powers criticism levied against public bureaucracies is often based on "an excessively rigid interpretation of this venerable doctrine" (p. 18). In a careful examination of the Constitution as well as the *Federalists Papers*, Rohr demonstrates that the founders applied a much more relaxed standard in their interpretation of the separation-of-powers doctrine. Public bureaucracies' exercise of combined executive, legislative, and judicial powers is not, in and of itself, unconstitutional. Rohr believes that the founders would not have been disturbed by the existing administrative arrangements.

Rohr (1986) advances his discussion by arguing that the upper echelons of the career civil service fulfill many functions the framers originally proposed for the Senate. The Senate was designed to be part of the executive establishment as well as a legislative body. After reviewing several attributes of the Senate considered by the founders (e.g., expertise, stability, permanency, and combined executive, legislative, and judicial powers), Rohr concludes that "today's Senate is not the sort of institution that the Federalists wanted and the Anti-Federalists feared" (p. 39). He further states that "the closest approximation to such an institution today is the career civil service, especially its higher reaches" (p. 39).

Rohr (1986) ends the first part of his argument by suggesting that the administrative state corrects a constitutional defect with respect to representation. He suggests that the modern career civil service best reflects the representation scheme advocated by the Anti-Federalists. Rohr offers evidence that the Anti-Federalists believed the House of Representatives "should be a microcosm of the society as a whole" and that "representatives should be close to and resemble the people they represent" (p. 41). He also points out that the Constitution makes it difficult to put this theory into practice because of the restrictions placed on the number of representatives that compose the House of Representatives. Rohr asserts, however, that the "personnel distribution" of public bureaucracies "comes much closer to the microcosm the Anti-Federalists had in mind than the House of Representatives ever could" (p. 45). Thus, he concludes that the career public service remedies the representation defect in the Constitution.

The second part of Rohr's (1986) argument is devoted to what he refers to as "Founding the Administrative State in Word" (p. 55). Rohr critically examines the works of Woodrow Wilson and

Frank Goodnow, leading theoreticians of the self-conscious public administration movement. Rohr argues that the constitutional theories of both Wilson and Goodnow are "fundamentally at odds with the principles of the founding of the Republic" because they favored legislative supremacy and, therefore, rejected the separation-of-powers doctrine (p. 56). Because of the tendency to rely on the works of Wilson and Goodnow as the founding philosophy of public administration in the United States, Rohr argues that Americans have developed a tradition that is founded on principles that are inconsistent with our constitutional heritage. This partially explains the administrative state's recurring legitimacy crisis. Administrative practice is not in line with the theory that legitimates this practice. Rohr's goal is to alter the legitimating theory rather than to hopelessly try to bring practice into conformance with an unrealistic theory.

The third part of Rohr's argument focuses on the New Dealers of the 1930s and their attempts to build a modern administrative state. He suggests that the actions and views of these founders in deed were compatible with original constitutional principles.

Rohr concludes that the role of public bureaucracies in the structure of American government is consistent with the intentions of the founders. In pursuing this argument, he offers a normative theory of public administration that is grounded in constitutional principles. Rohr's theory is of special interest because it provides a foundation on which to build my theory of bureaucratic leadership.

Rohr's (1986) constitutional theory of public administration revolves around three major themes. First, public administrators have a moral obligation to *preserve* and *sustain* constitutional principles because they took the oath of office to "uphold the Constitution of the United States" (p. 181). Second, public bureaucracies occupy a subordinate, yet autonomous position with respect to the Congress, president, and the courts. Finally, public bureaucracies, similar to the Senate envisioned by the framers, exercise all three powers of government without violating the framers' understanding of separation of powers. Unlike powers of the Senate envisioned by the framers, however, these powers should be exercised in a subordinate capacity. Public bureaucracy should exercise such powers by

... choosing which of its constitutional masters it will favor at a
given time on a given issue in the continued struggle among the
three branches as they act out the script of *Federalist 51,* wherein
ambition counteracts ambition and "the interest of the man . . . [is]
connected with the constitutional rights of the place." (p. 182)

Rohr's (1986) constitutional theory of public administration
gives public administrators an active leadership role in governance. Public administrators are not passive instruments who
exercise little, if any, power, authority, and strategic discretion in
pursuit of the public interest. As Rohr points out, the ongoing
process of choosing which constitutional master to favor to maintain the "constitutional balance of power in support of individual
rights" is anything but passive (p. 181).

The Representative Function of Bureaucracy

Cook (1992) provides additional arguments that seek to legitimate the role of public bureaucracies in the American system. In
his article "The Representative Function of Bureaucracy: Public
Administration in a Constitutional Perspective," Cook seeks to
legitimate public bureaucracies by drawing on Nancy L. Swartz's
(1988) constitutive theory of representation as well as on arguments offered by Rohr and others. The constitutive perspective
focuses on what makes a polity. As such, this perspective addresses the question, "How do you frame and form a people,
making them what they are?" (Swartz, 1988, p. 128). Cook's main
thesis is that although political foundings and popular representative elections have constitutive qualities, it is important to
acknowledge that all political institutions, including public bureaucracies, possess such qualities as well. To illustrate this point,
Cook argues that administrative institutions of government fulfill
the representation and separation-of-powers doctrines of the Constitution and assist in defining the polity on an ongoing basis.

With respect to representation, Cook (1992) concentrates on the
Federalists' conception of representation and their preoccupation
with designing political institutions that ensured serious and sustained deliberations on public policy issues. According to Cook,
the Federalists feared that the citizenry would succumb to passion

and demagoguery rather than retain reason during heated debates on public policy issues. They were also concerned that such passion would make the people extremely vulnerable to the influences of those whose self-interests were not aligned with the polity's larger interest. The Federalists feared that this would produce public policies that undermined the long-term interest of the political community. Cook asserts that because of their participation in public policy debates, public bureaucracies help ensure that reason will prevail. They do so through a variety of activities ranging from holding public hearings to conducting research on proposed policy initiatives.

> A modern executive establishment that participates in, indeed adds to, reasoned deliberation and "sedate reflection" on major public issues is quite consistent with the theory of representation embodied in the Constitution. More fundamentally, the republicanism of the Constitution holds that the people, who are the ultimate sovereigns, and the institutions of government in their representative and governing capacities, *together* constitute the regime. If Congress, the president, and the judiciary can be said to be constitutive of the American regime, then that must also be said of the bureaucracy. (pp. 420-421)

Cook then proceeds to illustrate the constitutive qualities of public bureaucracies by linking administration to the separation-of-powers doctrine as interpreted by Jeffrey K. Tulis (1987) in his work *The Rhetorical Presidency.* Guided by Tulis's arguments that the founders divided powers among the three branches of government to equip them to perform different functions and to make effective governance more likely, Cook (1992) concludes that public bureaucracies are best suited to fulfill the function of ensuring "steady administration of law" (p. 422). According to Tulis, this function is assigned to the presidency along with security and self-preservation of the nation. As Cook sees it, the "presidency cannot give first priority to both self-preservation and steady administration" (p. 422). He suggests that public bureaucracies are best equipped to give priority to this function because of their stability and permanence.

Cook (1992) argues that public bureaucracies have constitutive qualities because they "help form or define the polity on an ongoing basis" (p. 422). They do so in at least two ways. First, public bureaucracies contribute to the continuous process of determining and defining citizenship in our liberal democratic society. Second, public bureaucracies give "substance and an organized existence to the values, aspirations and purposes they help the citizenry articulate" (p. 427).

Cook makes a persuasive argument. The role he describes and prescribes for public bureaucracies makes it clear that public administrators share with all others in governing the American Republic. The continuing process of fostering citizenship, increasing opportunities for citizens to participate in policy deliberations, and assisting elected political officials and the citizenry determine what is in the public interest requires more than a mere preoccupation with the coordination of means or specialized activities. These regime-sustaining tasks dictate that public administrators become actively involved in governance, the exclusive domain of leadership. (For discussion of leadership and governance, see Selznick, 1992, chap. 11.)

The Logic of a Constitution:
Public Administration and the Checking of Power

In our recent article "Legitimacy, History and Logic: Public Administration and the Constitution," Spicer and I (1993) seek to legitimate the administrative state in terms of the "logic of a constitution" (p. 242).[8] We construct an argument that the "method of empathetic understanding" (p. 240), an approach to historical explanation used by Rohr and others to legitimate the administrative state, is problematic because it fosters an incomplete and romanticized view of the founders.[9] Such romanticization inevitably leads to questions about the founders' conduct and character. Spicer and I assert that this poses a problem for Rohr and others because of the founders' position on slavery, the moral issue of their day. Although Spicer and I are critical of Rohr's romanticization of the founders, we do see our work as an extension of his efforts. Instead of relying solely on a historical approach to legitimate public administration, Spicer and I offer an alternative approach that concentrates on the logic of a constitution. We explain our approach this way:

An alternative approach is to make explicit the central logic of a constitution in general and to see to what extent the constitutional argument of the founders reflects that logic. Implications of the logic can then be derived. This approach differs from that taken by the Constitutional School, which draws on a variety of arguments made by the founders to legitimize public administration. Whereas the Constitutional School seeks simply to develop an argument about the constitutional role of public administration that is consistent with arguments made by the founders, our approach seeks to examine the role of public administration in light of the logic or purpose of a constitution. In short we seek to explain the logic rather than the history of constitutions. (p. 242)

What is the "logic of a constitution"? Spicer and I (1993) suggest that it is the "reason or reasons why a community of rational individuals would agree in the first place to develop a constitution to guide their political order at all" (p. 242). Guided by classical constitutional theory, we offer two primary reasons why rational individuals would establish a constitution. First, because constitutions by their very nature determine the ground rules and structure the dialogue of the political process, rational individuals agree to be bound by such rules because they want to limit the discretion of government officials. Spicer and I contend that limits are needed because government officials are inclined to pursue their own economic self-interest and to engage in other opportunistic behaviors. This poses a threat to the citizenry because government officials may use their powers to exploit them. The second reason relates to the unanticipated consequences of public policy errors. Because a great deal of uncertainty surrounds the effects of public policies, rational individuals prefer constitutional rules that restrict the discretionary power of government officials. These rules minimize the cost that citizens must bear because of significant public policy errors.

Spicer and I (1993) continue by demonstrating that the arguments made by the founders, both the Federalists and the Anti-Federalists, are concerned with checking the abuse of political power and, thus, are consistent with the logic of a constitution. With the preceding discussion as a backdrop, Spicer and I conclude that public administrators have an active and legitimate role in governance. This role, grounded in the logic of a constitution, permits public administrators to use their discretion to check the power of elected political officials, especially if the exercise of such power leads to exploitation of citizens or results in public policy errors. Spicer and I state:

> If it is accepted that the logic of a constitution is about restraining discretionary power, then an active role for public administration may be justified on the constitutional grounds that it sometimes enables public administrators to modify, delay, or resist the directives of political leaders in a lawful manner. . . . If checks on the power of political leaders are justified because even leaders are prone to human weaknesses, then there is no *a priori* reason why such checks should not include the exercise of significant administrative discretion. (p. 244)

Although the logic of a constitution sanctions checking the power of elected political officials, Spicer and I quickly point out that this does not necessarily mean that public administrators should disregard the dictates of political superiors. Nor does this mean that the discretion of public administrators should go unchecked. Both instances would undermine the legitimacy of public administrators in our democratic system.

A Synthesis of Prescriptive Elements

By combining the important prescriptive elements contained in the works of Rohr (1986), Cook (1992), and Spicer and myself (1993), I draw the following conclusions with respect to the problem of legitimizing the role of public bureaucracies in the American political system:

1. The role of public bureaucracies in the structure of American government is compatible with original constitutional principles.
2. The role of both public bureaucracies and career civil servants is to sustain and preserve constitutional principles. Public administrators have a moral obligation to sustain such principles because they took an oath to uphold the Constitution of the United States.
3. Although public bureaucracies must occupy a subordinate yet autonomous role with respect to other democratic institutions and processes,

the performance of this role does not mean that career civil servants should become passive participants in governance. Guided by classical constitutional theory and, in turn, the logic of a constitution, public administrators have a legitimate right to check the power of elected political leaders.

4. Public bureaucracies heal the constitutional defect with respect to representation. They also serve as a representative institution that participates in and ensures reasoned deliberations on public policy issues.

5. Although public bureaucracies exercise combined executive, legislative, and judicial powers, the exercise of such powers in a subordinate capacity is consistent with the framers' relaxed interpretation of the separation-of-powers doctrine. Public bureaucracies also fulfill the constitutional design with respect to separation of powers because of their permanency and stability; they are equipped to give priority to "steady administration of law" (Cook, 1992, p. 422).

6. Public bureaucracies play an important role by helping form the character of citizens by contributing to the ongoing process of making the American regime what it is.

With these conclusions in mind, it is now possible to make some statement of theory about leadership in the administration of public bureaucracies. Because (a) the role of public bureaucracies in the American political system is consistent with original constitutional principles, (b) public bureaucracies perform an important role in sustaining such principles, and (c) public bureaucracies help form the character of the citizenry as well as contribute to the continuous process of shaping a political way of life that is unique to the American regime, I argue that public bureaucracies must be preserved so that they can serve the public good. Thus, the *primary function of bureaucratic leaders is to protect and maintain administrative institutions in a manner that promotes or is consistent with constitutional processes, values, and beliefs.* If this is indeed the case, then leadership in administration of public bureaucracies is similar to what Carl J. Friedrich (1961) describes as "maintaining leadership," a type of political leadership concerned with stability of the regime and based on authority—authority defined as the "capacity for reasoned elaboration based upon the recognized beliefs, values, and interest of the community" (p. 21). According to Friedrich, the maintaining leader is a *conservator* because his or her primary function is to protect and preserve the existing government and its traditions.

The concept of maintaining leadership, when applied to public bureaucracies, sheds some light on the notion of bureaucratic leadership. Grounded in this concept, then, public administrators are administrative conservators. As such, they are actively engaged in a special type of leadership: *administrative conservatorship.*

The Concept of Administrative Conservatorship

The concept of administrative conservatorship is consistent with the American constitutional tradition and provides a perspective for conceptualizing the leadership role of career executives in governance. Administrative conservatorship is statesmanship in the tradition of Edmund Burke, the 18th-century British politician and philosopher, because it requires a "disposition to preserve and an ability to improve." Administrative conservatorship is also an intellectual progeny of the institutional leadership school in sociology, particularly as manifest in the work of Philip Selznick (1957).

The term *conservatorship* was coined to characterize an active leadership role for public administrators in governance. The term is derived from the Latin word *conservare,* meaning to preserve. Someone who engages in the act of preserving is defined as a conservator. More specific, a conservator is a guardian, someone who conserves or preserves from injury, violation, or infraction. From an institutional perspective, administrative conservatorship is an active and dynamic process of strengthening and preserving an institution's special capabilities, its proficiency, and thereby its integrity so that it may perform a desired social function.

Administrative conservatorship is not an attempt to preserve a comfortable or static state and should not be confused with administrative *conservership* as described by Anthony Downs (1967, chap. 8 & 9). Rather, controlled adaptation to changing circumstances is obviously an ongoing necessity. As prudently stated by Selznick (1957), "To the essentially conservative posture of the responsible leader we must add a concern for change and reconstruction" (p. 149).

Because it is linked to much broader considerations, administrative conservatorship concentrates on more than solely fulfilling
the needs of organizational members. Properly conceptualized,
administrative conservatorship is the willingness of *administrative
elites*, out of traditional loyalty and moral principles, to preserve
authority and distribution of power with regard to the propriety of
an *institution's* existence, its functional niche, and its collective
institutional goals. In the final analysis, administrative conservatorship is concerned with the preservation of *institutional integrity*.

The significance and meaning of the terms *institution, institutional integrity,* and *administrative elites* used in the above definition of administrative conservatorship must be clarified. The term
institution as conceptualized here is consistent with the definition
offered by theorists of the institutional school in sociology and is
best represented by the works of Selznick. For analytical purposes,
the institution is differentiated from an organization, which is a
rational, means-oriented instrument guided by the "cult" of efficiency. In contrast, the institution is considered a creation of social
needs and aspirations; it is an adaptive, responsive, cooperative
system that embodies cultural values. The cultural values and
moral commitments of a society are implanted in its institutions.
In short, institutions represent the "ethos of the culture, its particular way of self fulfillment" (Selznick, 1952, p. 295).

Although some critics, most notably Charles Perrow (1986),
question Selznick's distinction between organization and institutions, their criticisms are weak. Perrow argues that Selznick's
distinction was the product of an era (1950s) preoccupied with
order and stability. He does not, however, address the substance
of Selznick's conceptualization of the institution. Moreover, a
careful review of Perrow's overall critique suggests that he may
have ignored the original purpose of the organization/institution
distinction. Selznick (1957) explicitly states that the distinction is
a "matter of analysis and not direct description" and was not
intended to suggest that any cooperative system is exclusively one
or the other (p. 5). In fact, it is quite possible for the social entity
to be a combination of both. This distinction was offered as an
alternative to the rationalist school of organization theory that
embraced efficiency as its dominant value.

The next term, *institutional integrity*, is central to the concept of administrative conservatorship. The idea of institutional integrity has not received the scholarly attention it deserves. Chester I. Barnard (1948) alludes to this:

> The primary efforts of leaders need to be directed to the *maintenance* and guidance of organizations as whole systems. I believe this to be the most distinctive characteristic sector of leadership behavior, but it is the least obvious and least understood. The leader has to guide all in such a way to *preserve* organization as the instrument of action. (p. 89; italics added)

Institutional integrity is related to the notion of "distinctive competence" (Selznick, 1957, p. 139), the special capacities, abilities, and proficiencies possessed by an agency in the performance of particular functions. An institution's distinctive competence is developed by a combination of value commitments made by administrative conservators. Value commitments are decisions that obligate and bind institutional activities and processes to specific courses of action. They are "choices that fix the assumptions of policymakers as to the nature of the enterprise" (p. 55). Administrative decisions relating to institutional purpose, the means for its accomplishment, and the social composition of the members are examples of areas bound by value commitments. Value commitments vary in terms of their importance to the formation and maintenance of an institution's distinctive competence. Because they provide the foundation of an institution's distinctive competence, some value commitments may be considered hypersensitive.

The notion of distinctive competence is the heart of *institutional integrity*. The word *integrity* refers to the completeness, wholeness, and intact quality of an entity. In the context of administrative conservatorship, institutional integrity refers to the completeness, wholeness, soundness, and persistence of administrative processes, value commitments, and unifying principles that determine an institution's distinctive competence. The preservation of institutional integrity is an important area of administrative concern. As noted by Selznick (1957), "the protection of integrity is more than an aesthetic or expressive exercise, more than an attempt to preserve a comforting, familiar environment. It is a practical concern of the first importance because the defense of integrity is also a defense of the organization's *distinctive competence*" (p. 139).

The final term, *administrative elites*, does not necessarily mean or imply aristocrats in the traditional sense; rather, it refers to those individuals or groups who are responsible for the promotion and conservation of social values. Although egalitarians may find the term *elite* somewhat unsettling, I advocate that elites are essential to the perpetuation and preservation of society because they are the bearers and conservators of cultural values.

In the context of administrative conservatorship, elites are public officials who are neither elected nor politically appointed but who hold administrative positions by virtue of a merit system. These officials influence public policy by exercising their administrative discretion. Administrative elites are *bureaucrats* as honorably defined by Rohr (1978). As administrative elites, career civil servants are responsible for the perpetuation and conservation of "regime values," that is, "values of the political entity that [was] brought into being by ratification of the Constitution that created the present American republic" (p. 59). The Constitution is the foundation of our society and symbolizes the society's frame of mind. According to George Will (1983):

> The Constitution does not just distribute power, it does so in a cultural context of principles and beliefs and expectations about appropriate social outcome of the exercise of those powers. . . . A Constitution not only presupposes a consensus of "views" on fundamentals; it also presupposes concern for its own continuance. Therefore, it presupposes efforts to predispose rising generations to the "views" and habits and dispositions that underlie institutional arrangements. In this sense, a constitution is not only an allocator of power; it is also the polity's frame of mind. (p. 79)

When public administrators take an oath to uphold the Constitution, they are making a moral commitment to the continuance of constitutional processes that encompass particular values, beliefs, and interests. This commitment is expressed in practical terms through their fidelity to duty in the administration of governmental institutions, including the values embodied in the Constitution.

Through such institutions, the authoritative allocation of resources is made to sustain the Republic's cohesion and moral balance. As a repository of regime values, governmental institutions must be conserved especially because the strength of cultural values is contingent on the capacity of primary institutions to transmit them without serious distortion.

The perpetuation of cultural values depends on the security of key institutions. Security in this context implies stability, strength, and overall integrity. Ensuring security of governmental institutions is, to a large extent, the responsibility of public administrators because they are vital in providing continuity and stability. This role is especially important in a democratic system in which political appointees are merely temporary custodians of governmental institutions (see Heclo, 1977).

The efforts of administrative executives to preserve the integrity of public bureaucracies afford them the distinction of being called administrative conservators. As conservators of public bureaucracies, administrative executives are active and legitimate participants in "statecraft." Statecraft, as coined by Will (1983), is "soulcraft" in that it involves the "conversation of values and arrangements that are not subjects of day-to-day debate" (p. 156). Soulcraft does not imply the conservation of values espoused by a particular political party, nor does it suggest the preservation of passing whims. Rather, soulcraft entails the conservation of regime values, which is a moral obligation. The preservation of public bureaucracies and, in turn, regime values reflects the normative quality of administrative conservatorship.

If a regime is fundamentally unjust and even immoral, it will be difficult for the public administrator to be a "good human being and a good citizen [of that regime] at the same time" (Rohr, 1978, p. 61). Nazi Germany's Third Reich was an extreme case. Not all regimes are so unjust. It is also possible for administrative executives to circumvent regime values, as illustrated by the actions of J. Edgar Hoover at the end of his reign and of Anne Burford during her tenure as administrator of the U.S. Environmental Protection Agency. Their actions did not constitute administrative conservatorship.

Administrative conservatorship may be regarded as a type of statesmanship. It requires balancing the inherent tension in the political system between the need to *serve* and the need to *preserve*. Public administrators must be responsive to the demands of political cal elites, the courts, interest groups, and the citizenry and at the same time must preserve the integrity of public bureaucracies. Public administrators must not be weak or subservient, nor must they be empire builders or public entrepreneurs conceptualized in a pejorative sense. Rather, public administrators must honorably hold up the administrative side of the governance equation. Paul Appelby (1949) said it best:

> Administrators share with all others in places of special responsibility the special obligation of *leadership*. They can, in all innocence, contribute to organizational practices and form elements that are inimical to popular government. They can help "take things out of politics"—or take themselves too far out of politics. They, like citizens and legislators, are capable of yielding too much to the prestige of military or other experts, too little to the politician who is the central factor in civilian control and popular government. By dealing with the legislature too directly, they may undermine and confuse executive responsibility; by the same tactics they may inadvertently substitute control by members of Congress for control by Congress as a body. By failing to be imaginative about legislative needs, attitudes, and prerogatives, they may overburden, and thus degrade the legislature. Their *special duty* is in part to help clear the way so that other parts of government and the other political processes may function well. (p. 199; italics added)

The concept of administrative conservatorship provides a valuable perspective in which public administrators and others may view their administrative leadership role in the American political system. It is offered as a means of restoring respectability to public administrators and the public service. The concept of administrative conservatorship is also offered as a framework for measuring administrative leadership effectiveness.

Notes

1. The term *institutional leadership* is used in the manner suggested by Philip Selznick (1957, 1992). According to Selznick (1992), "institutional leadership" is

concerned with governance. The institutional leader is responsible for "the whole life of the institution" and "takes account of all the interests that affect the viability, competence, and moral character of an enterprise" (p. 290). Quotations from Selznick (1992), *The moral commonwealth: Social theory and the promise of community* are reprinted by permission of the University of California Press, Berkeley.

2. Recent works include Doig and Hargrove (1987), Meier (1989), and Hargrove (1989). Herbert Kaufman (personal communication, May 28, 1992) brought to my attention that some commentaries on bureaucratic leadership go back at least half a century. I agree with this basic point. The type of active leadership stressed here, however, is seldom explored in the literature.

3. As noted by Rohr (1986), the Federalists used the term *leadership* in a pejorative manner. The term was closely associated with *favorite* or *demagogue*.

4. James Stever points out that the Progressives were not in total agreement in their diagnosis of the ills afflicting the quality of American institutions. According to Stever (personal communication, May 26, 1992), some Progressives believed that there were moral problems, whereas others such as the pragmatists held that institutions were poorly structured. Stever (1990) devotes considerable attention to this issue. See also Douglas Morgan (1994).

5. I have benefited from J. P. Burke's (1986) discussion and critique of the hierarchical and pluralist approaches (see *Bureaucratic Responsibility*, esp. chap. 1).

6. For a discussion of the different value orientations of bureaucracy and democracy, see David Nachmias and David H. Rosenbloom (1980, chap. 2). Also see Douglas Yates (1982, chap. 2).

7. The famous Friedrich-Finer debate is illustrative. See Carl J. Friedrich (1940) and Herman Finer (1941). Later contributions to this debate include Kenneth Cup Davis (1969) and Theodore Lowi (1969).

8. Rejoinders (to Spicer & Terry, 1993) by John A. Rohr, Kenneth Warren, Camilla Stivers, Charles Wise, and Theodore Lowi are also included in the same issue of *Public Administration Review*.

9. This method, often used by those described as the "Idealists," requires that the historian "seek to understand the motives, intentions, and in turn the character of persons involved in the events they wish to explain." This necessitates that historians "imagine themselves in the place of the person involved in the event; try to realize as completely as possible the circumstance under which they acted, and the motives that influenced their actions" (Spicer & Terry, 1993, p. 240).

A Model of Administrative Conservatorship

DESPITE A FEW notable exceptions (Chester I. Barnard, Philip Selznick, and, most recently, James Q. Wilson, among them), the idea of *conserving* public bureaucracies has not been welcomed with enthusiasm by many who study organizations and administrative leadership. It is difficult to explain why scholars have given conservation such a lukewarm reception. Very likely it has something to do with the emphasis Americans place on growth, the anticonservative bias of public administration and organization theory, and the widely held heroic view of leadership. From the perspective of administrative leadership theory, each

AUTHOR'S NOTE: Some of the material in this chapter has been drawn from my article "Leadership in the Administrative State," *Administration & Society*, Vol. 21, No. 4 (1990), pp. 395-412, copyright © 1990 by Sage Publications, Inc.

factor has done much to diminish the importance and value of conservation. In the sections that follow, I explore these factors in greater detail.

Growth as a Secure Social Value

Many Americans typically think of growth with the concepts of progress and change in mind. Growth is often equated with progress, and progress seems to imply beneficial changes or improvements in the way of life. Indeed, this understanding of growth and progress has changed little since the Progressive Era. We often long for and feel good about news relating to growth. Whether such news pertains to economic growth or to one's spiritual and emotional growth, the concept is still held in high regard in the United States.

Organization theorists also find growth attractive. David A. Whetten (1980) noted that "organizational theories in general are based on the assumption of growth and hence researchers are preoccupied with studying growth and its effects" (p. 577). Whetten offers several other reasons. First, growth is a desirable organizational goal because it reinforces the notion that "bigger is better." Second, growth is a commonly used measure of organizational effectiveness. Third, growth is a prevailing ideology in American society, and thus it has a significant influence on how theorists perceive and interpret organizational phenomena.

When juxtaposed with growth, conservation is viewed unfavorably by organization theorists. There is a perception that the concept of conservation embodies values in conflict with the progrowth, utilitarian beliefs held by many American scholars (see Scott, 1974). Because conservation involves the act and process of preserving tradition, it is criticized for favoring stability at the expense of change and progress. To many leadership theorists, stability is a pejorative term. Critics contend that stability conveys an image of a static, unalterable entity. Stability is also criticized for its inherently conservative qualities. As a consequence, scholars have not felt an urgent need to write about the virtues of stability. In fact, anyone contemplating such a task would most likely be accused of professional heresy, as Scott seems to think.

In a critique of the premises and values underpinning the classical management paradigm, Scott concludes that one is hard-pressed to find any serious discussion in the professional literature extolling the virtues of organizational stability. Why? Because the concept of organizational stability "reflect[s] values that are foreign to American expectations, and thereby are foreign to the mainstream of management thought and practice" (p. 247).

Contrary to what many writers propound, conservation is *not* antithetical to growth, progress, or change. When viewed in a broader context, conservation incorporates each of these concepts. Conservation is based on the premise that traditional values, beliefs, and customs do not remain the same: They evolve gradually over time as Edmund Burke, Joseph de Maistre, and other traditionalists so wisely point out. This suggests that preserving traditional views and values is, to a large extent, an evolutionary process. The key word here is *evolutionary*. Placing the concepts of growth, progress, and change under a microscope soon brings into focus that evolution is a unifying theme. For example, organization theorists acknowledge that growth has both quantitative and qualitative dimensions (see Ford, 1980). Quantitative dimensions are classified under the heading *size*, which refers to an increase in "physical capacity, number of people, inputs or outputs, or discretionary resources" (p. 590). The qualitative dimension of growth focuses on the organization's gradual process of historical development. More specifically, it examines an organization's development as it moves from "earlier to later or from simpler to more complex stages of evolution" (*American Heritage Dictionary*, 1982, p. 389).[1] Because organization theorists have focused almost exclusively on the quantitative dimension of growth, it is not difficult to understand why conservation is considered at odds with growth.

Conservation and progress are also linked together by evolution. Progress is defined as "development, unfolding; steady improvement; to advance toward a more desirable form" (*American Heritage Dictionary*, 1982, p. 990). James March and Johan P. Olsen (1989) criticize the contemporary use of the term *progress* because it is thought to imply that institutions "evolve through some form of efficient historical process" (p. 7).[2] Progress should be understood neither in this way nor as "historical efficiency" (p. 7) but rather, as March and Olsen observe, that institutions are not always efficient in their response to historical change.

Conservation does not necessarily suggest an antagonism toward change. In fact, conservation may require change, as Edmund Burke (1789/1987) advised. A fierce defender of tradition, Burke recognized the need and importance of gradual, evolutionary change. This is reflected in his distinction between reform and change. Burke favored reform and defined it as the preservation of tradition by *necessary* change. In contrast, change (especially change for the sake of change) can destroy an institution and thus should be avoided at all cost. The essential link between necessary change and conservation is revealed in Burke's oft-quoted statement: "We must all obey the law of change. A state without some means for change is without the means for its *conservation*" (p. 19; italics added).

The Anticonservative Bias of Public Administration and Organization Theory

The anticonservative bias of public administration and organization theory also explains why scholars have not devoted much time to conserving public bureaucracies. The act and process of conserving public bureaucracies is by its very nature a conservative enterprise. As I argued in the previous section, many scholars who write about public organizations in general and leadership in particular regard conservatism as something to be avoided, much like the plague. There is an anticonservative bias among many public administration and organization theorists. This bias is reflected in scathing critiques of conservative scholarship and in negative characterizations of conservative bureaucratic officials. Sheldon Wolin's (1960, chap. 10) critique of Philip Selznick's theories of organization and leadership and Theodore Lowi's (1993a) critical commentary on the 1993 article by Michael W. Spicer and myself provide excellent examples of the former. Anthony Downs's (1967, chap. 9) description of the "conserver" is a classic example of the latter.

In a caustic critique of organizational theories, Wolin (1960) attacks Selznick for his "fondness for large scale organization"

(p. 427) and for relying on philosophical organicism and the ideas of Edmund Burke to develop theories of organization and leadership.[3] Wolin is convinced that Selznick's treatment of large and powerful bureaucracies as evolving, natural communities with specific needs is misguided. He contends that the use of Burkean language and concepts such as spontaneity, natural processes, adaptive organism, and nonrational behavior is odd, especially when used to describe large bureaucracies such as General Motors and the Pentagon.

Wolin (1960) also criticizes Selznick's theory of *elite autonomy*, which he directly links to Burke's idea of a natural aristocracy. In his book *Leadership in Administration*, Selznick (1957) argues that elites must be protected because they are responsible for maintaining and protecting social values. Although Selznick is careful to define elites as "any group responsible for a social value" (p. 120), Wolin (1960) ignores this definition and offers his own. He argues that Selznick's notion of elite appears at first glance related to Platonism, which suggests that "those few who have the qualifications for exercising the highest social functions should be in the positions of highest authority" (p. 420). But on close inspection, says Wolin, another dominant form of elitism becomes apparent—a form that conceptualizes an elite as "a group whose superiority rests on its excellence in manipulation" of the masses (p. 420). According to Wolin, Selznick's work and other "conservatively-oriented literature of organization theory" (p. 427) provide a blueprint for elite manipulation of the masses. As complex systems of domination, large bureaucracies are instruments of control; they are used by elites to shape the behavior of the masses. Wolin considers this dangerous because Selznick's conservative theories are nothing more than "Leninism clothed in the language of Burke" (p. 427). Wolin continues by asserting that the "conservative cast to the thought of Selznick and, earlier, Elton Mayo suggests how hopelessly anachronistic are the contemporary romantic conservative writers" (p. 510, n. 283).

It is obvious that Wolin has difficulty with the inherent conservatism of Selznick's work. It is no stretch to say that this pronounced anticonservative bias has an influence on his interpretation of Selznick's theories. The same can be said about Lowi's (1993a) critique of the article by Spicer and myself.

As I discussed in Chapter 1, Spicer and I (1993) attempt to legitimate the role of public administrators in governance by grounding our arguments in classical constitutional theory.[4] In the tradition of the Federalists, Michael Oakeshott (1975), James Buchanan and Gordon Tullock (1962), and Friedrich A. Hayek (1944), among others, Spicer and I argue that an important purpose of a constitution is to limit the abuse of political power and that public administration has a rightful place in governance if it performs this regime-sustaining function.

Lowi (1993a), "disturbed" by this argument, counters with two main criticisms.[5] First, Lowi makes his familiar argument that the discretion and power of administrative officials has increased immensely since the New Deal largely because of poorly crafted and imprecise laws. This has created a situation that shakes the foundation of the American political system. To suggest that public administrators should have more discretion, especially when such discretion is used to check the power of elected political officials, undermines the values and principles of the American democratic form of government.

Lowi's (1993a) second major criticism pertains to the conservative nature of the article by Spicer and myself. He views our work as representative of a band of conservative scholars who seek to establish public administration as the "core of modern government" and of the "constitution itself." Lowi argues that our approach to public administration is "totally bizarre"; it is "pessimistic about democracy—if not downright hostile to it." Lowi suggests that our approach is "farther to the right wing side of American politics than the New Deal was to the Left." He also states that our position is "not libertarian but genuinely *conservative*" (pp. 263-264; italics added). In short, it is the conservatism that annoys Lowi the most, as the following statement reveals.

> The position of Spicer and Terry in this article is neither ludicrous nor, in its own way, illogical. It is to me frightening. . . . Conservatism has emerged and is coalescing around an effort to provide America with a new approach to public administration as the core of a new, more conservative regime. We see elements of this effort in Spicer and Terry and in Rohr, despite some disagreements

between them. Taking the whole group together, they are pushing us in theory, and eventually in practice, toward the Third Republic. It is a republic that I would like even less than the second. (p. 264)

In addition to the attacks on conservative scholarship by Wolin, Lowi, and others, the anticonservative bias of public administration and organization theory is reflected in the negative portrayal of administrative officials who actively seek to maintain public bureaucracies and, in turn, the American regime. Nowhere is this more obvious than in the work of Anthony Downs (1967). In building a theory of bureaucratic decision making, Downs describes five ideal types of bureaucratic officials: "climbers," "conservers," "zealots," "advocates," and "statesmen" (p. 88). Each type is driven by a range of self-interested motives and behaviors. According to Downs, climbers and conservers are the most self-interested because they are not "altruistic" nor do they have any "loyalty to larger values" (p. 88). Of interest here is Downs's characterization of the conserver, which should not be confused with the administrative conservator.

Downs paints an unflattering portrait of the conserver and acknowledges that his characterization of the conserver is based in part on Robert Prethus's (1975, chap. 7) concept of "indifferents" (p. 185). This alone warns of the inherently negative quality of Downs's conserver concept. Prethus's description of the indifferents indicates a prejudice against bureaucratic officials from working and lower middle backgrounds. The following comments by Prethus certainly lead to this conclusion:

> Turning to the indifferents' accommodation to the bureaucratic situation, we find that they are typical of working-class or lower-middle class origin. This implies a distinctive style of early socialization. Not only will they rarely have been inculcated with the desire to excel, but class status and limited education have not usually prepared them for the graceful acceptance of authority which has become so critical for organizational mobility. Whereas middle-class child training has emphasized self-direction, respect for authority, and the muffling of aggression, lower-class socialization has stressed conformity and been rather more tolerant of fighting, truancy, haphazard toilet training, and the like. (p. 196)

Under the influence of Prethus's concept, Downs (1967) proceeds to demean bureaucratic officials who perform the valuable function of maintaining administrative institutions of government. The conserver is portrayed as a pathetic bureaucratic official who is afraid of and resists most, if not all, types of change. Downs's conservers are "timorous, self-effacing, extremely cautious, plagued by inferior feeling or just indifferent about their occupations" (p. 97). They also have a defeatist outlook on life, possess "mediocre abilities," and are confined to their official positions because of a lack of ambition.

Downs's description of the conserver has successfully created what Doris Graber (1976) describes as "reality-sleeves"—"conceptual straightjackets which tightly enclose the minds of individuals or groups and prevent them from accepting conflicting perceptions" (p. 53). Consequently, it should come as no surprise that Downs's negative image of the conserver has had a profound influence on how theorists perceive bureaucratic officials who preserve the integrity of public bureaucracies. Unfortunately, administrative officials dedicated to this regime-sustaining function are viewed, more often than not, with a jaundiced eye.

The Heroic Conception of Leadership

The heroic conception of leadership may explain why scholars have shied away from the idea of conserving public bureaucracies. Conserving the organization does not conform with the heroic image of leaders promoted by many theorists. Writers tend to overemphasize the importance of leaders, creating what is nearly a "great man" theory of administration (see Meindl, Ehrlich, & Dukerich, 1985).

The business management literature, in particular, is saturated with images of a powerful, heroic leader (e.g., Bass, 1984, 1985; Bennis, 1989; Tichy & Devanna, 1986; Tichy & Ulrich, 1984). This literature contains several dominant themes. One readily apparent theme is that leaders of private sector institutions are cast in a role larger than life. These leaders are viewed as having (or as those who should have) enormous power, derived primarily from charisma, to alter organizational events at their discretion. Lee Iacocca, the former chairman of the Chrysler Corporation, and Michael Blumenthal, the head of Burroughs Corporation, are offered as illustrations. Implicit in this heroic view of leadership is a coercive conception of authority that is based on domination and forced submission.

A second theme found in business management literature relates to the measurement of leadership effectiveness. Leaders are considered effective if they successfully implement revolutionary changes that result in the radical reconstruction of an organization's technical, political, and cultural systems. A propensity for risk taking, opportunism, and innovation is also factored into the effectiveness equation. Leaders who fulfill these requirements are said to have "made a difference."

A third theme found in the business management literature revolves around the concept of tradition. The term *tradition* has ecclesiastical roots and is defined as a "set of established values and beliefs having persisted over several generations" (C. J. Friedrich, 1972, p. 18). Contemporary organization theorists tend to portray leaders as antitraditionalists. Organizational values and traditions that have endured through time are viewed with disdain and suspicion. Heroic leaders are encouraged to abandon tradition in their urgent search for new ways of doing things.

As has often been the case, public administration theorists have borrowed concepts from the business management field. Most, if not all, of the aforementioned themes have surfaced in recent discussions concerning leadership in public bureaucracies. For example, Jameson Doig and Erwin Hargrove (1987), in an edited volume on leadership in public bureaucracies, seek to counteract what they call a "pessimistic view" that leaders of public agencies "make very little difference" (p. 4). They adopt a conceptual framework governed by the principles of entrepreneurship and innovation. Leaders of public bureaucracies are characterized as entrepreneurs.

Given the conceptual framework employed by Doig and Hargrove (1987), it is no surprise that they emphasize many of the dominant themes found in the business management literature. For example, leaders of public agencies are depicted as individuals who possess unusual powers and qualities that enable them to dominate and conquer others:

Our thirteen entrepreneurs were strongly motivated to place their imprints on the complex world of public policy. For some such as Nancy Hanks and Elmer Staats the personal style was low-keyed but assertive. Others like Lilienthal and Rickover were more competitive, even combative reminding us of Schumpeter's characterization of the entrepreneur as a person who has the "will to conquer: the impulse to fight, to prove oneself superior to others." For all of our chosen leaders, probably the will to conquer was there; some sought to only conquer challenging political and technical problems; while others were motivated as well by the need to dominate people inside and beyond their organization. (p. 12)

Doig and Hargrove (1987) also imply that leadership effectiveness is measured by the leader's ability to reconstruct organizational structures, functions, and processes. Effective leaders, that is, those who make a difference, "identify new missions and programs," "create and nourish external constituencies to support new goals," "create internal constituencies through changes in organizational structures," and "enhance the organization's technical expertise to implement new goals and programs." (p. 8). The emphasis on *new* can be interpreted to mean that existing organizational structures, functions, and processes are inadequate and thus require radical reconstruction.

The notion that effective bureaucratic leaders are risk takers and opportunists is central to Doig and Hargrove's (1987) conception of leadership. Leaders are viewed as high-stake players in the organizational game who are willing to sacrifice everything to "make a difference." They are said to have a burning desire to throw their "energies and personal reputations into the fray in order to bring about change" (p. 11). The organization's established value system is perceived as a formidable foe that challenges the creation and institutionalization of innovation. Entrepreneurial leaders are encouraged to disassociate themselves with established traditions and reformulate their self-concept in terms of a new value system. In other words, effective leaders must destroy organizational traditions in order to "make a difference." In quoting Schumpeter, Doig and Hargrove state:

In one sense, he may indeed be called the most rational and most egotistical of all . . . and the typical entrepreneur is more self-centered than other types, because he relies less than they do on

> tradition and connection with the past and because his charac-
> teristic task—theoretically as well as historically—consists of pre-
> cisely in breaking up old, and creating new, traditions. (p. 11)

Innovative leaders are almost always needed at some point in an organization's history. Nevertheless, the depiction of these leaders as heroes and high-flying risk takers is a distortion of reality. The heroic conception of leadership is dangerous for several reasons. First, the heroic conception perpetuates a romanticized view of leadership. The view that leaders of public bureaucracies must impose their will on the world to make a difference is a myth, a reflection of "poetic exaggeration" better suited for song and legend (C. J. Friedrich, 1961, p. 21). Bureaucratic leaders are not obliged to accept the challenges of fulfilling unrealistic role expectations that require that they become a "cross between superman and knights of the Round Table" (Drucker, 1985, p. 139).

Second, the heroic perspective focuses exclusively on the radical reconstruction of public bureaucracies. Although drastic changes may be necessary at times, such changes are the exception rather than the rule. Bureaucratic leadership more often requires the ongoing management of evolutionary and incremental changes.

Third, the heroic view depreciates the valuable contributions made by many bureaucratic leaders. The so-called nonheroic leader is ridiculed and labeled a manager. Unfortunately, the manager is seen as an ineffective individual who is threatened by change and whose main calling in life is to defend the status quo, regardless of changing circumstances. Surely it is possible that something more exists between the "great man" who is capable of heroic acts and the pathetic, unimaginative technocrat incapable of taking risk, who avoids conflict and is driven by narrow purposes. The heroic view of leadership makes it virtually impossible to conceive of other possibilities.

Last, the heroic conception of leadership encourages the abandonment of tradition, the normative anchor that governs the rational action of administrative officials. This is especially troublesome because, as Selznick (1987) writes, "the rational action of individuals must be anchored in some way" (p. 458). Consistent with the views of Edmund Burke, Selznick argues that rational action must be grounded in tradition. When public administration theorists encourage bureaucratic leaders to disregard tradition, they are in a sense asking them to abandon their rational basis of authority. Authority in this context is defined as the "capacity for reasoned elaboration" grounded in the funded experience or tradition of the political community (C. J. Friedrich, 1958a, p. 39).

The heroic conception of leadership deflects attention from the importance of conserving public bureaucracies. Conserving viable and legitimate governmental institutions is equally important to transforming bad institutions or building new ones. Meindl et al. (1985) are correct in asserting that leadership theorists have "elevated the concept [leadership] to a lofty status and level of significance. . . . It has gained a brilliance that exceeds the limits of normal scientific inquiry" (p. 78).

The Preservation of Institutional Integrity

In light of the heroic model's commitment to radical change and the conserver's opposition to any change at all, the notion of institutional integrity, at the core of the theory of administrative conservatorship, has both heuristic as well as practical value. As indicated in Chapter 1, institutional integrity is related to the concept of distinctive competence. Administrative agencies, like all other institutions, develop special capabilities and proficiencies in the performance of their tasks. Through time, these proficiencies solidify into a distinctive competence that is maintained by a combination of value commitments made by institutional leaders concerning the nature of the enterprise. To say that an institution has integrity is to suggest that it is faithful to the functions, values, and distinctive set of unifying principles that define its special competence and character (Morgan, 1990; see also Morgan & Kass, 1991).

The term *preservation* has special significance when discussed in relationship to institutional integrity. Preservation, according to *Webster's Tenth Collegiate Dictionary* (1993), involves the process of keeping from injury, destruction, or decay or the protection or maintenance of an entity. In the context of administrative conservatorship, the preservation of institutional integrity involves protecting from injury, destruction, or decay those processes, values, and unifying principles that determine an institution's distinctive competence. For example, if a university develops a distinctive competence as an institution dedicated to teaching, the administrative conservator must protect values, processes, and activities relating to the teaching function. Functions and processes relating to recruitment and selection of faculty members are a case in point. The administrative conservator must ensure that recruitment and selection processes and procedures are governed by values that consistently result in the hiring of faculty members who have a demonstrated commitment to teaching. The conservator must also pay close attention to other institutional policies and procedures (i.e., those relating to faculty evaluation, faculty/student ratio, classroom size and design, and so forth) that may have a direct bearing on the teaching function.

Selznick (1957) pointed out that "few aspects of organization are so important, yet so badly neglected by students of the subject, as the problem of institutional integrity" (p. 130). He also stated that the defense of institutional integrity is "one of the most important and least understood functions of leadership" (p. 63).[6] Since Selznick wrote these words, little has changed. Organization and leadership theorists continue to devote scant attention to this important concept. Because institutional integrity occupies a central place in the theory of administrative conservatorship, I will discuss the concept in more detail. I review Selznick's treatment of the subject in two prominent works, *Leadership in Administration: A Sociological Interpretation* (1957) and *The Moral Commonwealth: Social Theory and the Promise of Community* (1992). I then draw on Selznick's conceptualization to advance this discussion of administrative conservatorship.

Selznick's Theory of Autonomy and Responsiveness

Selznick (1952) introduced the concept of *institutional integrity* in a study of communist organization. But not until the publication of *Leadership in Administration* (1957) did the concept attract serious attention. In describing what he means by the "institutional embodiment of purpose" (p. 90), Selznick explains the meaning and importance of institutional integrity. He suggests that it is the responsibility of the leader as statesman to protect the "institution's distinctive values, competence and role" (p. 119). This is what he means by the defense of institutional integrity. Selznick contends that an institution's integrity is vulnerable to corruption when its values are "tenuous or insecure" (p. 120).

Selznick (1957) draws attention to the dangerous internal forces that undermine institutional integrity. He also discusses strategies that institutional leaders can use to prevent or minimize the destruction by such forces. A viable strategy is elite autonomy. When Selznick speaks of autonomy, he is referring to "a condition of independence sufficient to permit a group to work out and maintain distinctive identity" (p. 121). As indicated earlier, elites are responsible for the preservation of the institution's distinctive competence, values, and role. To effectively perform this function, they must be protected from dangerous extraneous pressures. According to Selznick, autonomy can be achieved through the *isolation of elites.*

Thirty-five years later, in *The Moral Commonwealth: Social Theory and the Promise of Community*, Selznick (1992) offers a more complex and developed notion of institutional integrity. Although the essence of the concept remains the same, Selznick examines integrity from the perspective of the "moral institution" (p. 229). After discussing the concepts of identity and character and their relationship to institutional integrity, Selznick carefully explains the idea of integrity this way:

> A test of moral character is the idea of *integrity.* This idea brings morality to bear in a way that respects autonomy and plurality of persons and institutions. The chief virtue of integrity is fidelity to self-defining principles. To strive for integrity is to ask: What is our direction? What are our unifying principles? And how do these square with the claims of morality? . . . Integrity involves both wholeness and soundness. It is something we associate with moral coherence, not with coherence of every sort. Integrity has to do with principles, and therefore with principled conduct. Not every belief is a principle, nor may every action in the name of belief be considered principled conduct. A political, administrative or judi-

cial decision is principled if it is guided by a coherent conception of institutional morality, that is, of appropriate ends and means. . . . What counts as integrity, and what affects integrity, will be different for a university press and a commercial publisher; for a constitutional court and a lower court; for a regulatory agency and a highway department. Each institution, or type of institution, has special functions and values; each has a distinctive set of unifying principles. When a lack of integrity is charged, there is always an explicit conception of what the institution is or should be. (pp. 322-324; italics in original)[7]

As he had done in previous discussions of institutional integrity, Selznick addresses the notion of autonomy. But this time the emphasis is on institutional autonomy rather than elite autonomy. The theory of elite autonomy is not discarded; many of its elements remain intact and are embodied in the idea of institutional autonomy. Instead of explicitly discussing elite autonomy *within the institution*, Selznick shifts the discussion to institutional autonomy *within the larger community*. This is a subtle but important shift because now the dialogue focuses on a different level of analysis (institutional vs. group) and addresses both external and internal forces that threaten institutional integrity.

In Selznick's (1992) recent formulation, autonomy and integration are viable strategies for preserving institutional integrity. "Autonomy," writes Selznick, "safeguards values and competencies by entrusting them to their most committed agents and by insulating them from alien pressures and temptations" (p. 334). In contrast, institutional integration builds and "widens support for the institution and provides opportunities for growth and adaptation." It also checks the power of institutions and serves as a buffer against "perverse and self-defeating isolation" (p. 334).

The idea of responsiveness and its bearing on institutional integrity is also moved front and center in Selznick's recent work. In the earlier work *Leadership in Administration* (1957), responsiveness is discussed in the concluding chapter under the heading of the "responsible leader." A responsible leader is one who understands, among other things, the dangers of both opportunism and utopianism. Opportunism is the "pursuit of immediate, short-run advantage in a way inadequately controlled by considerations of principle and ultimate consequence" (p. 143), whereas utopianism is the avoidance of difficult institution-sustaining decisions because of a "flight to abstractions" (p. 147; i.e., the overgeneralization of mission and an overreliance on technical solutions to resolve institutional problems).

In *The Moral Commonwealth* (1992), responsiveness is examined in a much broader context as Selznick once again shifts the level of analysis to the institution. The responsive institution is one that "avoids insularity without embracing opportunism"; it preserves institutional integrity "while taking into account new problems, new forces in the environment, new demands and expectations" (p. 336). Selznick emphasizes that the responsive institution is "selective" in its adaptation to external demands; the institution must resist pressures and demands that weaken institutional integrity. This is a complex task for the threat of opportunism is always present. He also stresses that the responsive institution is a "responsible institution" (p. 338). The moral institution is responsible to the extent that it is open to changes and revisions in its functions and process. Such changes are and should be guided, however, by a fidelity to the values and unifying principles that determine institutional integrity.

Selznick's discussion of institutional integrity and, in turn, autonomy and responsiveness is relevant to the theory of administrative conservatorship. To examine administrative leadership in public bureaucracies and the distinctions between public institutions and the modern business enterprise, Selznick's notion of autonomy and responsiveness requires some additional clarification.

Institutional Autonomy and Administrative Conservatorship

The concept of autonomy raises several important questions in connection with public bureaucracies. The first question relates to the meaning of autonomy. What does the term mean when used in relation to public bureaucracies? Does it mean, as Herbert Kaufman (1981a) asks, that career administrative officials and public bureaucracies have the freedom to do whatever they desire, regardless of what others want? Does it mean that public bureaucracies have the ability to "act independently of some of or all of the groups that have authority to constrain it?" (J. Q. Wilson, 1978, p. 165; quoted in Kaufman, 1981a, p. 161). Does it mean protecting the "relatively undisputed jurisdiction" or turf of public bureaucracies? (J. Q. Wilson, 1989, p. 183). Or does autonomy mean institutional insulation from political intrusion? It appears that autonomy has a variety of different meanings and, thus, is subject to multiple interpretations.

The second question relates to the so-called bureaucracy/democracy problem. Is there, or should there be, a legitimate place for autonomous administrative institutions in the American democratic form of government? This important question goes straight to the heart of our constitutional system of government. The American political regime is founded on principles that emphasize the checking of political power. The separation of powers among the three political institutions is intended, in part, to achieve this purpose. If one accepts the argument of Rohr (1986) and others that public bureaucracies should be subordinate yet autonomous institutions, does this not undermine the rationale and principles of our constitutional democracy? Is it possible for administrative institutions to be subordinate and autonomous at the same time? In other words, is there an inherent contradiction in the notion of subordinate-autonomous? The answers to these and related questions are no doubt complex. Nevertheless, it is necessary to deal with the autonomy issue directly if the theory of administrative conservatorship is to have any persuasive appeal.

The moral and political philosopher, Gerald Dworkin (1988, chap. 1), traces the etymology of the term *autonomy* back to the Greek city-state. According to Dworkin, a city had *autonomia* when the citizenry made and administered their own laws. He points out that because *auto* means self and *nomos* refers to rule of law, *autonomy* embodies the concept of self-rule or independence. The operative word here is independence. *The Compact Oxford English Dictionary* (1991) defines independence as the "condition or quality of being independent" (p. 847). The term *independent* means "not depending on the authority of another, not in a position of subordination or subjection; not subject to external control or rule, self governing, autonomous, free" (p. 847).

When the meaning of autonomy is based on a strict and literal interpretation of the term, it is easy to understand why political theorists such as Herbert Kaufman, Theodore Lowi, Herman Finer, and Charles Hyneman, among others, vehemently opposed any theory that advocates the autonomy of public bureaucracies. It is also easy to understand why organization theorists such as Philip Selznick, James D. Thompson, Jeffrey Pfeffer, and Gerald Salancik view autonomy as a desirable and valuable organizational quality. The holding of different views by political theorists and organization theorists regarding the desirability of autonomy is, in and of itself, an issue to ponder. Why do political and organization theorists have diametrically opposing views on autonomy? One answer might be that theorists are caught in what Gary L. Wamsley (1990) describes as the "conceptual no-man's-land" that exists between political theory and organization theory (p. 127). This answer has merit and seems plausible, but it appears incomplete. I argue that there is something more to this notion of autonomy: *The meaning of autonomy is contextual, that is, the condition of independence or self-rule is conditioned by the context.* Literary, legal, and philosophical scholars concerned with the interpretation of texts offer persuasive arguments that the complete meaning of words and phrases cannot be ascertained without regard to their context. This so-called contextualist doctrine applies here as well.

Autonomy has particular meaning within the context of the American political system. The executive, legislative, and judicial branches of government are autonomous only insofar as they have primary (but not exclusive) responsibility for specific functions as well as the protection of values related to such functions. From a constitutional perspective, each political institution is independent, but not one has absolute autonomy in the strictest sense of the word. Because of the interdependency of constitutional functions and the sharing of power among the three branches, one must speak of a *measure* or *degree* of autonomy. This suggests that autonomy is a relative state; it is not an all-or-nothing condition. The lack of complete independence does not necessarily prohibit an entity (in this case, political institutions) from acquiring some degree of autonomy. It is difficult to determine how far one can stretch the concept before crossing the line of demarcation separating autonomy from dependence. One suspects that this critical point is contingent on the context as well as on the specific circumstances occurring within that context. For example, the executive branch can lose a significant amount of autonomy because of the action or inaction of a weak president. If a president concedes to Congress on a majority of substantive foreign policy and military matters, the executive branch loses autonomy as the principal political institution responsible for security or self-preservation of the Republic.[8] The legislative branch can also lose autonomy if Congress, because of a lack of political will to make difficult decisions, continuously delegates its policy-making powers to administrative agencies as a means of resolving important or fundamental policy issues (McGowan, 1977).[9]

Returning to public bureaucracies and the question of autonomy, I concur with Rohr (1986) that "the public administration neither constitutes nor heads any branch of government, but is subordinate to all three of them" (p. 182). The constitutional democracy demands no less. I also agree that public bureaucracies require and indeed should have a sufficient amount of autonomy to exercise delegated authority within a specific realm of social action. This leads back to the subordinate-autonomous question: Does the subordinate-autonomous concept, when used to describe the role of public bureaucracies in the American political system, pose a threat to constitutional democracy? My answer to this question is no. The subordinate-autonomous concept is no more problematic than the idea of superior-autonomous (or some other variation) used to describe the role of the three political institutions. I have already mentioned that autonomy in the strictest sense does not and cannot exist within the American political system.

The basic tenets of Rohr's (1986) subordinate-autonomous concept are useful for advancing the theory of administrative conservatorship, but some clarification is in order. Rohr views autonomy as the freedom to choose among competing constitutional masters. Although some scholars incorporate the term *freedom* as part of a baseline definition of autonomy, Rohr's use suggests a *benefit of the condition* rather than a *precise statement of the essential nature of the condition,* a requirement for any definition. (For a discussion of the various meanings and definitions of autonomy, see G. Dworkin, 1988.) In other words, autonomy is an advantage; it gives public administrators the *flexibility* (a benefit and the freedom) to choose among the three constitutional masters. But knowing the benefits of autonomy does not indicate much about the essential nature of the condition. Needed is a definition that captures the essence of the phenomenon.

Selznick's (1957) definition, with minor modifications, is helpful here. Autonomy, as used in relation to administrative conservatorship, is defined as a *condition of independence sufficient to permit public bureaucracies to preserve their distinctive values, competence, and role.* To create and sustain this condition of independence and, in turn, to preserve the integrity of public bureaucracies, the administrative conservator must engage in a wide range of actions that address both the internal state of the institution and its position in the larger political community.

This discussion thus far suggests that institutional autonomy is a complex, multifaceted concept with fine and subtle distinctions. As previously indicated, there are the *essential properties* of the condition itself (i.e., independence and self-governing). There are also a range of *strategies* for achieving and maintaining institutional autonomy (i.e., insulation from dangerous external pressures and the protection of jurisdictional boundaries) and the *benefits* of institutional autonomy: "long range, flexibility, purposive nonpolitical management" (Selznick, 1992, p. 344). The different aspects of autonomy should be kept in mind throughout this discussion.

I must emphasize once again that the autonomy of public bureaucracies is contextual. The condition of independence sufficient for public bureaucracies to preserve their distinctive value, competence, and role is determined by the overarching framework of the American political system in general and the specific public policy domain in particular. To drive this point home, I use two concrete examples; one involves the Federal Reserve Bank and the other, the National Endowment for the Arts (NEA).

The Federal Reserve (the "Fed," as it is commonly called) is often characterized as the "independent" central bank of the United States—a designation its governing board is quick to clarify. In referring to the Fed's independent status, an official publication states: "Because the Federal Reserve works within the framework of the overall objectives of economic and financial policy established by the government, it is more accurate to characterize the System as 'independent within government' " (Board of Governors of the Federal Reserve System, 1985, p. 2).

The Fed is primarily responsible for fostering a "flow of money and credit that will facilitate orderly economic growth, a stable dollar, and long-run balance in our international payments" (Board of Governors of the Federal Reserve System, 1963, p. 1). The dominant value governing the Fed's operation is the economic and financial security and stability of the United States. Because the Fed's policies and actions have a significant influence on the U.S. economy, the institution is insulated from extraneous political pressures. Although the Fed was established by an act of the Congress in 1913, it is a privately owned nonprofit institution. Private ownership was established to eliminate political control of the Federal Reserve system. The central bank's seven-member governing body and its chair are appointed to fixed terms by the president of the United States with the advice and consent of Congress (the chair and vice chair serve a 4-year term; other board members serve 14-year terms). The appointment process and tenure of the Board of Governors buffers the Fed from political interference. The Fed generates income from services offered to banks and thus does not depend on Congress for budgetary appropriations.

The Fed's insulation from extraneous political pressures gives the Board of Governors and its chair the flexibility to establish long-range monetary policy. It also allows the Fed to effectively administer its other responsibilities such as supervision of member banks and custodianship of required reserves without direct involvement of partisan politics ("nonpolitical management").

The public policy domain or institutional context of the NEA is different from that of the Federal Reserve Bank. Consequently, the condition of independence sufficient for the NEA to preserve its distinctive values, competence, and role is also different. The NEA is and should be concerned with the *degree of control it exercises over decision-making processes in awarding financial support to art institutions and individual artists.* A core value governing this process is artistic freedom. Consequently, matters concerning NEA's autonomy are inextricably interwoven with functions and processes that promote and protect this value.

Since its establishment in 1965, the NEA has relied on a grant-making process that uses peer review panels. The peer review panel's structure and composition are intended to ensure that grants are awarded on the basis of artistic quality rather than their content. The NEA's autonomy (and possibly survival) is threatened when policies or actions interfere with its capacity to award grants on the basis of the peer review panel's judgment of artistic quality. This became readily apparent in the late 1980s when the NEA became embroiled in a bitter controversy over the works of two artists who received financial support from the agency.[10]

In the spring of 1989, Senators Alfonse D'Amato (R-New York), Jesse Helms (R-North Carolina), and several other lawmakers waged a widely publicized campaign against government involvement in funding art. The lawmakers attempted to restrict the NEA's ability to give grants to artists whose work they considered indecent or obscene. Senator Helms severely criticized the NEA in particular for supporting the works of Andres Serrano (whom he characterized as a jerk) and Robert Mapplethorpe. Serrano's work *Piss Christ*, a photograph illustrating a crucifix immersed in a vessel filled with urine, was described as offensive, blasphemous, and a form of religious bigotry. Mapplethorpe's traveling exhibition of photographs, *Robert Mapplethorpe: The Perfect Moment*, created a stir because it included many homoerotic and sadomasochistic images. Anti-NEA forces in Congress characterized the photographs as antifamily and threatened to prohibit the NEA from providing financial support to any art institution that showed the exhibition. (Apparently the Corcoran Gallery in Washington, D.C., took this threat seriously; it canceled an announced showing of the exhibition.)

In the NEA 1990 appropriation bill, Senator Helms introduced an amendment that prevented the agency from funding

1. obscene or indecent materials, including but not limited to depictions of sadomasochism, homoeroticism, the exploitation of children, or individuals engaged in sex acts;
2. materials which denigrate the objects or beliefs of the adherents of a particular religion or non-religion; or
3. material which denigrates, debases, or reviles a person, group, or class of citizens on the basis of race, creed, sex, handicap, age, or national origin. (*Congressional Record*, 1989, S. 8806)

After a heated debate in Congress and an intense lobbying effort on the part of the art community, the Helms amendment was defeated. A watered-down version of the Helms amendment became law as Congress reached a compromise and substituted the Supreme Court's obscenity standard handed down in *Miller v. California* (1973).[11] To comply with Public Law 101-121 (the 1990 NEA appropriation bill), the NEA stipulated that grant recipients sign a statement pledging not to use public funds for the creation of obscene works of art. (This requirement was abandoned a year later after a successful court challenge.) Congress also adopted a modified provision contained in the Senate version of the bill that reprimanded the Institute for Contemporary Art and the Southeastern Center for Contemporary Art for showing the Serrano and Mapplethorpe exhibits. The Senate bill denied both art institutions NEA funding for 5 years. In the compromise bill, the NEA was required to inform Congress 30 days in advance before awarding grants to either institution.

The NEA case is illuminating in several respects. First, it illustrates that the condition of independence necessary for an agency to preserve its distinctive competence is intimately related to its public policy domain or institutional context and the prevailing values operating within that domain. For example, by the very nature of its function, the NEA is embedded in the public cultural policy domain, which is governed by values related to artistic freedom. The NEA case also provides additional evidence that insulation from political interference is a common strategy for achieving and maintaining institutional autonomy and that this strategy is operationalized in a variety of ways. The way that the NEA attempts to insulate itself from political pressures is distinct from that of the Federal Reserve. The Fed's autonomy was achieved through its private nonprofit status, the appointment process and long-term tenure of its governing board, and its independent funding status. In contrast, the NEA tries to achieve and maintain political insulation by adopting a narrow set of artistic criteria for renewing funding alternatives and by using a peer review panel that consists of professionals within the various art disciplinary forms.

The NEA case demonstrates that institutional autonomy is not permanent or guaranteed. Consequently, the administrative conservator should carefully monitor and evaluate strategies used to acquire and maintain institutional autonomy. Such actions are needed on an ongoing basis to buffer public bureaucracies against what Selznick (1992) referred to earlier as "perverse and self-defeating isolation" (p. 334).

Institutional Responsiveness and Administrative Conservatorship

Similar to other complex organizations, public bureaucracies must *adapt* to a constantly and rapidly changing political, economic, and social environment to prosper. The term *adapt* is emphasized because it has special meaning in organizational analysis. In the business management literature, for example, *adapt* and its cognates (*adaptation* and *adaptiveness*) typically refer to an organization's capacity and willingness to respond to environmental changes that threaten its survival. The key word here is *survival*. Business management scholars speak a matter-of-fact language and make no apologies that long-term organizational survival is the bottom line; organizational adaptiveness and, in turn, responsiveness are merely means to achieve this end.

There is some merit to this purely instrumental mode of thinking. Organizations do perish in large numbers, as Herbert Kaufman (1991) observes:

> There is no doubt that organizations do, in significant numbers, cease to exist. We know that business failures in thousands occur every year. We know that government agencies, such as those that flourished in the days of the New Deal . . . and World War II . . . are no longer around. Indeed, whole civilizations have virtually disappeared. Small wonder that eminent students of organizations, such as Chester Barnard, concluded that long-lived organizations are atypical and that most organizations disintegrate after comparatively short periods of existence. To be sure, there is some evidence that long life may not be quite as unusual as is commonly assumed; the weight of the evidence and of informed opinion, however, is on the other side. (p. 12)

But an overemphasis on organizational survival can lead down the dangerous path of opportunism. As Selznick (1957) cautions, the perils of traveling down this path are real. The shortsightedness and recklessness that is so much a part of opportunism poses a serious threat to institutional integrity. The institution's character may become "attenuated and confused" (p. 145); its leadership cadre may allow the institution to drift by relinquishing policy- and decision-making authority to powerful external forces; and foreign elements may infiltrate the institution and eventually control major functions and processes, thus leading to a complete lose of autonomy. Any one of these events could undermine institutional integrity. For example, during the 1989 controversy, the leadership of the NEA could have easily pursued opportunistic strategies that undermined the agency's integrity. If the NEA's leadership had succumbed to political pressures exerted by Senator Jesse Helms and others and had allowed Congress to determine the aesthetic quality and content of art in exchange for guaranteed statutory reauthorization and a substantial budget increase, the agency could have more easily survived but would have sacrificed its integrity in the process. The NEA also would have seriously undermined its integrity if the agency's leadership surrendered all of its authority over determining the composition and structure of the peer review panels.

I noted earlier in the discussion of Selznick's theory of autonomy and responsiveness that selective adaptation is needed to avoid opportunism and its destructive consequences. Selective adaptation requires that those entrusted with the preservation of institutional integrity resist the temptation to respond to every environmental pressure. All environmental pressures are not created equal when measured against their effect on institutional integrity. The determination of which pressure to seriously consider and when to do so is a complex process that should be guided by a fidelity to the institution's distinctive competence, values, and role. When successful, selective or controlled adaptation translates into responsiveness. In this context, responsiveness refers to the "reconstruction of self and outreach to others" (Selznick, 1992, p. 338). For example, the Federal Reserve is responsive when the chair of the Board of Governors reaches out to the president, the Congress, the secretary of the Treasury, and the Council of Economic Advisers in an effort to provide and solicit information that assists in the development of long-term (and in some instances short-term) monetary policy objectives.

It is obvious that the Federal Reserve example addresses only the outreach component of the responsiveness definition. But what about the reconstruction of self, the other essential component of responsiveness? When should administrative officials make substantive revisions in established institutional structures, processes, policies, and rules? This question is controversial, especially when raised in connection with the topic of bureaucratic responsiveness.

Writers concerned with the role of public bureaucracies in American constitutional democracy have passionately debated for some time the question of bureaucratic responsiveness (see Saltzstein, 1985).[12] The line of demarcation is sharply drawn between two opposing factions. On one side are the traditional hierarchical theorists. As mentioned in Chapter 1, scholars such as Theodore Lowi, Herman Finer, and Charles Hyneman argue that administrative officials are responsive to the extent they strictly follow the dictates and commands of *elected officials.* Traditional hierarchical theorists operate under the assumption that elected political officials (especially legislative officials) have a privileged or superior role in the American political system because they are elected by the people.

On the other side of the line are scholars who reject the idea that supremacy rests with elected political officials. Scholars such as David Truman, Norton Long, Robert Dahl, Herbert Storing, and John Rohr argue that public bureaucracies and their administrative officials are responsible for, as well as accountable to, the *public.* In describing the public-oriented perspective, Grace Hall Saltzstein (1985) writes that "supremacy rests with the people and the object of their choice as sovereign people is [quoting Rohr] not a group of legislators who will carry out their will, but rather a constitutional order which balances the powers they have delegated to all three equal branches" (p. 290).

Despite the fundamental differences that exist between the hierarchical and nonhierarchical conceptions of bureaucratic responsiveness, there are several important similarities. For example, implicit in each conception is the principle of *immediate action.* Public bureaucracies and administrative officials are considered responsive if they take immediate action to address the expressed needs, wishes, and desires of either elected political officials or the public. Each conception also places a heavy emphasis on the willingness and capacity of public bureaucracies to respond to *current* or popular policy initiatives.

The similarities between the two dominant conceptions of bureaucratic responsiveness are far more revealing than their differences. By overemphasizing immediate action and a receptiveness to current policy initiatives, each approach ignores or downplays the significance of preserving past public policy commitments that have been translated into law and entrusted to public bureaucracies for their care. This is unfortunate because public bureaucracies and administrative officials should be sensitive to both current and past public policy commitments. B. Dan Wood (1988) makes a similar point:

> Theories of bureaucracies must make clear the dual capacity in which administrative institutions operate. Bureaucracies translate current events and ideology into change, making government responsive to popular initiatives. They also manifest past events and ideologies, thereby insulating government from the continual progression of passing stimuli. They are reflections of both policy in the present and in the past. In this dual role, they operate as agents of the law who, by virtue of delegated authority, are transformed into quasi principals.
>
> Public bureaucracies are legitimate principals charged with the obligations of providing responsiveness and stability. Like elected institutions of government, they have representational tasks. They represent all of those static coalitions from the past that successfully had their policy ambitions transformed into law. Bureaucracy derives its legitimate claim to principality from the laws and regulations that flowed from past coalitions. (p. 231)

If public bureaucracies have, to use Wood's words, a "dual capacity" as presumably they do, then it is possible to conclude that *preserving institutional integrity is and should be another form of bureaucratic responsiveness.* Thus, there are now three dominant conceptions of bureaucratic responsiveness: (a) responsiveness to elected political officials, (b) responsiveness to the public, and (c) responsiveness to an institution's legally embodied practices and

traditions. Administrative conservatorship not only involves outreach to others but also entails a receptivity and openness to
changes in established institutional functions and processes as
prescribed by elected political officials and the public, while at the
same time remaining faithful to the values and unifying principles
that define an agency's distinctive competence. This conception
of bureaucratic responsiveness is complex and captures the essence of the necessity of balancing the inherent tension in the
political system between the need to serve and the need to preserve. Different orientations may at times conflict. In such situations, what is the administrative conservator to do? The answer
to this question is this: *The Conservator should take orders from the
situation: The "law of the situation" governs what should be done.*[13]

The previously discussed case regarding the NEA provides a
concrete example that helps make my point. The NEA seeks to
preserve institutional autonomy by exerting as much control as
possible over the grant decision-making process. During the Serrano and Mapplethorpe controversy, critics attacked the agency's
system of peer review panels. Critics charged that NEA's peer
review panels were exclusive and incestuous because they con-
sisted of "individuals from a small number of cultural centers who
share similar aesthetic values and who promote each other's artistic interests and careers" (Mulcaly, 1992, p. 78). This charge led to
related questions concerning panel representation and the public
interest.

To respond to the desires and criticisms of elected political
officials, segments of the American public, and the independent
commission established by Congress, the NEA's leadership revised
established policies and procedures relating to the peer review
panel. Peer advisory panels now consist of informed laypersons as
well as discipline-based artists. By changing the composition of
the peer review panels, the NEA's leadership was responsive to
elected political officials and to the public. The agency's leadership was also responsive from the standpoint of the institutions
because they successfully resisted attempts to diminish the role of
peer review panels in determining artistic excellence. In doing so,
the NEA's leadership protected the value of artistic freedom and
preserved the agency's integrity.

The Continuum of Leadership Roles and
the Preservation of Institutional Integrity

As the preceding discussion suggests, the preservation of institutional integrity is a complex process that involves maintaining institutional autonomy while at the same time remaining responsive to elected political officials, the public, and the institution itself. The preservation of institutional integrity may be best understood by examining leadership in public bureaucracies from a historical perspective, focusing on the evolution of institutions during long periods. Special attention is devoted to the critical tasks and roles performed by leaders in response to prevailing historical conditions (see March & Olsen, 1989; Selznick, 1957; Tushman, Newman, & Nadler, 1988).

As public bureaucracies evolve and develop through time, the administrative conservator is called on to perform different leadership roles. These roles may be placed along a continuum and differentiated by the type and scope of institutional change involved. At one end of the continuum is what Carl J. Friedrich (1961) describes as "initiating leadership" (p. 21). The initiating leadership role requires that the administrative conservator pursue innovative courses of action to preserve institutional integrity. When it is essential for conservation of the principles underlying its distinctive competence, the conservator seeks to create or establish a new system of institutional values. The institution builder, innovator, and transformational leader are identifiable forms of initiating leadership discussed in the literature.[14] Change and innovation sought by the administrative conservator is not the same as the heroic administrator's reckless abandon because it is done not for its own sake or to boost the administrator's image as a "mover and a shaker" but to respond to new forces and demands in the environment and to preserve an institution's integrity. This type of change is equivalent to the Burkean notion of reform. The change and innovation initiated by the administrative conservator is guided by a fidelity to the institution's values and unifying principles.

Initiating leadership is concerned primarily with *strategic change*. This type of change addresses the entire institution, including its mission, values, personnel, and technologies. Strategic change consists of two analytically distinct types: *frame breaking* and *frame bending* (see Tushman et al., 1988). Frame-breaking changes are initiated in response to internal pressures and external events that threaten the institution's integrity. These changes require a radical break from an institution's established conduct. Because frame-breaking changes are revolutionary, they are hard to implement and are inherently shattering to the organization. They should probably be carried out quite rarely. The administrative conservator who breaks frames will realize that great costs are incurred. Public agencies, like private organizations, tend to resist innovations that are inconsistent with the performance of existing tasks, and overcoming this resistance will drain energy in and of itself (see J. Q. Wilson, 1989, chap. 12). In addition, revolutionary changes are often close to impossible to implement because of the far greater number of external constraints (laws, regulations, rules, interest groups, legislative committees, etc.) that govern the activities of public agencies.

Frame-bending changes are also made in response to external events. These events, however, are typically seen coming over the horizon. Frame-bending changes differ from frame-breaking changes in that they do not require a drastic departure from the past. Rather, these changes build on tradition as they "emphasize continuity with the past, particularly values of the past" (Nadler, 1988, p. 72). Frame-bending change may be large scale and may be made within the existing institutional frame. Public bureaucracies are more inclined to implement frame-bending changes for the same reasons that prompt them to resist frame-breaking changes.

At the other end of the continuum is *protecting leadership,* another leadership role discussed by C. J. Friedrich (1961). Protecting leadership provides *security* for an institution and its "particular way of life, its culture, its values, beliefs, and interest" (p. 21). Protecting leadership seeks to strengthen institutional functions, processes, and values and at the same time guards against excessive opportunism. This form of leadership is best reflected in Selznick's institutional leader who defends the institution's integrity after it is firmly established over time.

Protecting leadership concentrates on either *incremental change* or what I call *zero-change.* Incremental change addresses specific aspects of the institution and also consists of two types: fine-tuning

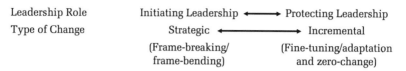

Figure 2.1. A continuum of leadership roles performed by administrative conservator and corresponding types of change.

and adaptive (Nadler, 1988). Fine-tuning changes are designed to increase efficiency and coordination of institutional functions and processes as well as to reinforce values, beliefs, and myths. Such changes are made on an ongoing basis. For example, the administrative conservator might seek to refine existing policies and procedures relating to the hiring and promotion of personnel.

Adaptive changes are pursued in response to external events. These changes are relatively minor in the scheme of things because they require small-scale adjustments in how the institution performs its existing tasks. Both fine-tuning and adaptive changes are add-ons—they are "added on to existing tasks without changing the core tasks" of an institution (J. Q. Wilson, 1989, p. 225).

Zero-change means exactly what the term implies. Strategic or incremental changes are resisted, especially if such changes threaten to undermine an institution's integrity and result in opportunism. Many writers tend to labor under the erroneous assumption that change is inherently good. Sir Francis Bacon's dictum "He who will not apply new remedies must expect new evils, for time is the greatest innovation" deserves attention, but we must remember that some changes may do more harm than good.[15] The continuum of leadership roles performed by the administrative conservator and the types of change associated with each are shown in Figure 2.1.

The effective performance of both the initiating and protecting leadership role is not necessarily contingent on particular personality orientations or traits. Although it is true that some individuals may possess certain personality characteristics that favor one role over another, they may be capable of effectively performing both. Nor am I ruling out the possibility that some individuals may be overly committed to particular outlooks and orientations and thus are less adaptable to changing conditions.

Yet there is a dark side to both the initiating and protecting leadership roles. Each role can undermine an institution's integrity if taken to extremes or employed at inappropriate times in an institution's history. For example, scholars have documented that institutions experience "relatively long periods of stability (equilibrium) punctuated by compact, qualitative, metamorphic change (revolution)" (Gersick, 1991, p. 12).[16] From these findings, one can conclude that the role of initiating leadership may not be well suited for periods of relative stability. Stable conditions require a different role orientation, as Chester I. Barnard (1948) suggests:

> Stable conditions . . . may be complex and very large scale; but they are comparatively free from violent changes and extreme uncertainties of *unusual* character or implying important hazards. The behavior of leaders under such conditions may be calm, deliberate, reflective, or anticipatory of future consequences. . . . Leadership . . . must be carried on without the aid of emotional drives and obvious necessities and against the indifference often accompanying lack of danger, excitement and sentiment. Stable conditions call for self-restraint, deliberation, and refinement techniques, qualities that some men who are good leaders under tense conditions are unable to develop. (p. 91)

In contrast, the role of protecting leadership may be destructive during periods of instability and uncertainty. Because protecting leadership entails guarding traditional views and values that exist at a particular time, the leader may resist all types of change, even though some form of change is needed to address internal and external events that threaten institutional integrity. Moreover, the leader may rely on past strategies and practices that are no longer appropriate for changing conditions. The lesson here is that the forces that preserve an institution through time may be the same ones that undermine its integrity.

The Functions of Administrative Conservatorship

The foregoing discussion suggests that the administrative conservator is summoned to perform different leadership roles ranging from initiating to protecting as a means of preserving institutional integrity. These roles specify, in a general way, the behaviors and orientations needed to address conditions and problems associated with a given institution's stage of historical development. How these roles relate to the preservation of institutional integrity becomes more apparent when examining some of the critical functions performed by the administrative conservator.

Conserving Mission

The concept of mission occupies a central place in the analysis of complex organizations. It is indeed rare to find any serious discourse on executive leadership that does not pay homage to the mission's special function in organizational affairs. Although theorists employ a multitude of terms to describe the concept (e.g., purpose, official goals, etc.), mission in its most basic form determines the institution's reason for existence.

The symbiotic relationship between the task of mission definition and responsible leadership behavior is well documented. Writers discuss at great length the connection between mission definition and leadership effectiveness. Selznick (1957) writes that "leadership is irresponsible when it fails to set goals and therefore lets the institution drift" (p. 25).

The concept of mission takes on significant and complex meaning when discussed in the context of public bureaucracies, especially because administrative executives are not given the responsibility for mission definition. They "may have no presumptive right to set purpose" (Bower, 1977, p. 132). The mission of administrative institutions is supposedly determined by legislative mandate, judicial decisions, and executive orders that delegate authority to administrative officials to act as agents in the administration of policy objectives. Administrative officials must, of necessity, use their discretion to make concrete decisions that provide meaning to a multiplicity of diverse, conflicting, and ambiguous policy objectives. It is the responsibility of administrative executives to ensure that the spirit as well as the letter of statutory mandates, executive orders, and judicial decrees is fully realized. In other words, administrative executives have an obligation to preserve the values that the constitutional masters have granted legitimacy by enshrining in law, albeit vague and contradictory. With this in mind, conserving the mission of public bureaucracies is a critical function of administrative conservatorship.

Conserving Values

The second function performed by the administrative conservator involves conserving the values of public bureaucracies. The conservator is responsible for the protection of values that help establish and maintain an agency's distinctive competence and role. Conserving the values of public bureaucracies is largely the responsibility of the executive cadre, that group of individuals who "reflect the basic policies of the organization in their own outlooks" (Selznick, 1957, p. 105). Selznick describes the executive cadre as the institutional core. The executive cadre performs a vital function in preserving the integrity of public bureaucracies because its members are entrusted with the transmittal and protection of core agency values. Because the executive cadre members have an indispensable role in preserving core institutional values, maintaining their viability is a critical function of administrative conservatorship. The term *viability* refers to the executive cadre's strength and thereby capacity to protect core institutional values that are intensely held and widely shared from serious corruption. The maintenance of a viable executive cadre requires that the administrative conservator control the members' demographic composition, protect their autonomy, and maintain their commitment to core agency values.

Conserving Support

The maintenance of both external and internal support is the third critical function performed by the administrative conservator. The preservation of external support is of great importance. Public bureaucracies are influenced by an external environment composed of individuals, groups, and organizations of stakeholders interested in and affected by the activities of bureaucracies. These stakeholders represent a variety of actors who may be either allies or adversaries. Moreover, stakeholders differ in the amount of influence and control they exert on the institution. Because the survival of public bureaucracies is contingent on the steady flow of needed resources, the administrative conservator must develop and sustain good relationships with stakeholders who provide resources and necessary support for institutional activities (see March & Simon, 1958; Pfeffer & Salancik, 1978; Thompson, 1967).

To secure and preserve external support, the administrative conservator must provide inducement for stakeholders to participate actively in advancing institutional goals (see Barnard, 1938; March & Simon, 1958). In exchange for these inducements, stakeholders make contributions in the form of behaviors, resources, and capabilities necessary to sustain the institution's integrity—and thereby distinctive competence. As a result, the administrative conservator is continuously involved in both formal and informal exchange relationships with external stakeholders to secure and maintain resources and support for institutional activities. These relationships are evaluated, renewed, honored, and serviced on an ongoing basis to ensure that they are in the long-term interest of the agency. Although external support is critical to agency survival, securing it can also lead to a loss of discretion and limited autonomy (see Selznick, 1957; Thompson, 1967; J. Q. Wilson, 1989, esp. chap. 4). The administrative conservator must continually monitor and evaluate external arrangements and inducements offered to secure contributions from influential stakeholders without losing autonomy.

The administrative conservator must also sustain support among internal interest groups for larger institutional aims. Because organizations are composed of a multitude of formal and informal groups seeking to promote their own vested interests that may or may not be consistent with larger organizational goals, this is not an easy task. Internal interest groups are not "wholly controllable by official authority" and thus may "subvert the enterprise or lend it strength" (Selznick, 1957, p. 94). The administrative conservator must constantly engage in activities that instill in organizational members a sense of loyalty and identification with the enterprise. In other words, he or she must "bind parochial group egotism to larger loyalties and aspirations" (p. 94).

Notes

1. For a discussion of the distinction between the quantitative and qualitative dimensions of growth, see Starbuck (1965), who describes changes in an organization's qualitative dimension as development.

2. March and Olsen (1989) describe an efficient historical process as "one that moves rapidly to a unique solution, conditional on current environmental conditions, and is thus independent of the historical path" (p. 8). For an excellent critique of progress, see Lasch (1991).

3. Wolin (1960) specifically attacks Selznick's works of 1948, 1952, and 1957.

4. Because Spicer and I (1993) ground our arguments in classical constitutional theory, it makes sense that we are labeled (and rightly so) conservative. Classical constitutional theory has been criticized by some political scientists for its inherent conservatism. See, for example, James W. Ceaser, 1993.

5. Many of the ideas expressed by Lowi (1993a) in this article are included in several of his other works (1979, 1993b).

6. I use the word *preservation* instead of *defense* because of its proactive (as opposed to reactive) qualities.

7. From *The Moral Commonwealth: Social Theory and the Promise of Community,* pp. 322-324, by P. Selznick, 1992, Berkeley: University of California Press. Copyright © 1992 by University of California Press. Reprinted by permission granted by the Regents of the University of California and the University of California Press.

8. I would like to thank John Rohr (personal communication, n.d.) for suggesting this example concerning his use of the term *autonomy.*

9. The debate among legal scholars concerning the "delegation doctrine" suggests that there is a genuine concern about the legislative branch's potential loss of autonomy. In April 1986, the journal *American University Law Review* organized a symposium on this subject (see "Symposium on Administrative Law: The Uneasy Constitutional Status of Administrative Agencies," 1987). Symposium participants included, among others, Theodore Lowi, Ernest Gellhorn, David Schoenbrod, and Richard Pierce.

10. For excellent discussions of the NEA controversy, see Andrew Buchwalter (1992) and Richard Bolton (1992). My discussion of the NEA controversy draws heavily on these works.

11. For discussion of the *Miller v. California* (1973) decision and its bearing on the NEA, see Carole S. Vance (1992) and Gloria C. Phares (1992).

12. Saltzstein (1985) analyzes how scholars use the concept of bureaucratic responsiveness as well as the difficulties associated with such use.

13. The idea of the "law of the situation" was developed by Mary Parker Follett. See Henry C. Metcalf and L. Urwick (1940).

14. For a discussion of leaders who effectively performed the "initiating leadership" role, see Terry L. Cooper and N. Dale Wright (1992) and Jameson Doig and Erwin Hargrove (1987). Although Doig and Hargrove describe the leaders in their book as entrepreneurs (a concept I have criticized on numerous occasions), some of the figures profiled in the book seem to fit the description of the administrative conservator. Nancy Hanks, the former director of the National Endowment for the Arts, and Elmer Staats, former Comptroller General, General Accounting Office, are cases in point.

15. I am indebted to John Gardner (personal communication, August 8, 1986) for bringing this quote to my attention.

16. Gersick's (1991) "punctuated equilibrium" paradigm is currently challenging the traditional, Darwinian notion of gradual evolution. Although I agree with proponents of punctuated equilibrium that institutions experience relatively long periods of stability punctuated by abrupt change, I do not, however, agree with the contention that such change is always revolutionary. Abrupt changes can produce reforms. Reform and revolution are not synonymous.

3

Conserving Mission

I DOUBT THAT ANYONE who studies administrative leadership would voice much opposition to the statement that leaders have primary responsibility for the organization's mission. But when there is serious discussion about the exact nature and scope of this responsibility, the silence abruptly ends. Many of those who write about private business leadership assert that administrative leaders are responsible for defining and redefining the organization's mission as well as for ensuring its acceptance by employees (see Bennis & Nanus, 1985; Tichy & Devanna, 1986). The mission is considered a cornerstone in the formulation of a competitive organizational strategy and thus demands the undivided attention of administrative leaders. Leaders who fail to define what business the enterprise should be in and why it exists are harshly criticized and accused of defaulting in their responsibility (see Drucker, 1985; Selznick, 1957).

Scholars of public administration and political science voice a different opinion. They contend that administrative executives do not, and should not, have responsibility for defining the mission of public bureaucracies: The Constitution assigns this responsibility primarily to elected political leaders (for discussion, see Perry & Kraemer, 1983). Through legislative mandates and other legally binding acts, political leaders determine the mission of public bureaucracies, their reason for existence, and their principal products and services. This line of argument leads many writers to the seemingly inescapable conclusion that administrative executives are delegated authority and responsibility for simply *interpreting* the mission of public bureaucracies in relating appropriate means to ends. Although this idea informs the thinking and theorizing of many scholars, it must be viewed with a degree of skepticism for several reasons.

First, the assertion that administrative executives are responsible simply for mission interpretation reflects the influence and limitations of the traditional hierarchical view of public administrators in the American democratic system. Unfortunately, the task of mission interpretation from this traditional view is misconceived as a simplistic, instrumental, and mechanical exercise. There is an underlying assumption that the intentions of political leaders are (or should be) clearly stated in legal mandates and, thus, all administrative executives need to do is to "read the text" and act accordingly. They are not to assume an active role by reading anything into the text of mandating statutes because the interpretive enterprise is merely a matter of doing what the law says. In this view, mission interpretation is guided by the same logic and rationale used to justify what constitutional law scholars describe as mechanical jurisprudence and others refer to as "originalism." In its most extreme forms, originalism suggests that strict adherence to the text and intentions of the Republic's founders is necessary to constrain the discretion of decision makers and to guarantee that constitutional interpretations remain consistent over time. Strict originalism has been rejected by constitutional law scholars because the approach fails to consider the "open-textured quality of language" and its "social and linguistic context"

(Brest, 1980, p. 223). Moreover, strict originalism is based on a flawed assumption that one can interpret the intentions of the founders with a certain degree of mechanical precision (I will return to this matter shortly). Public administration scholars should also question this narrow, instrumental view of mission interpretation for similar reasons.

The second reason that the purely instrumental view of mission interpretation is problematic results from the complexity of mission interpretation. Implicit in the instrumental notion of mission interpretation is the assumption that the task of mission definition is more complex and thus holds a more prominent position in the realm of administration. It is true that the mission cannot be interpreted if it is not defined. But the ordering of a task is not, and should not be, the sole criterion for deciding its importance and complexity. The tasks of mission definition and mission interpretation are equally important and inherently complex in nature. Interpreting the intent of political leaders as embodied in legal mandates is extremely important in a representative democracy because such mandates reflect the values and aspirations of the citizenry. Furthermore, the act and process of interpreting legal mandates with any degree of certainty and precision is a complex and difficult undertaking. As scholars from a variety of disciplines have argued, interpreting the text of any document is a complicated intellectual endeavor because of the ambiguous, incomplete, and contradictory nature of most, if not all, texts and because of the difficulty of determining an author's intent and purpose. Legal scholar James Boyd White (1982) makes the argument that "there are in both legal and nonlegal texts enough real ambiguities and uncertainties to make it . . . absurd to speak as if the meaning of a text were simply there to be observed and demonstrated in some quasi-scientific way" (p. 417). He further observes:

> Intention can, after all, be stated with generality or particularity, as a matter of motive or a matter of aim; and we are always subject to conflicts in our intentions, many of which are somewhat unconscious and out of our control. To try to follow the intention of the writer seems an inherently unstable procedure, leading to a radical conceptual collapse. (p. 419)[1]

The complexity of the interpretive task is also compounded because the "one best way" to interpret the textual meaning of a document does not exist. A text is subject to multiple interpretations, each guided by different theories, schools of thought, and traditions of interpretation (see Brest, 1980; R. Dworkin, 1982). Authors can neither control nor predict all the various ways a text may be interpreted. This applies to the text of mandating statutes drafted by political leaders. It is true that the intents of political leaders, once embodied within the text of a statute, determine the ground rules about how the text may be interpreted. This does not, however, lead to the foregone conclusion that they have a monopoly on knowledge or superior insight into the "correct" reading of the statute. The very nature of legal statutes precludes such possibilities. Austin Sarat (1987) makes a cogent argument along these lines. In quoting Stanley Fish, the English and humanities scholar who has written extensively in the area of legal and literary theory, Sarat states:

> Any text, whatever its conditions of production, is capable of being appropriated by any number of persons and read in relation to concerns the speaker could not have foreseen. Indeed, it is standard strategy in literary criticism to detach a text from what might have seemed to be its severely limiting original situation and turn it into the kind of text that speaks to all men in all circumstances. The author and his intentions are not ignored, but neither are they accorded primacy. Texts are not owned by their authors. Indeed, authors assume the position of participants in a discourse about textual meaning and significance. Texts invite and provoke interpretive disputes; authors provide no final resolution. Legal texts in general, and the Constitution in particular, are no exception although they, perhaps somewhat more than other texts, are invested in the effort to manage the terms on which such disputes occur. (pp. 257-258)

The third reason that the narrow view of mission interpretation is flawed relates to the idea of *authority*. When writers say that public administrators are "delegated authority" for mission interpretation and implementation, they often rely on the hierarchical model's prescription of how authority and responsibility are transferred, delegated, and exercised within the American political system (see DeGeorge, 1985, esp. chap. 5). This is understandable considering the structure of our constitutional government. Although the hierarchical model of authority has been criticized by legal scholars, it is generally accepted because the courts have traditionally used the model in "adjudicating the legitimacy of administrative authority" (Bayles, 1987, p. 290). Unfortunately, the same cannot be said with respect to how public administration scholars apply the model to explain the responsibility and actions of administrative executives.

When discussing delegated authority, it is not uncommon for public administration theorists to focus exclusively on the notion of *delegation*, that is, "the act of empowering to act for another" (*Merriam Webster's Collegiate Dictionary*, 1993, p. 305), ignoring the idea of *authority*. This error is committed by a broad cross-section of scholars, especially those who champion a hybrid version of economic agency theory to legitimate the role of public administrators in governance.[2] In its purest form, agency theory suggests that social relationships can be explained as a series of contractual arrangements involving two parties: a principal and an agent. The agent acts for and on behalf of the principal who delegates some of his or her authority to the agent. Because it is only a matter of time until the agent resorts to his or her natural self-serving behaviors, agency theorists assert that specific mechanisms should be adopted to ensure that the agent continues to act for and on behalf of the principal. If cleverly designed and instituted, these mechanisms can minimize "agency loss," that is, the degree to which the agent deviates from adhering to the desires of the principal (Donaldson, 1990, p. 369; Perrow, 1986).

Despite agency theory's heavy emphasis on methodological individualism, its narrow view of human behavior and motivation, and its predominantly negative moral characterization of the individual, a cadre of public administration scholars has borrowed the theory to explain the role and responsibilities of public administrators in democratic government (Donaldson, 1990). In transferring agency theory to the public sector, theorists have created a hybrid version of the theory by modifying several of its basic assumptions. The "acting for" relationship has been extended beyond the individual level of analysis to include organizations and society. And the inherently negative, self-serving view of the administrator has been replaced with the Hegelian notion that public administrators are (or should be) trustworthy and noble individuals who work for the good of society.[3]

Both the pure and hybrid forms of agency theory concentrate on the agent's obligation in fulfilling his or her responsibility with respect to acting for and on behalf of the principal. In the purest form, the relationship is viewed primarily from the vantage point of the principal. In the hybrid form, the relationship is viewed from the agent's perspective. Little, if any, systematic attention is devoted to the concept of authority, although it is central to the principal-agent relationship. If the concept of authority is discussed, it is often confused with related concepts, especially power.[4] Writers take for granted that the agent must have a sufficient amount of authority to fulfill the responsibilities to the principal. Consequently, there is no need to focus on the concept of authority. This is an egregious error because the concept of authority is too important from a practical and theoretical perspective to be given passing attention.

I am not objecting to the assertion that public administrators act for and on behalf of others, because obviously they do. My point is that acting for another is only one component of the administrative leadership equation. Another significant part of the equation relates to the concept of authority. When political leaders delegate authority to public administrators, they are not only empowering them to act for and on behalf of others but also conferring the responsibility to preserve and nurture the authority of public bureaucracies to act within a specific realm of social action and to pursue specific policy objectives. In other words, public administrators are also entrusted with the responsibility of preserving and nurturing the authority embodied in legal mandates that determine the mission of public bureaucracies. This is what I mean when I speak of conserving the mission of public bureaucracies. Because the concept of authority is central to the notion of conserving mission, it is necessary to explain what authority is and how the concept relates to the preservation of institutional integrity and, in turn, administrative conservatorship.

The Authority of Public Bureaucracies

Scholars across a spectrum of disciplines have attempted to discover the hidden secrets of the phenomenon known as authority (see DeGeorge, 1976; C. J. Friedrich, 1958b; Pennock & Chapman, 1987; Raz, 1979). They have attempted to define and describe the nature of authority as well as identify its various types, sources, and functions. These scholarly efforts have produced a vast and impressive body of literature on authority, in general, and political authority, in particular. The lack of consensus on a single definition, theory, or classification scheme of authority should not be interpreted to mean that scholars know little about authority. In fact, we know a great deal about authority. We know that authority embraces several other concepts such as power, reason, legitimacy, obedience, and consent, as well as advice and command. We also know that authority can be vested in an impersonal entity such as a constitution or in a person by virtue of his or her knowledge, competence, or position within a particular system. We know that authority must be justified and recognized as legitimate if it is to be accepted by those subject to it. Therefore, it is possible to clarify the nature and types of authority vested in public bureaucracies. Several scholars, including C. J. Friedrich and Richard T. DeGeorge, have organized this knowledge into various coherent frameworks.

Friedrich (1958a, 1963, 1972) argues that the prevailing view of authority is erroneous, resulting in confusion and misunderstanding. He asserts that the contemporary view of authority and its preoccupations with power, domination, and forced submission have led scholars astray from its ancient and meaningful origin. Friedrich is critical of writers who attempt to build a concept of authority based solely on power.[5] As far as he is concerned, they have missed the point because authority on the basis of power alone is weak and unlikely to endure through time. Friedrich makes a convincing argument that authority must be grounded in *reason.* He goes to great lengths to illustrate how reason and authority are wedded together and that any effort to divorce the two concepts is profoundly misguided.

In building his case, Friedrich examines the etymology of *author-ity*, which he traces to the Latin word *auctoritas* (meaning to enlarge, augment). The term is linked to the Roman Senate, which used its wisdom, guided by superior knowledge, insight, and experience, to enlarge and augment the popular will through reasoning. Friedrich observes that the Romans were a conservative people who relied on tradition—the values, beliefs, and disposition of the community—to guide policy decisions. Tradition constituted the foundation on which reasoning was based and provided a means for determining the acceptability of popular will. Once the Senate bestowed its blessings on the popular will, it became law and thus acquired authority. In noting the important role of reason in the ancient conception of authority, Friedrich (1972) writes:

> The ancient connotation brings out the crucial role of reasoning in situations where men follow other men without being compelled to do so. When there are good reasons for doing or believing something, such actions or thought gets a quality that is otherwise lacking; it becomes "authoritative." What makes a particular course of action authoritative, that is to say, vested with authority, is that convincing reasons may be offered in support of it. (p. 48)

Friedrich underscores the importance of putting reason back into the concept of authority and offers his assistance in this effort. According to Friedrich, "authority rests upon the ability to issue communications which are capable of reasoned elaboration" (p. 46). He adds:

> What we must ask is what enables a man to get his proposal accepted, that is to say, "to gain another's assent." Our reply would be that when such ability to gain assent springs from his capacity for reasoned elaboration we have authority. It inheres in his communication! Only when what is commanded is asserted can be reasoned upon and defined is authority real. . . . He who obeys authority does so because he who orders him to obey appears to have a very sufficient reason to do so. Authority is not an alternative to reason, but is grounded in it. (p. 55)

Friedrich makes it clear that commonly the actual giving of reasons need not occur, only the potentiality for doing so must be present and recognized as such.

Friedrich's conception of authority is illuminating in two significant respects. First, it reveals that *acceptance* is the central criterion of authority. Second, it helps in understanding that authority requires *justification* to be seen and accepted as legitimate by those subject to it. The giving of reasons by definition is an act or process of justification because it is intended to show that a communication, law, or decision rendered is just, rightful, and reasonable. Friedrich makes an important contribution by observing that authority must be justified, that is, those persons affected by it have good reasons for accepting it. He does not, however, say much about the different types of authority. Because all authority is not the same, one can assume that there are differences in the types of justifications offered. Other scholars, particularly DeGeorge (1985), have illuminated the relationship between the different types of justification and the different forms of authority.

DeGeorge (1985) begins his in-depth analysis by reviewing the ordinary uses of the term *authority*. He concludes that any discussion of authority must take into consideration the types of authority and their different kinds of justifications. He argues that one must differentiate between a "person or a thing that is an authority and the authority—that is, the quality or power—that he has or exercises" (p. 13). He also argues that a "person may be an authority within a certain field of knowledge, or he may occupy a certain position which carries with it certain powers" (p. 13). With these preliminary observations as a backdrop, DeGeorge offers a general working model of authority that he schematically presents in the time-honored philosophical tradition: "Someone or something (X) is an authority if he (she, it) stands in relation to someone else (Y) as superior stands to inferior with respects to some realm, field, or domain (R)" (p. 14). The model accentuates two prominent attributes of authority: (a) It involves some type of relational quality, and (b) it is limited to a particular realm or context. DeGeorge uses the model as a foundation for differentiating between two types of authority that he describes as *executive* and *nonexecutive* authority.

DeGeorge (1985) defines an executive authority as someone having the "power and right to act for and on someone else" (p. 22). A nonexecutive authority lacks this right or power. Executive authority is further divided into imperative and performatory authority. Imperative authority "involves the right or the power of some bearer to command someone who is subject to authority to act or to forbear from acting in certain ways." In contrast, performatory authority is the "right or power of someone to perform some action, sometimes on or for another person" (pp. 63-68). Stated more succinctly, executive authority encompasses the right and power to issue commands as well as to perform specific acts.

DeGeorge (1985) argues that the very nature of executive authority suggests that it must be linked to some system or context to make any sense. This context or system may be established by a "set of laws, a constitution, a tradition, a position or a set of personal qualities that are appropriate for a set of circumstances" (p. 64). Specific rules govern the context or system and, in turn, determine the scope and limits of executive authority. For example, Congress, by enacting tax laws, determines the context for the Internal Revenue Service (IRS). The IRS has the right and power to command and perform specific acts within the realm of revenue collection. Congress not only specifies the context but also determines the rules concerning the scope and limits of the IRS's executive authority. The agency does not have the right or power to issues directives and perform specific acts within the realm of foreign policy, for example. To do so would be a violation of its executive authority.

DeGeorge (1985) also divides nonexecutive authority into two types, epistemic and competence. Epistemic authority is based on superior knowledge in a particular field or area. Epistemic authority is considered legitimate if what someone says is *believed* and, therefore, *accepted* by those for whom that person is an authority. For example, the general public is likely to believe officials of the U.S. Food and Drug Administration (FDA) when they report that a drug is unsafe because of its potential side effects. FDA officials are believed because they are presumed to have specialized knowledge that is relevant in judging the safety of the drug in question. It is also presumed that FDA officials are telling the truth and are accurately reporting test results.

Authority based on competence is closely related to epistemic authority. Officials have competence authority if they have the capacity or ability to perform certain tasks in a particular field or area. DeGeorge (1985) quickly points out that a thin line exists between epistemic authority and competence authority and that their relationship may be examined from a couple of different perspectives:

> According to one view, epistemic authority is a broad type of authority, and competence authority is one kind of epistemic authority. The argument in support of this view holds that implicitly Y believes that X has the requisite knowledge in R [realm] to do *a* [a specific action]. . . . According to the other view, competence authority is a broad type of authority of which epistemic authority is one kind. Thus someone is competent in R if he has knowledge of it. His knowledge may be theoretical or practical. (p. 44)

When consolidated, the works of Friedrich and DeGeorge provide a coherent conceptual framework for understanding the authority of public bureaucracies. With benefit of the previous discussion, I draw the following conclusions: The mission of public bureaucracies is established by legislative mandates and other legally binding acts that grant authority to administrative agencies to act within a designated realm or field of action and to pursue specific policy objectives. This authority must be justified; those persons affected by an agency's authority must have good reasons for accepting it. The authority vested in public bureaucracies consists of two mutually reinforcing types, executive and nonexecutive. Because public administrators are entrusted with the responsibility of preserving the authority of public bureaucracies, administrative conservators should preserve both executive and nonexecutive authority as a means of conserving the missions of administrative agencies and their capacity to act. By doing so, administrative conservators are preserving the integrity of public bureaucracies because the mission represents the institution's "true commitments" (Selznick, 1957, p. 73). These internal and external commitments determine an agency's distinctive competence and character.

Administrative conservators may use a variety of strategies to preserve the authority of public bureaucracies. In the remainder of this chapter, these strategies are discussed within the context of preserving both executive authority and nonexecutive authority.

Preserving Executive Authority

As previously discussed, executive authority involves the right and power to issue commands and to perform certain acts in a given realm. As with other types of authority, there are limits to the scope of executive authority vested in public bureaucracies. These limits vary according to the specific realm or field of action, the purposes of administrative activity, and the types of acts performed by the agency. For example, the executive authority of the National Park Service is (or should be) restricted to the realm of park preservation and public recreation because these two functions are a part of the agency's legally mandated mission. Administrative officials of the Park Service should sanction and engage in only those activities that achieve these purposes. Activities such as stocking the streams with game fish and restricting the use of certain areas of the park are certainly acceptable. There are limits to how far the National Park Service can and should go in performing these acts. Park officials should not, for example, go overboard in encouraging park development and ignore park preservation.

The administrative conservator should be sensitive to the limits placed on the executive authority of public bureaucracies. The conservator should remember that gross or consistent violations of these limits can erode an agency's executive authority and thus render such authority unacceptable to those subject to it. The administrative conservator should prevent or reduce violations directly related to the law(s) granting an agency its executive authority. These include violations of the spirit of the law and violations of the letter of the law.

The Spirit of the Law

It is not uncommon in political circles to hear policymakers, scholars, and others refer to "the spirit of the law" when discussing the actions of governmental agencies. This phrase is used so often that people seldom give it a second thought. *The Compact Oxford English Dictionary* (1991) defines spirit as the "broad or general intent of meaning of a statement, enactment, etc." (p. 1855). Another definition suggests that spirit is the "real sense or significance of something; the spirit of the law" (*American Heritage Dictionary*, 1982, p. 1178). Using these definitions as a guidepost, one can say that an agency has violated the spirit of the law when its actions and activities are unfaithful to the broad purposes, intent, and unifying principles that provide the basis for the law that determine its reason for existence. Note that administrative officials can violate the spirit of the law without violating the letter of the law.

Violations of the spirit of the law consist of at least three different types. First, an agency may violate the spirit of the law when its activities cease to make sense and thus are unacceptable to its employees and/or external stakeholders because they are perceived as inconsistent with the agency's reason or purpose for existence. For example, the U.S. Department of Agriculture's Co-operative Extension Service has been aggressively attacked by politicians and agricultural interest groups for expanding its programs and activities into urban areas. Critics charge that the Cooperative Extension Service has violated the spirit of the Smith-Lever Act of 1914, which established the nationwide system, because Congress did not intend for the Extension Service to become involved in urban areas. When Congress instructed the Extension Service to "give good leadership and direction along all lines of *rural activities*," this is exactly what they meant (U.S. Congress House Committee on Agriculture, 1913, p. 5; emphasis added). The image of a 4-H youth specialist teaching an inner-city youth how to raise a prize-winning steer for the county fair conflicts with images of the Extension Service held in the minds of many Americans. Activities of this nature do not seem to make a lot of sense in view of the reasons given for the Extension Service's existence. It seems that neither the American public nor agricultural interests as a whole willingly accept the notion that rural, agriculturally based programs are legitimate in the urban environment. This may partially explain why the Extension Service has experienced a weakening of popular support for its programs and services throughout the country.[6]

The second type of violation of the spirit of the law relates to the manner in which the agency fulfills its mandated responsibilities. An agency can violate the spirit of the law when it is overly zealous in carrying out statutory provisions. Herman Finer (1941), the distinguished British political scientist, labels this type of violation "overfeasance." He suggests that overfeasance occurs when "a duty is undertaken beyond what law and custom oblige or empower" (pp. 337-338). Finer further states that "overfeasance may result from dictatorial temper, vanity and ambition of the jack in office, or genuine, sincere, public-spirited zeal" (pp. 337-338). When critics say that an agency has exceeded, overstepped, or overreached its authority, they often mean that its officials have engaged in some form of zealotry. The following cases involving questionable tax collection activities of the IRS illustrate overzealousness.

The Internal Revenue Code of 1954 gives the IRS the executive authority for the collection of taxes in the following words: "The Secretary shall collect taxes imposed by internal revenue law" [26 U.S.C.A. § 6302(b) (West 1989)]. In carrying out tax collection activities, the IRS has the right and power to use discretionary methods, that is, those methods not specifically outlined in the tax law, to collect unpaid taxes:

> Whether or not the method of collecting any tax imposed by Chapter 21, 31, 32, 33, § 4481 of Chapter 36, [or] § 450(a) of Chapter 37, is specifically provided for by this title, any such tax may, under regulations prescribed by the Secretary, be collected by means of returns, stamps, coupons, tickets, books, or other such reasonable devices and methods as may be necessary or helpful in securing a complete and proper collection of the tax. [26 U.S.C.A. § 6302(b) (West 1989)]

Thus, the IRS possesses wide discretion, as evidenced by the phrase "other such reasonable devices and methods." But even with such broad authority, unreasonable methods of collection can be used, as was revealed when the press reported that the IRS, as a common practice, intercepts and cashes the personal checks of delinquent taxpayers sent through the mail and made payable to other parties. Letters with enclosed checks were confiscated from U.S. post offices, opened, altered, and deposited by IRS agents into U.S. government bank accounts. The legitimacy of such practices has been questioned on the grounds that the IRS is exceeding its statutory authority because Congress did not intend for the agency to go to such extremes in collecting delinquent taxes.

Other collection practices of the IRS have also been called into question, most notably those pertaining to the seizure of bank accounts as payment for back taxes. The Internal Revenue Code authorizes the agency to levy the account of individuals as a means of collecting unpaid taxes:

> The Secretary may authorize Federal Reserve banks, and incorporated banks, trust companies, domestic building and loan associations, or credit unions which are depositories or financial agents of the United States, to receive a tax imposed under the internal revenue laws. . . . He shall prescribe the manner, times, and conditions . . . which the receipt of such tax . . . is to be treated as payment of such tax to the Secretary. [26 U.S.C.A. § 6302(c) (West 1989)]

This provision essentially means that the IRS has the executive authority to seize bank accounts to collect back taxes. The agency has been accused of being overly zealous in using this aspect of the law. One such accusation stemmed from the IRS's seizure of bank accounts held by children as a means of collecting back taxes of their parents. A stir was created when the *Washington Post* reported that the IRS seized the life savings ($694) of a 10-year-old girl and wanted proof that the money was not her father's, an unemployed carpenter (see "IRS Seizes Life Savings," 1987). In another case, the agency seized the savings account of a young boy who raised money by recycling aluminum cans. The actions of the IRS, in both cases, were perceived by the public as unacceptable and well beyond the limits of the spirit of the law. As a result of widespread public opinion against such actions, the IRS instituted a new policy that bans the seizure of bank accounts containing $100 or less.

The third type of violation of the spirit of the law is closely related to the second in that it also pertains to the manner in which the agency fulfills its statutory responsibilities. An agency can violate the spirit of the law if it is "un-energetic," "inattentive," or "negligent" in carrying out its legally mandated responsibilities. Finer (1941) calls this type of violation "nonfeasance" (p. 337). Nonfeasance occurs when administrative officials "have not done what law or custom required them to do owing to laziness, ignorance, or want of care for their charges, or corrupt influence" (p. 337).

The Occupational Safety and Health Administration's (OSHA) management of its whistle-blowers protection program illustrates nonfeasance. OSHA is required by law to investigate complaints from employees of interstate transportation companies who claim that they were retaliated against for refusing to violate or for reporting that their employer disobeyed federal motor vehicle safety regulations. After an internal investigation, the U.S. General Accounting Office (GAO, 1988b) criticized OSHA for not devoting "enough management attention to the whistle-blowers protection program for employees in the interstate motor vehicle industry" (p. 1) as mandated by law. The GAO reported that OSHA "did not investigate and issue findings on 56 percent of the whistle-blower cases in 1986 and the first eight months of Fiscal 1987 within the 60 days required by law" (p. 1).

In another case, the GAO was critical of the Department of Justice's management of defense procurement fraud investigations. In 1982 the department's criminal division was given responsibility for prosecuting fraud cases within the defense establishment. As a means of fulfilling this responsibility, the criminal division established the defense procurement fraud unit. At the request of Senator William Proxmire, the GAO was called in to investigate the department's handling of procurement fraud cases. The GAO (1988a) report portrayed an administrative agency that was extremely "negligent" in fulfilling its responsibilities. The Justice Department was criticized for not having "complete or timely information on a significant number of defense procurement fraud referrals" and for not knowing "the amount of attorney resources spent in the effort" (p. 2).

So far I have focused exclusively on violations of the spirit of the law. Although important, this is only one aspect of a complex process required to preserve an agency's executive authority. As I mentioned earlier, the administrative conservator should also ensure that the agency's actions and activities do not violate the letter of the law. But what exactly does this mean?

The Letter of the Law

The administrative conservator should ensure that the agency's actions and activities consistently comply with the primary, ordinary, and plain meaning of the language used in mandating statutes and other legally binding acts that specify its field of action, the purpose of its activity, and the type of tasks it is designated to perform. Unlike violations of the spirit of the law, violations of the letter of the law may be illegal. This alone necessitates that the law's language be observed. Despite lengthy discussions by public administration theorists on the problems posed by the ambiguous language contained in statutory mandates and other legally binding acts, the language is for the most part quite clear. If this were not the case, administrative agencies would be paralyzed and unable to perform their functions. Consider the following section of the Aviation Safety Research Act of 1988:

> The Administrator shall prepare, review, revise, publish, and transmit a national aviation research plan to the Committee on Commerce, Science, and Transportation of the Senate and the Committee on Science, Space, and Technology of the House of Representatives no later than the date of the submission to Congress of the President's budget for fiscal year 1990, and for each fiscal year thereafter. The plan shall describe, for a 15 year period, the research, engineering, and development considered by the Administrator necessary to ensure the continued capacity, safety, and efficiency of aviation in the United States, considering emerging technologies and forecasted needs of civil aeronautics, and provide the highest degree of safety in air travel. The plan shall cover all research conducted under this section and section 316 of this Act and shall identify complementary and coordinated research efforts conducted by the National Aeronautics and Space Administration with funds specifically appropriated to such Administration. [49 App. U.S.C.A. § 1353(d)(1) (West 1994)]

This language is relatively straightforward. The administrator of the Federal Aviation Administration (FAA) is required (as indicated by the word *shall*) to prepare, publish, and submit a national aviation research plan to specific committees of Congress every fiscal year beginning with fiscal year 1990. The act is also explicit about the nature and contents of the plan. If the FAA administrator failed to comply with directives specified in the act, the administrator would be accused of violating the letter of the law. This is exactly what happened to officials of the Office of Human Development Services (OHDS).

An agency within the Department of Health and Human Services, OHDS is responsible for awarding grants related to prevention of child abuse and neglect. The National Center on Child Abuse and Neglect is the agency's vehicle through which such grants are awarded. OHDS became the focus of an investigation because of accusations that it had engaged in arbitrary and inequitable decision making in awarding nearly $37 million in discretionary grants. These charges were substantiated because OHDS "frequently did not justify in writing its decisions to approve applications out of ranking order" (GAO, 1987, p. 20). Moreover, "none of the applications rejected within ranking order was justified in writing, nor were 93 percent of the decisions to select grant applicants for administrative review rather than competitive review" (p. 20). In this case, officials of OHDS violated provisions of the Administrative Procedures Act of 1946, which specifically states that "[a]n agency or commission must articulate with clarity and precision its findings and reasons for its decisions" (§ 71). This is especially so in cases in which there appears to be a difference in treatment among interested parties.

Similar to violations concerning the spirit of the law, violations of the letter of the law may occur as a result of overfeasance or nonfeasance. The covert activities of Lieutenant Colonel Oliver L. North, the so-called action officer on President Reagan's National Security Council staff, is a classic case of overfeasance in violation of the letter of the law.[7] North managed both the Iran and Contra affairs, which involved secret arms transactions with the government of Iran and secret military assistance to the Nicaraguan Contras (the armed opposition to the Sandinista regime in Nicaragua). North diverted funds, generated from profits made on the sale of arms to Iran, to the Contras, despite congressional mandates prohibiting such activities. The Defense Appropriations Act (1984) specifically stated:

> No appropriation or funds made available pursuant to this joint resolution to the Central Intelligence Agency, the Department of Defense or any other agency entity of the United States involved in intelligence activities may be obligated or expended for the purpose of which would have the effect of supporting, directing or indi-

rectly, military or paramilitary operations in Nicaragua by any nation, group, organization, movement or individual. (Boland II amendment)

It is clear from this language that North's clandestine activities violated the letter of the law. Whether North's actions and activities were a result of "vanity and ambition" or "genuine, sincere, public-spirited zeal" (driven by the desire to secure the release of American hostages held by Islamic fundamentalist groups) is still an open question (recall Finer, 1941, pp. 337-338). One thing is certain: His covert activities were contrary to authorized congressional policy.

The actions and activities of Anne M. Gorsuch, administrator of the Environmental Protection Agency (EPA) during the first Reagan administration, provide an illustration of nonfeasance. Gorsuch was criticized for the performance of one of her subordinates, Rita M. Lavelle, an assistant administrator of the EPA, for the manner in which she enforced the Resource Conservation and Recovery Act. This act covers the handling and disposal of toxic wastes and the so-called superfund for cleaning up abandoned hazardous waste sites. Lavelle was sharply criticized by members of Congress and environmentalists because she failed to "vigorously" enforce the letter of the law.[8]

Maintaining Compliance With Spirit and Letter of Law

To say that the administrative conservator should prevent violations of the spirit and letter of the law indicates *what* must be done to preserve an agency's executive authority. But this does not say much about *how* the administrative conservator should minimize or prevent such violations. Certainly there is something more than merely knowing the different types of violations and their possible causes. The administrative conservator may employ a variety of strategies, the more important of which are discussed below.

Strategy: The Interpretation of Legal Mandates

The administrative conservator should *develop the capacity to interpret the text of legal mandates in a consistently meaningful and responsible manner.*[9] This requires a sophisticated understanding of mandating statutes and other legally binding acts that grant the agency its executive authority. Such an understanding should be based on extensive knowledge in several areas.[10] First, the administrative conservator should become familiar with the meaning of the language used in the text of legal mandates because this will aid in the interpretive endeavor. The conservator should be "sensitive to any special senses the words have acquired, and should also consider the placement of words in the sentence, and even the punctuation of the sentence" (Eskridge & Frickey, 1990, p. 355). The administrative conservator should also have a clear idea of the general structure of legal mandates and how the various provisions of the law fit together.

Second, the administrative conservator should know the specific and general legislative history of an agency's legal mandates. This will provide important insights into the original intent and purpose of the legislative body that enacted the law. The administrative conservator can discover such information by reviewing various versions of the law prior to its enactment, legislative committee reports, and other public records such as the *Congressional Record*. For example, evidence of what the authors of the previously mentioned Aviation Safety Research Act of 1988 intended can be found in the House of Representatives Bill 4686 (1988); Senate Bill 2746 (1988); House Report No. 894 (1988), prepared by the Committee on Science, Space, and Technologies; Senate Report No. 584 (1988), prepared by the Committee on Commerce, Science, and Transportation; and the *Congressional Record* (1988).

The administrative conservator should remember that interpretations of the law evolve over time and thus are subject to change. These changes are desirable and necessary to conform with the changing habits, dispositions, and values of the constitutional order. Hence, the administrative conservator must, of necessity, adjust the interpretation of legal mandates to conform with changing circumstances. Such adjustments require the prudent use of administrative discretion,[11] as illustrated by the following case involving the IRS and Bob Jones University.

The Internal Revenue Code of 1954 permits tax-exempt status for "corporations . . . organized and operated exclusively for religious, charitable . . . or educational purposes . . ." [26 U.S.C.A. § 501(c)(3) (West 1988)]. In 1970, 6 years after the passage of the Civil Rights Act, the IRS abandoned a long-standing policy of granting tax-exempt status to private schools that practiced racial discrimination. This action was instituted in response to a court injunction that prohibited the agency from granting tax-exempt status to private schools in Mississippi that denied African Americans admission because of their race. In light of changing societal values and public policies that prohibited racial discrimination, officials of the IRS issued the following revised policy statement:

> Both the courts and the Internal Revenue Service have long recognized that the statutory requirement of being "organized and operated exclusively for religious, charitable, . . . or educational purposes" was intended to express the basic common law concept [of charity]. . . . All charitable trusts, educational or otherwise, are subject to the requirement that the purpose of that trust may not be illegal or contrary to public policy. (*Bob Jones v. United States*, 461 U.S. 574, 579, 1983).

IRS officials justified the policy change on the grounds that private schools that practiced discrimination in admissions did not meet certain common law requirements of charity. As such, these educational institutions did not serve the public good because their policies were inconsistent with the national policy to discourage racial discrimination. Bob Jones University was immediately affected by this interpretation because of its policy that discriminated against unmarried African Americans and those who condoned interracial dating or marriages. The IRS revoked the university's tax-exempt status. The university then challenged the IRS's modified interpretation of Section 501(c)(3) of the Internal Revenue Code in court and argued that the agency had exceeded its statutory authority. The case was eventually heard by the U.S. Supreme Court, which upheld the IRS's interpretation of the law. The Court stated that Congress grants the IRS the authority and responsibility to interpret the tax laws to "meet changing conditions and new problems" (*Bob Jones v. United States*, 596). Moreover, the Court indicated that the change in policy was consistent with the intent of Congress.

Strategy: The Education of Personnel

The administrative conservator must understand the nature and limits of the agency's executive authority. But this is not enough to ensure compliance with the spirit and letter of the law; he or she must help others understand their mandated responsibilities as well. Such an understanding may be achieved through education. The term *education* as used here encompasses more than what is normally associated with socialization. Education includes those processes that are not only "socializing but personalizing and humanizing as well" (C. J. Friedrich, 1972, p. 19). In conjunction with other strategies, education may be used to cultivate a nourishing sense of purpose by instilling important organizational values.

The administrative conservator may use an assortment of educational strategies ranging from formal institutionalized training programs to informal on-the-job experience. For example, the Federal Bureau of Prisons (1985) conducts an institution familiarization program for new employees. The 4-week program is designed to "give new employees critical skills which they must have before receiving a specific job assignment" (p. 5). The bureau's institution familiarization program is a means of educating new employees to the agency's reason for existence and of conveying what actions are acceptable in this context.

The U.S. Fish and Wildlife Service has a long-standing policy of requiring all prospective regional directors to spend several months at the Washington headquarters as condition for promotion. This policy is designed to "sensitize would-be directors and to assist them to acquire a greater appreciation of activities at the national level" (F. E. Hester, former deputy director of the U.S. Fish and Wildlife Service, personal communication, January 9, 1987). This essentially means that would-be regional directors are made aware of the acceptable boundaries of administrative action. In other words, they are educated on the nature and limits of the agency's executive authority. In a study of federal bureau chiefs,

Herbert Kaufman (1981a) alludes to the value of this type of education:

> A host of understandings develop inside a bureau, and between the people with whom it comes in contact, regarding the course the bureau will follow—the practices it will render—in its job. So long as everybody involved, including the chief, remains within the boundaries of those understandings, things tend to go on routinely and quietly. But let anyone step over the boundaries, and the reactions—of employees, other officials, politicians, interest groups, or the press—are likely to be explosive. (pp. 126-127)

Kaufman's comments also point to another significant role of employee education: It helps (or should help) employees understand and avoid those actions and behaviors that will undermine the agency's credibility and incur high political costs. Once again, the acceptability of an agency's actions and activities is determined by its specific field of action, the purpose of its activities, and the type of acts performed. For example, inadequate safety procedures in launching manned space vehicles can cause a credibility problem for the National Aeronautics and Space Administration (the explosion of the space shuttle *Challenger* immediately comes to mind); the publication of inaccurate and biased investigative reports by the GAO can undermine its credibility; and widespread corruption in the form of drug smuggling by Drug Enforcement Administration officials can have an adverse effect on the agency's reputation.

Strategy: The Judicious Use of Rule Making and Adjudication

A final strategy for preserving executive authority involves *agency rule making and adjudication*. Legislative bodies grant most administrative agencies executive authority for rule making and adjudication. These two analytically distinct yet mutually reinforcing functions give governmental agencies their quasi-legislative and quasi-judicial qualities.[12]

According to Cornelius M. Kerwin (1994), "rulemaking is the single most important function performed by agencies of government" (p. xi). Rule-making activities entail the development of broad policies that may be consistently applied to all within a designated category. As stated earlier in the discussion of the Bob Jones University case, the IRS's Revenue Ruling 71-447, 1971-1972 (which addresses racially discriminatory practices of "charitable" organizations) denies tax-exempt status to "all charitable trusts, educational or otherwise" if their purposes are "illegal or contrary to public policy" (*Bob Jones v. United States*, 596).

Agency rule making consists of two types, formal and informal. Formal rule making mandates that an agency conduct a public hearing, whereas informal rule making does not impose this requirement. Administrative officials may, unless mandated otherwise by law, use their discretion to determine whether a public hearing is necessary. If it is determined that a formal hearing would enhance fair and effective administration of a law, then administrative officials must follow the rule-making provisions outlined in the Administrative Procedures Act of 1946.

Adjudicatory action taken by an agency is "directed at least in part at determining the legal status of persons who are named as parties, or of the acts or practices of those persons" (Shapiro, 1965, p. 924). Adjudication differs from rule making in several ways. First, adjudicatory proceedings are comparable to those used in the courtroom and thus are more formal than rule-making proceedings. Second, decisions emerging from adjudicatory proceedings can establish a precedent that can be applied to others in similar situations. Third, "rules made in adjudicative proceedings are retroactive and those made in rule making are prospective only" (p. 933). The administrative conservator often has a choice of using either rule making or adjudication in giving content to general statutory provisions. Decisions regarding which approach to use require careful consideration. There are advantages to each, conditioned by prevailing institutional circumstances. Hence, the administrative conservator must be a good diagnostician as well as an adept strategist. For example, the administrative conservator may wish to use formal rule making to provide all interested parties an opportunity to voice their opinion, especially if it is anticipated that a proposed policy will cause controversy or affect a large number of groups or individuals. Agency rule making may also be used to generate support for proposed policies, as A. Lee Fritschler

(1989) points out in his book *Smoking and Politics.* Fritschler illustrates how the Federal Trade Commission (FTC) frequently used formal rule making to establish policy regarding cigarette labeling and advertising. According to Fritschler, administrative officials of the FTC "knew that if they adopted the rule without hearings, the cigarette manufacturers could seize upon the secretiveness of their action to argue that the FTC was undemocratic, arbitrary and dangerous" (p. 69).

In some instances, the administrative conservator may decide to use informal rule making if substantial agreement exists that the proposed policy is not contrary to public policy or if the policy is routine and relatively benign. The conservator may also use informal rule making for another reason: to change existing policies that are, for one reason or another, no longer applicable because of changing circumstances. The previously mentioned IRS rule that denied tax-exempt status to so-called charitable institutions that adopted discriminatory policy is a case in point.

The administrative conservator could elect to use adjudication if a case-by-case approach is sufficient for establishing policies. This decision is largely influenced by the nature of the problem (e.g., industrywide vs. specific activities or practices of selected parties) and the scope of the policy needed. For example, the FTC had to abandon the adjudicatory approach in addressing the industrywide problem of deceptive cigarette advertising. The agency could not "state authoritatively a general policy of what constituted deception in cigarette ads for all advertisers" because the "procedures employed in adjudicatory actions narrowly defined the scope of admissible evidence" (Fritschler, 1989, p. 61).

Regardless of the approach selected, the administrative conservator must ensure that the end results of rule making and adjudication proceedings are consistent with the spirit and letter of the law. With respect to federal agencies, Congress made this clear in the Administrative Procedures Act of 1946, as the following statement indicates: "Although weight must be given to an administrator's interpretation of a particular statute, where an administrative regulation is plainly inconsistent with the statute and operates in a manner which frustrates congressional intent, it can be given no force and effect and must be declared invalid" [5 U.S.C.A. § 557, n. 80 (West 1977)].

Beyond Compliance

To preserve an agency's executive authority, the administrative conservator must do more than ensure that its actions and activities comply with the spirit and letter of the law. Other areas of administrative concern must be considered. These include, among others, being responsive to the various constitutional masters and the citizenry as well as protecting the agency's jurisdictional boundaries.

Strategy: Responsiveness and the Exercise of Strategic Discretion

Public administration scholars are quick to note that legislative mandates and other legally binding acts that grant authority to public bureaucracies contain a multitude of diverse, conflicting, and ambiguous policy objectives. These unique characteristics are perceived by many scholars as a constraint or burden that makes administration of public bureaucracies more difficult and complex. In this context, complexity is considered a serious problem. It is true that the distinctive character of mandating statutes contributes to administrative complexity, but it does not necessarily follow that complexity is a serious problem (see H. Wilson, 1975). Indeed, the multifaceted and complex nature of mandating statutes can be viewed as an asset because it is a manifestation of the constitutional tradition of a compound democratic republic and an opportunity that broadens the administrative conservator's discretion. This discretion must be prudently and strategically exercised to be responsive to the executive, legislative, and judicial branches as well as to those interest groups that are committed to the common good. The administrative conservator's responsiveness strengthens communal bonds and loyalty to the agency and thereby to the constitutional order.

To be responsive to the constitutional masters and the citizenry, the administrative conservator must exercise strategic discretion to *shift the relative emphasis placed on different policy objectives (contained in legal mandates) to correspond to changing priorities.* This does not imply that the administrative conservator should abandon certain policy objectives because of changing political priorities. To do so would undermine the agency's executive authority and, in turn, its integrity. As C. J. Friedrich (1958a) states, "no authority can be legitimate that fails to fulfill the function for which it has been created—the public good" (p. 40). The administrative conservator must act responsibly when shifting the emphasis placed on different policy objectives. This requires ongoing attention to those policy objectives deemphasized during the changing political climate.

The importance of shifting the emphasis on policy objectives to accommodate the changing political climate is often reflected in the language of governmental administration. Phrases such as "change the thrust," "make important course correction," "change the focus," and "make programmatic adjustments" are a few of those commonly heard expressions that reflect sensitivity to the larger political forces at work in society. The statements of F. Eugene Hester (1981), former acting director of the Fish and Wildlife Service, illustrate the point. In a memorandum distributed to all agency employees at the outset of the first Reagan administration, Hester states:

> The new administration came to Washington recognizing a mandate from the public. It was a mandate for a new beginning, for a stronger national economy, for less Federal regulation and bureaucratic red tape, for a better partnership and good neighbor attitude and less Federal domination, unresponsiveness and arrogance. . . . The Federal Government had been perceived as burdensome, overly restrictive and high-handed and political leaders were elected and appointed to overcome these problems. . . . So, the administration came to town with a purpose . . . and a determination to take bold action that would be required to make the change. . . . Changes in government are sometimes thought of as like the pendulum. If it gets too far from center, it then swings back in a corrective action. I think that is a good analogy. I like to compare it to a sailboat. It can't sail directly into the wind, but it can definitely go on that general course by sailing to one side and then the other in a somewhat zig-zag course, with the net effect being progress in the desired course. I believe government sometimes makes progress in a similar manner, and a parallel type of course correction is essential to keep us, as a Nation, headed in the right direction. (p. 2)

Examining public bureaucracies from a historical perspective makes it readily apparent that the emphasis placed on different policy objectives does shift from time to time. For example, the National Park Service is mandated to pursue two seemingly contradictory policy objectives: (a) to promote public use of the parks and (b) to preserve the parks. Alston Chase (1987) demonstrates that the agency has throughout its history shifted back and forth between the two policy objectives:

> During the periods when the Service was most anxious to please the recreation industry and serve the public, it tended to encourage park development, stocking the streams with game fish and building hotels, resorts, and even golf courses. This emphasis on public use inevitably affected the wildlife. Seeking to please the public, the Park Service immediately after its creation inaugurated a program to exterminate the "bad" animals, predators such as wolves and mountain lions, in order to increase the number of "good" animals, such as elk and bison, that the new agency believed would bring in more people. But when conservationism was ascendent in America, the Service tended to put higher value on preservation. During the 1930s, for example, when the railroads—once a potent influence in national park policy—were declining and environmentalism was on the rise, the Park Service terminated the predator-control program and established an ecological think tank known as the Wild Life Division. (p. 36)

The foregoing discussion suggests that the administrative conservator's responsiveness to the constitutional master and the citizenry is a requisite for preserving an agency's executive authority.

Strategy: The Protection of Jurisdictional Boundaries

When an agency is granted executive authority, its officials are given the legal right and power to perform certain acts within some designated realm. The concept of realm implies that an agency's actions are restricted to a specific area of interest, that there are "boundaries." Although these boundaries define the agency's jurisdiction, they are *not*, however, rigid, permanent, or clear-cut lines of demarcation. Rather, they are permeable, fuzzy, and constantly changing. The administrative conservator should be sensitive to the agency's jurisdictional boundaries and aggressively defend them against encroachment by bureaucratic rivals. This may be accomplished by developing and maintaining a high degree of agency *autonomy*. According to James Q. Wilson (1989), autonomy is an agency's "relatively undisputed jurisdiction" (p. 183). He goes on to say that "agencies ranking high in autonomy have a monopoly jurisdiction (that is, they have few or no bureaucratic rivals and a minimum of political constraints imposed on them by superiors)" (p. 183). Wilson offers several strategies for achieving agency autonomy, many of which may be used by the administrative conservator.

First, the administrative conservator should "fight other organizations that seek to perform" the agency's tasks (J. Q. Wilson, 1989, p. 189). This is exactly what administrative officials of the Federal Bureau of Investigation (FBI) did when the U.S. Marshals Service (USMS) became more aggressive in federal fugitive investigations. At one time, the FBI had a monopoly jurisdiction over pursuing federal fugitives. But as the USMS became more active in hunting key narcotic fugitives, the FBI had to fight this new bureaucratic rival to protect its jurisdiction (the FBI lost).

Second, the administrative conservator should "avoid taking on tasks that differ significantly from those that are at the heart of the organization's mission" (J. Q. Wilson, 1989, p. 190). Officials of the U.S. Department of Agriculture's Cooperative Extension Service did just the opposite when they took on social welfare programs in urban areas. As previously mentioned, this decision has caused the agency to lose a great deal of autonomy.

Third, the administrative conservator should not participate in joint or cooperative ventures with other agencies unless such arrangements protect the agency's autonomy. But this can be done. For example, the USMS uses both its Boeing 727 aircraft as part of the National Prison Transportation system to assist other agencies in the long-distance movement of prisoners. The agency coordinates and schedules the majority of long-distance prisoner transfers between institutions operated by the Federal Bureau of Prisons. The USMS also transports prisoners for the Immigration and Naturalization Service as well as for a variety of state and local agencies. These cooperative ventures do not pose a threat to the agency's autonomy because of the nature of the relationships. The

other agencies depend on the USMS for their transportation services. The USMS gains much and loses nothing by cooperation.

Fourth, the administrative conservator should "avoid tasks that
will produce divided or hostile constituencies" (J. Q. Wilson, 1989,
p. 191). This may be difficult to do because legislative bodies are
prone to draft mandating statutes in such a manner to appease
multiple and distinct interests. But in most instances, the various
stakeholders who have a history of working out formal and informal arrangements or "rules of the game" tend to get along quite
well until other players enter the game. This changes the nature of
existing relationships by creating a degree of suspicion and increased speculation about the allocation of scarce agency resources.
The administrative conservator should not consciously pursue
additional tasks that will bring with them a different set of stakeholders whose interests are totally foreign to those who have a
traditional stake in the agency's product or services. Returning to
the example of the National Park Service, it is safe to assume that
the agency's two traditional constituencies—environmentalists and
those who represent the recreation industry—have learned to live
together. This does not mean that they will agree on all issues. It
does mean, however, that they have agreed to disagree and that the
manner in which disagreements are handled is most likely governed by a set of ground rules. These ground rules structure the
actions and behavior of environmentalists and the recreational
industry as they compete for benefits accrued from the allocation
of the agency's resources. But if the National Park Service were to
add, for example, the task of managing the use of public parks for
fossil fuel exploration, then an entirely different set of players
enters the game—each with a different agenda. Possible players
would include the oil, natural gas, and other interests related to
the fossil resource industry; the Departments of Defense and Energy; the Bureau of Land Management, the U.S. Geological Survey,
and the Fish and Wildlife Service, to name a few. This does not
include the various congressional committees and subcommittees
who have oversight responsibility. The ground rules established
by environmentalists and those representing the recreational industry may not be honored by the new players who have entered
the game.

Preserving Nonexecutive Authority

As stated earlier, nonexecutive authority is distinguished from executive authority in that it "does not involve any right to command or to act on or for another" (DeGeorge, 1985, p. 22). Nonexecutive authority consists of two different types, epistemic and competence. Epistemic authority consists of superior knowledge in a particular area, whereas competence authority results from the ability to perform certain tasks in a given area. Because the relation of epistemic and competence authority can be viewed in different ways, it is necessary to clarify how the concepts are used here. For purposes of this discussion, epistemic authority is viewed as a "broad type of authority and competence authority is one kind of epistemic authority" (p. 44). An administrative agency has legitimate epistemic authority if it possesses and is perceived by others to have superior knowledge and competence in a particular field or realm. The belief that administrative agencies have (or can acquire and develop) such knowledge and competence is one of the primary reasons they are delegated authority to perform certain tasks. For example, the National Aeronautic and Space Administration (NASA) has and is perceived by Congress and the American people to have superior knowledge and competence in the realm of space exploration.

As with executive authority, there are limits to an agency's epistemic authority. And, as noted by DeGeorge (1985), violation of these limits "help[s] erode the general justification of such authority and undermines the use of authority in the specific instances in question" (p. 46). The administrative conservator should be cognizant of these limits and guard against violations. Violations of an agency's epistemic authority tend to revolve around questions concerning the *public trust.*

Violations of the Public Trust

Legitimate epistemic authority is based on the notion that what someone says is believed and therefore accepted by those for whom that individual is an authority. In this formulation, the concept of *belief* is central to the notion of epistemic authority.

Belief is a spacious concept because it embraces several other concepts such as confidence, faith, and trust. Consider the following definitions (*Merriam-Webster's Collegiate Dictionary*, 1993):

> *Belief*—"a state or habit of mind in which trust or confidence is placed in some person or thing; something believed" (p. 104)
>
> *Confidence*—"faith or belief that one will act in a right, proper, or effective way; reliance on another's discretion" (p. 241)
>
> *Faith*—"allegiance to duty or person; fidelity to one's promises; firm belief in something for which there is no proof; complete trust" (p. 418)
>
> *Trust*—"one in which confidence is placed; a charge or duty imposed in faith or confidence or as a condition of some relationship; something committed or entrusted to one to be used or cared for in the interest of another" (p. 1269)

Guided by these definitions, I can say that violations of an agency's epistemic authority occur when there are sufficient reasons *not to believe* what is said by administrative officials because of a loss of public confidence, faith, and trust. Thus, it is possible to conclude that violations of an agency's epistemic authority involve those infractions that undermine the public's trust in the agency's capacity to serve the common good. These violations tend to be of at least two types: (a) the deliberate deception of those for which the agency is an epistemic authority (i.e., legislative, executive, and judicial bodies as well as the general public) and (b) the use of epistemic authority for personal or group benefit.[13] The administrative conservator should be concerned with both types of violations.

Violation: Deliberate Deception

The administrative conservator must remain trustworthy and honest in carrying out his or her official duties and must ensure that agency employees do the same. This simple, seemingly self-evident statement should not be taken lightly. Deliberate acts of deception can undermine an agency's epistemic authority and create a credibility gap between the agency and those for whom it is an epistemic authority. The concept of a *credibility gap* has special significance because of its etymological link to the concept of belief. *The Compact Oxford English Dictionary* (1991) says that a credibility gap is the difference between what is presented as truth and the amount of it believed to be true by the public. The word *credibility* is derived from the Latin term *credere*, meaning to believe. One who is capable of being believed is described as credible, or worthy of trust and confidence. This is what journalists often mean when they speak of a "credible source." Credibility implies truth, "one of the key values to which authority in many contexts is vitally linked" (C. J. Friedrich, 1958a, p. 46).

When a credibility gap exists between governmental agencies and those for whom they are an epistemic authority, what administrative officials say is received with a degree of skepticism and doubt. When communications or decisions by administrative officials are consistently questioned or openly challenged, then the agency's epistemic authority is weakened. Because an agency's epistemic authority is inextricably interwoven with its executive authority, the latter is also eroded. When this occurs, the agency is apt to experience a "legitimacy crisis"—the loss of public confidence, faith, and trust in the agency's ability to perform the functions for which it was established (D. O. Friedrich, 1980). Thus, it is easy to understand why deliberate acts of deception are viewed as betrayals of the faith, confidence, and trust placed in administrative agencies and, in turn, in those entrusted with the responsibility for their care.

The administrative conservator should institute preventive measures to ensure that agency functions and processes adhere to standards and practices that sustain the public's trust in the agency's capacity to perform its delegated function. The conservator must inspect, monitor, and adjust the agency's functions and processes as the need arises. For example, consider the bureaucratic propaganda activities of governmental agencies.

As a standard practice, government agencies issue official reports documenting activities and accomplishments. These reports perform an important function in articulating, reinforcing, and shaping the perceptions of those who have an interest in the agency's programs, services, or activities. They are also useful in creating a favorable public image that may be transformed into prestige, a viable strategy for controlling external dependencies (see Perrow, 1961). Official documents transmit information that engenders confidence in stakeholders by assuring them that the agency's activities are legitimate and, thereby, consistent with the spirit and letter of the law.

The institutionalized dissemination of information in the form of official reports is often referred to as "bureaucratic propaganda" (Altheide & Johnson, 1980). Such propaganda is intended not only to inform but also to convince relevant audiences of the legitimacy of an agency's activities. According to Altheide and Johnson:

> The purpose of modern propaganda is to maintain the legitimacy of an organization and its activities. The practical and day-to-day aspects of the organization are well understood by their workers but all actions are symbolically changed when placed in the context of an official report. These accounts, subject to evaluation by superiors and other organizations, are constructed to reflect what an organization is presumed to do and how well it does it. In hoping to satisfy evaluations and thereby legitimize the organization's activities and purposes, official reports have inadvertently presented contrived, managed, and essentially decontextualized pictures of their respective portions of social life. Thus, the overriding purpose of bureaucratic propaganda is not to dupe everyone, but it is intended to convince relevant persons. (p. 18)

Official documents disseminated by the GAO illustrate the type of propaganda activities carried out by governmental agencies. The GAO was established by the Budget and Accounting Act of 1921 for the explicit purpose of investigating "all matters relating to the receipt, disbursement and application of public funds" (p. 25).

Under the leadership of Comptroller Elmer Staats, the agency expanded its conception of auditing to include program evaluation. In documenting its audit and evaluation activities, the GAO issues a series of official documents through its Office of Public Information, ranging from an annual report to a *Congressional Source Book*, which includes information prepared by the agency to assist Congress and other relevant audiences. In its monthly publication, *Reports Issued*, the GAO documents audit and evaluation activities as well as congressional testimony given by agency officials. The publication is complete with reports whose titles reflect the agency's responsibilities, thus further reinforcing the perception that it is adhering to the spirit and letter of the law. For example, reports cited in the June 1987 issue of *Reports Issued* include "Financial Audit: Commodity Credit Corporation's Financial Statement for 1986 and 1987" (p. 15), "School Lunch Program: Evaluation of Alternatives to Commodity Donations" (p. 15), "Small Business: Evaluation of a Study on Access to Capital" (p. 16), and "Aviation Safety: Needed Improvements in FAA's Airline Inspection Program Are Underway" (p. 17).

Official documents issued by the GAO are believed and therefore accepted by Congress, the news media, and the general public because they are presumed to be accurate and objective, that is, true. Comptroller General Charles A. Bowsher (1992), the agency's current chief executive, is very attentive to internal standards governing the accuracy of official documents prepared for public consumption:

> GAO has rigorous standards. It checks and rechecks its facts carefully, and its employees report-review techniques to make sure that its reports will stand up to the closest scrutiny. The accuracy and objectivity of the agency's products are the major reason GAO enjoys widespread *credibility* [italics added] in an era when other agencies of the government are often subject to public distrust and suspicion. (p. 6)

Bowsher's comments are revealing because they emphasize the importance of establishing policies and procedures to maintain the truthfulness of information contained in official reports. His leadership of the GAO provides an example of what the administrative conservator should do. Another case involving the U.S. Army Armament Materiel Development and Readiness Command (DARCOM) demonstrates what the administrative conservator should *not* do.

DARCOM has jurisdiction over the nation's government-owned, contractor-operated facilities specializing in the production of propellants and explosives. DARCOM's largest ammunition plant for many years was the Radford Army Ammunition Plant (RAAP), located 40 miles southwest of Roanoke, Virginia. At one time,

RAAP produced about 98% of all propellants used for Army ammunition rockets. The plant is owned and operated by Hercules, Incorporated.

Because the risk of explosion is always present, the manufacture of explosives is a hazardous enterprise. Nitroglycerine, for example, is a highly volatile processing ingredient that is routinely used in the production of such ammunition. Because of the high probability of detonation, nitroglycerine is very unforgiving— there is little margin for error. Given the dangers associated with the production of explosives, safety is of utmost importance.

Many of its official public statements reflected that RAAP had made safety the cornerstone of its public relations campaign. According to an official plant document,

> During the 35 years of existence, RAAP's total commitment to safety has been magnified as compared with that of the U.S. chemical industry, as a whole. In the mid-1960's, RAAP recorded an 815-day period without an injury, an industry record. Recent years show an average of well below half an injury per million man-hours worked. (RAAP, n.d., p. 4)

RAAP measures safety in terms of lost-time injuries, excluding an explosion. The number of days linked without injuries that require time off is often well publicized in official documents. The *Powder Press*, the plant's internal newsletter, often carries a front-page column titled "Safety Scoreboard," which lists the number of days and hours worked without an injury requiring time off. The publication also frequently carries headlines highlighting its safety record, for example, "Proactive Safety Wins Again," "One, Two, Three, We Are Injury Free," and "Proactive Safety Has Won Us Another Award."

Over time, RAAP developed an impressive aerospace industry record of 18 million work-hours worked without a lost-time injury. This record ended in 1985 with an explosion that killed two workers and resulted in several million dollars in property damage. An Army investigation into the cause of the explosion revealed numerous safety violations ranging from the failure to follow safety procedures to faulty equipment. In an investigative report, the *Roanoke Times and World News* (a Virginia newspaper) questioned how RAAP could maintain its impressive safety record under such conditions. The article also questioned how, in view of the seriousness of reported violations, the plant maintained around-the-clock shifts with nearly 4,000 workers for 3½ years without a lost-time injury on the job ("Is the Arsenal Safe," 1986; see also "Arsenal's Lost-Time Injury Figures Vary," 1986).

The newspaper concluded, after interviews with plant workers, U.S. Army and Hercules officials, state safety officials, and others, that managers at the plant ignored injuries to workers as a means of maintaining the safety record. The highly publicized safety record was maintained despite employees receiving injuries that required them to miss work. In "When an Accident Isn't" (1986), the newspaper stated,

> Arsenal officials overlooked broken bones, torn ligaments, burns, and disabling injuries that occurred on the job over the past three and one half years. The record was maintained by the arsenal despite rulings by the Virginia Industrial Commission that the plant had to pay employees for work-related injuries that kept them off the job. The record was maintained even though some employees were required to report to work to avoid lost time after being seriously injured. The record was maintained even as some employees were required to schedule their surgery for job-related injuries on their days off in order to avoid lost time. (p. A1)[14]

The highly publicized safety record included in official plant publications and the actual day-to-day activities were inconsistent, resulting in a credibility gap. Since then, the news media, union officials, and the general public have expressed doubt about the plant's safety record-keeping procedures. Safety figures included in official documents and public pronouncements by RAAP officials are no longer considered a credible source of information. They are no longer believable.

Violation: The Use of Epistemic Authority
for Personal or Group Benefit

The administrative conservator should ensure that the epistemic authority acquired by virtue of his or her official position is exercised with the common good in mind. This is extremely important, because the *proper use* of epistemic authority (or any other type of authority, for that matter) is a prerequisite for its preservation. The phrase "proper use" is emphasized because it has direct bearing on this discussion. The word *proper* suggests appropriateness and correctness, whereas the term *use* (when employed as a noun) is defined as the "utilization or employment for or with some aim or purpose, application or conversion to some (especially good or useful) end" (*The Compact Oxford English Dictionary*, 1991, p. 2204). In relation to epistemic authority, proper use suggests that such authority must be appropriate and used for some good or useful end. It is reasonable to assume that the epistemic authority vested in public bureaucracies and exercised by those who occupy official positions should be employed for the common good. The failure to do so is a violation of the limits placed on such authority and is especially troublesome in a democratic society. Flagrant and widespread abuses provide constant reminders of how easy it is for legitimate authority to become perverted and thus transformed into a form of authoritarianism (see Henderson, 1991). People need not look beyond the regrettable actions and activities of J. Edgar Hoover, former director of the FBI, and Senator Joseph McCarthy, a member of the U.S. Congress (who persecuted citizens for their supposedly communist sympathies), to understand the dangers of authoritarianism.

The administrative conservator should be acutely aware that the abuse of authority is a proved formula for disaster. As a consequence, the conservator must be on the alert for any abuses that may undermine the agency's epistemic authority. Although there are different types of abuse, of special concern are those abuses that involve an official's use of specialized knowledge and competence (acquired largely as a result of or directly related to the formal position) for personal gain. This type of abuse is *malpractice*.[15]

The term *malpractice* as used here differs from the ordinary uses of the word. In common use, malpractice typically refers to the "failure to exercise an accepted degree of professional skill or learning by one . . . rendering professional services which results in injury, loss, or damage" (*Merriam Webster's Collegiate Dictionary*, 1993, p. 705). But there is another meaning of malpractice.

According to *The Compact Oxford English Dictionary* (1991), malpractice is "illegal action by which a person seeks to benefit at the cost of others while in a position of trust" (p. 1026). I will rely on this definition because of its relevance to this discussion, but a few modifications are in order. First, malpractice may or may not involve illegal acts. It is often possible for someone to find loopholes in a law that are, for all practical purposes, legal in that they do not violate the letter of the law. Whether such acts violate the spirit of the law is another question. Nevertheless, the action taken is suspect and likely to raise questions that can undermine the individual's epistemic authority exercised on behalf of the agency.

Second, administrators or other employees need not necessarily occupy official positions at the time they use their specialized knowledge and competence (derived from direct involvement with the agency) for personal benefit. For example, an individual may develop a sophisticated understanding of an agency's internal operation by having worked in an official position for an appreciable time. This understanding includes both the formal and the informal ways of getting things done. Such knowledge is invaluable to outsiders who have a vested interest in having access to key figures in the agency and in knowing how the agency operates. When an official decides to leave an agency, that individual should resist the temptation to use insider information for personal gain. Of course, the use of this knowledge cannot be realistically restricted or prohibited forever without violating an individual's rights. But there seems to be an acceptable time lapse between when a person leaves an agency and when that individual can do business with the agency without being perceived as engaging in influence peddling. The length of this period is an open question. Federal law, for example, uses 1 year as a benchmark, but there is nothing magical about this number (see Zimmerman, 1994, chap. 9). The acceptable time is influenced by a number of important considerations, such as the type of position held by the individual and the degree of access the individual had to privileged information. A scandal involving senior officials of the U.S. Department of Housing and Urban Development (HUD) provides an illustration. Established in 1965, HUD is the primary federal agency charged with addressing the nation's housing needs (see Office of the Federal Register, 1992).

Early in the administration of President George Bush, HUD Inspector General Paul A. Adams released the findings of an investigation focusing on several of the agency's programs. During the Reagan administration, Adams reported that the Section 8 Moderate Rehabilitation program, which provides developers long-term rent subsidies if they agree to bring substandard housing for low-income families up to acceptable levels, was rife with political favoritism. A substantial number of ranking Republicans and former HUD officials benefited financially from the program, either as developers or as high-priced consultants who lobbied senior HUD officials (see Kuntz, 1989). In view of these revelations and the speculation of a widespread scandal, HUD Secretary Jack F. Kemp ordered an investigation of the agency's 48 major programs. The preliminary results were not encouraging. It was disclosed that a majority of the programs were plagued by abuse or serious mismanagement during the Reagan administration. Although several officials and lobbyists were accused of influence peddling, a case involving Lance Wilson, a ranking HUD official and protégé of Samuel L. Pierce, Jr. (the former HUD Secretary), provides a textbook example of malpractice.[16]

Edward T. Pound (1989), a staff reporter for the *Wall Street Journal*, raised numerous questions about the conduct of Lance Wilson, a young, up-and-coming attorney who held a high-level political post at HUD. In his article "Good Connections: How HUD Aide Used Ties to Help Himself, Later PaineWebber," Pound paints a picture of a politically astute, wheeling-and-dealing public official who used his position and inside knowledge of the agency for personal advantage. Wilson's activities at HUD and later as a first vice president at PaineWebber (the billion-dollar financial services corporation) were the focus of congressional investigations into possible wrongdoings at the agency. Wilson was accused of using his influence while still at HUD to assist a developer (and later business partner) secure funds from the agency. He was also accused of making millions of dollars from HUD-related transactions shortly after he left the agency. Commenting on Wilson's questionable activities at HUD, Pound writes:

> What has most aroused congressional investigators about Mr. Wilson are his dealings . . . with Texas-based developer Leonard Briscoe.

In 1983, when Mr. Wilson was still at HUD, he supported $7 million in federal aid for a Briscoe apartment project in Texas, according to House investigators. Then in 1984, only a few months after he left the agency, Mr. Wilson and Mr. Briscoe formed a Texas consulting company, Urban Community Consultants. . . . In 1985, a little more than a year after leaving the agency, Mr. Wilson received a 15% interest—then valued at $750,000—in a HUD-backed Florida apartment project in which Mr. Briscoe was the general partner. (p. A4)[17]

Pound (1989) also portrays Wilson as an influence peddler who used his connections at HUD to assist PaineWebber make profitable business deals. One such deal involved assisting the firm in securing a contract to serve as a financial adviser for HUD as they sold off loan assets. Despite a review panel selecting another firm, PaineWebber was awarded the contract. Pound speculates that Wilson used his influence and inside knowledge to win the contract for the firm:

Mr. Wilson was opening other doors to help admit PaineWebber to a lucrative business involving the sale of HUD loan assets. The agency, under a mandate from the White House to sell off assets for cash to help reduce the federal deficit, wanted a financial advisor on hundred of millions in assets sales—an agreement potentially worth $1.3 million. Mr. Wilson provided "technical advice" on PaineWebber's 100-page proposal and kept the firm abreast of how the competition was going. . . . A seven-member HUD advisory panel recommended another concern, Chemical Bank. . . . The panel's choice, however, was rejected by Mr. Pierce's under-secretary, Carl Covitz, who in an April 1988 memo designated PaineWebber because of its "extensive, direct experience with HUD programs" and its financial expertise. Mr. Covitz says he doesn't remember whether Mr. Pierce ever voiced a preference on the matter. Mr. Covitz also says he doesn't recall ever being lobbied by Mr. Wilson for the job. But someone close to Mr. Wilson says that Mr. Wilson spoke to a Covitz aide shortly before Mr. Covitz picked PaineWebber over Chemical. (p. A4)[18]

The actions of Lance Wilson and others had a profound effect on HUD's integrity. The scandal raised serious questions about the agency's capacity to represent the nation's housing interest. The public's trust and confidence in HUD reached an all-time low.

Summary

Conserving the mission of public bureaucracies is a complex and multifaceted function. It requires that the administrative conservator devote energies to preserving both executive and nonexecutive authority vested in public bureaucracies. With respect to preserving executive authority, the administrative conservator must ensure that the agency's activities and actions do not violate the spirit or letter of the law. Strategies useful for this purpose include the responsible interpretation of legal mandates, the education of employees, and the judicious use of rule making and adjudication. The administrative conservator should prudently and strategically exercise discretion as a means of being responsive to the constitutional masters and the citizenry. The conservator should also protect the agency's jurisdictional boundaries.

The preservation of the agency's nonexecutive authority is also a requirement for conserving the mission of public bureaucracies. The administrative conservator should guard against violations of the public trust. These violations include deliberate deception and the use of epistemic authority for personal gain.

Notes

1. I first discovered this quotation in Austin Sarat (1987).

2. Although agency theory has its roots in commercial law, the theory has attracted a great deal of attention in recent years partly because of its identification as one of two models of competitive self-interest classified under the theoretical paradigm of organizational economics. See, for example, Lex Donaldson (1990) and Charles Perrow (1986, chap. 7).

3. These modifications are readily apparent in Henry D. Kass's (1990) work on stewardship. For a discussion of the Hegelian notion of the civil service, see Georg Wilhelm Friedrich Hegel (trans. 1952).

4. This is not surprising because agency theory owes much to the philosophy of Thomas Hobbes. In discussing authority, Hobbes uses the term *author* instead of *principal* and *actor* instead of *agent*. Hobbes defines *authority* as the actor's "right of doing an action." Hobbes does not make a distinction between right and authority. They are treated as synonymous concepts. See his *Leviathan* (ed. 1957, pp. 105-116). R. S. Peters (1967) also raises this point.

5. C. J. Friedrich uses Thomas D. Wheldon's (1953) *The Vocabulary of Politics* as an illustration.

6. Several state extension services have been the focus of intense criticism. For example, the Virginia Extension Service was severely criticized by the Joint Legislative and Audit Review Commission, an oversight agency of the Virginia General Assembly, for expanding its activities into urban areas. See Virginia Joint Legislative and Audit Review Commission (1979). The Georgia Cooperative Extension Service has also come under attack. In 1991, Governor Zell Miller recommended that the state reduce extension spending by 42%, or $13.9 million. Georgia's Agriculture Commissioner, Tommy Irvin, indicated that the Extension Service had lost a great deal of political support because it had "gotten into areas where it didn't belong." [See "Farm Extension Programs Withering," 1991, p. A12, in *The Plain Dealer*, a Cleveland (Ohio) paper.] In 1994, the federal extension service was abolished as part of the reorganizaton of the Department of Agriculture. See the U.S. Department of Agriculture Secretary's memorandum 1010-1, October 20, 1994, *Reorganization of the Department of Agriculture*, p. 8.

7. For a detailed description and analysis of the Iran-Contra affairs, see Theodore Draper (1991).

8. The EPA scandal and the dispute between the Reagan administration and Congress about turning over documents concerning the superfund program was headline news during the first half of 1982. The *Washington Post* and *New York Times* devoted considerable attention to this story.

9. In discussing the topic of statutory interpretation, I have benefited from the work of William N. Eskridge, Jr., and Philip P. Frickey (1990).

10. Knowledge and competence are integral components of nonexecutive authority. The argument advanced here does not undercut the analytical distinction offered by DeGeorge. According to DeGeorge (1985), the "possession of such authority [non-executive] is frequently the basis for conferring executive authority on an individual" (p. 26).

11. The term *discretion* as used here is consistent with the conceptualization offered by C. J. Friedrich (1972). He suggests that discretion generally involves a decision among alternatives that can and must be implemented. He further states that such decisions cannot be made "arbitrarily, wantonly or carelessly, but in accordance with the requirements of the situation" (p. 68).

12. My discussion on rule making and adjudication is based primarily on A. Lee Fritschler's (1989) book *Smoking and Politics: Policy Making and the Federal Bureaucracy* (esp. chap. 5) and David L. Shapiro's (1965) classic article, "The Choice of Rulemaking or Adjudication in the Development of Administrative Policy." Other works on rule making include Gary Byner (1987), Cornelius M. Kerwin (1994), and James O'Reilly (1983).

13. These violations are derived from DeGeorge's (1985, esp. chap. 3) discussion of the limits of nonexecutive authority.

14. From "When an Accident Isn't," March 30, 1986, *Roanoke Times and World News*, p. A1. Reprinted by permission of the *Roanoke Times and World News*.

15. I am indebted to Lawrence F. Keller (personal communication, n.d.) of Cleveland State University for suggesting the term *malpractice* during one of our discussions on epistemic authority.

16. Other key figures implicated in the HUD scandal include former Massachusetts Senator Edward W. Brook; Frederick M. Bush, former aide and fund-raiser to President George Bush (no relation); Deborah Gore Dean, former executive assistant to HUD Secretary Samuel Pierce; Paul J. Manafort, prominent Republican political

consultant; Richard Shelby, political director, Republican Senatorial Committee and former White House personnel aide; and James G. Watt, former Secretary of Interior, to name a few. See Kuntz (1989).

17. From "Good Connections: How HUD Aide Used Ties to Help Himself, Later PaineWebber," by E. T. Pound, September 22, 1989, *The Wall Street Journal*, pp. A1, A4. Reprinted by permission of *The Wall Street Journal*, © 1989 Dow Jones & Company, Inc. All rights reserved worldwide.

18. From "Good Connections: How HUD Aide Used Ties to Help Himself, Later PaineWebber," by E. T. Pound, September 22, 1989, *The Wall Street Journal*, pp. A1, A4. Reprinted by permission of *The Wall Street Journal*, © 1989 Dow Jones & Company, Inc. All rights reserved worldwide.

4

Conserving Values

◆ BECAUSE ADMINISTRATIVE LEADERSHIP and organizational values are closely linked in the leadership literature, it is difficult to discuss one without the other. This bond has been strengthened in recent years as scholars and practitioners have become enthralled with the idea of *organizational culture*. Many writers, especially champions of the so-called excellence theories of leadership, state with an evangelical zeal that successful executives know (or should know) how to create, manage, and manipulate their organization's value system. (See Bennis & Nanus, 1985; T. Peters, 1981; Zaleznick, 1989; for a critique of this literature, see Rost, 1991.) This value system or culture is said to consist of an assortment of elements, such as organizational myths, ideology, language, and rituals.

As one reads the voluminous literature on leadership and organizational culture, a recurrent theme emerges: Writers overestimate the amount of power that administrative leaders have with respect to managing an organization's culture. The organization's value system is treated much like clay in the hands of a skilled artist; it is to be molded and shaped in accordance with the wishes and desires of its creator. Administrative leaders are conferred the power to single-handedly create, transform, and protect core institutional values against all comers.

As noted in Chapter 2, this larger-than-life concept of leadership does not hold up under close scrutiny. Consequently, I reject the notion that administrative leaders have the power and intellectual ability to conserve institutional values alone; the task is too complex and exceeds the capacity and skill of any one individual. It is more realistic to say that conserving the values of public bureaucracies is a shared responsibility; a multitude of actors both inside and outside the agency play an important role in performing this function. These include, among others, agency personnel from the street-level bureaucrat to the executive cadre, members of Congress, individual citizens, and external professional organizations.

In this chapter, I examine the administrative conservator's role and responsibility for conserving the values of public bureaucracies. When I speak of values, I am referring to "objects of desire that are capable of sustaining group identity," including "any set of goals or standards that can form the basis of shared perspective and group feelings" (Selznick, 1957, p. 121).[1] This discussion concentrates on the conservator's relationship with the agency's executive cadre and examines strategies designed to maintain a viable executive cadre. Special attention is devoted to maintaining commitment among the executive cadre and to ensuring that it is appropriately composed in terms of skills, attitudes, and behaviors needed to preserve institutional integrity.

A Viable Executive Cadre

The executive cadre within most public bureaucracies consists of senior career executives representing various functional and administrative support areas. The exact composition and size of the executive cadre varies from agency to agency. The executive cadre is identified by several different names such as the "executive team," "chief and staff," "executive council," "management team," "administrative team," "executive cabinet," and "strategic management team."

The fascination that many organization and leadership theorists have had with the powerful heroic leader has contributed to the neglect of the executive cadre's role in preserving institutional values. This is an unfortunate oversight because the executive cadre plays an important role in preserving institutional integrity. Members of the executive cadre are "custodians of policy"; they are responsible for the "persistence of an organization's distinctive values, competence and role" (Selznick, 1957, p. 105). According to Selznick, the executive cadre can (and should) "perform the essential task of indoctrinating newcomers along desired lines." He also asserts that "they can provide assurance that decision making will conform, in spirit, as well as letter, to policies that may have to be formulated abstractly and vaguely" (p. 105).

Because of the central role in protecting the values of public bureaucracies, the administrative conservator should focus on maintaining a viable executive cadre. The term *viable* has special significance and refers to the executive cadre's strength and thereby capacity to protect the values of public bureaucracies from serious corruption. The maintenance of a viable executive cadre requires that the administrative conservator devote special attention to at least two important areas of concern. First, the conservator should maintain commitment among the executive cadre to core institutional values. Second, the conservator should ensure that the executive cadre is appropriately composed in terms of skills and perspectives.

Commitment and the Executive Cadre

The executive cadre is more inclined to protect the core values of public bureaucracies if it is committed to them. This commitment is evidenced by the willingness of cadre members to identify, accept, and devote personal energies to the protection of agency goals and values because of a strong sense of loyalty.[2] The administrative conservator should not take for granted that members of the executive cadre are, or will remain, committed to the goals and values of the agency. Indeed, there is too much at stake—namely, the integrity of public bureaucracies. The conservator should continuously explore ways to build and maintain commitment among the executive cadre to larger institutional aims. Although scholars have identified a wide range of useful strategies, of special interest are using inducements and persuasion, minimizing dissension among members of the executive cadre, and building and maintaining high levels of trust between the administrative conservator and members of the executive cadre.

Strategy: Using Inducements and Persuasion

The use of inducements and persuasion as a commitment strategy was given intellectual currency by Chester I. Barnard (1938) in his seminal work, *The Functions of the Executive*. Although organization theorists have attempted to extend Barnard's theory, I will rely on his original work for guidance.

Barnard (1938) suggests that securing cooperation (a prerequisite for building and maintaining commitment) from organizational members is achieved by "objective inducements" and by "changing states of mind." He refers to the former as the "method of incentive" and the latter as the "method of persuasion." Barnard asserts that the method of incentive consists of two analytically distinct types. The first type he calls *specific inducements* because they are addressed to the individual. Specific inducements include material things such as money and other forms of compensation; opportunities for acquiring personal power and prestige; "desirable physical working conditions" such as office space; and the satisfaction of "personal ideals relating to non-material, future, or altruistic relation" (pp. 142-146). The second type of incentive is termed *general incentives* because they are not offered to the individual as such. General incentives include providing opportunities for "social compatibility and comradeship" (pp. 147-148).

Barnard contends that organizations cannot offer all the necessary incentives needed to secure cooperation. Consequently, executives must use persuasion in conjunction with the incentives they can provide. He identifies three forms of persuasion. The first form is *coercion*. Coercion can be used to secure cooperation or to exclude an individual from participating as a member of the organization. Barnard concedes that coercion is not well suited for securing cooperation over time, especially if it is the only method employed. Forced exclusion appears to work quite well if used with some discretion. Exclusionary practices may include demotion, dismissal, the withholding of rewards, and excommunication for those who do not abide by the rules. Forced exclusion is a means of getting the message across that some modes of behavior are not acceptable.

The second mode of persuasion is the *rationalization of opportunity*. Using his characteristic style of presentation, Barnard separates this form of persuasion into two types, specific and general. Specific rationalizations are designed to persuade organizational members that cooperation is in their "best interest." General rationalizations appeal to high ideals reflected, for example, in political or religious doctrines.

The final method of persuasion cited by Barnard is the *inculcation of motives*. This refers to the indoctrination of organizational members with desirable behaviors. Indoctrination is accomplished through education and propaganda.

Barnard's (1938) reliance on incentives and persuasion provides important clues to how the administrative conservator might build and maintain commitment among the executive cadre. With the previous discussion in mind, I conclude the following: The conservator should offer a combination of incentives in conjunction with appropriate forms of persuasion as a central strategy for maintaining commitment among the executive cadre. In doing so, the administrative conservator should consider that members of the executive cadre are "moved by different incentives or combination of incentives, and by different incentives or combination of incentives at different times" (pp. 148-149). In other words, the use of incentives and persuasion must be well suited for the behaviors and dispositions of cadre members. They should also be employed at the appropriate time in relation to prevailing organizational circumstances. The following example examines the offering of financial compensation as a specific inducement to members of an executive cadre within a federal administrative agency.

Financial compensation, in and of itself, does not seem to be much of an incentive within federal administrative agencies. In his study of federal bureau chiefs, Herbert Kaufman (1981a) found that the chiefs he observed could not "rely on the pay structure to keep the work force at a high pitch intensity" (p. 79). The pay ceiling imposed by Congress on high-ranking, career civil servants, as well as extended periods of inflation, makes it virtually impossible to use financial compensation as an effective incentive. Other types of incentives, both specific and general, should be provided instead. For example, the administrative conservator could offer cadre members more opportunities for acquiring prestige by widening their discretion and participation in the decision-making process. This is a proved strategy, as Selznick (1957) points out: "Morale is closely related to the possibility of increasing participation as a way of developing personal commitment to the organization" (p. 98).

The administrative conservator should keep in mind that incentives must be used in conjunction with persuasion to secure cooperation. Again, in the federal government, the threat of dismissal (persuasion of a coercive nature) is not an effective method of securing cooperation. The chance of being dismissed from federal government services is relatively small (Kaufman, 1981a). Although the fear of dismissal may not work well, excommunication or ostracism from participation in high-level decision making is a viable alternative. In addition, other modes of persuasion such as rationalization of opportunities and the inculcation of motives are appropriate. For example, the U.S. Forest Service uses a rotation strategy as a means of educating personnel on what it means to be a member of the service. It is safe to assume that members of the Forest Service's executive cadre have held a variety of different field positions throughout the service and are well socialized in its traditions and values.

Strategy: Minimizing Dissension Within the Executive Cadre

The administrative conservator should also minimize dissension among members of the executive cadre to maintain commitment to larger institutional values. Conflict within the cadre, however, should not be suppressed or discouraged. A certain amount of conflict or creative tension is a normal state of organizational affairs. Students of organization theory and behavior have suggested that a degree of conflict is even necessary and useful for increasing organizational performance. But dissension within the executive cadre is an entirely different matter. By dissension I mean widespread dissatisfaction, petty jealousy, anger, discord, and strife. Dissension within the executive cadre is a sure way to circumvent commitment to larger agency goals and values.

The administrative conservator should be on the lookout for two common sources of dissension: (a) unhealthy competition among cadre members and (b) loss of faith in the agency's ability to perform its function. With regard to the first source, unhealthy competition is detrimental to cultivating a spirit of cooperation, an essential condition for building and maintaining commitment. The unhealthy competition among competing factions within the Bureau of Alcohol, Tobacco and Firearms (ATF) is a case in point.

The Bureau of Alcohol, Tobacco and Firearms (n.d.-a) is responsible for "law enforcement; regulation of the alcohol, tobacco and firearm industries; and ensuring the collection of federal taxes imposed on distilled spirits and tobacco products" (p. 1).[3] For most of its history, ATF was a division of the IRS. The agency achieved bureau status within the Department of Treasury in 1972. As such, ATF is a relatively new agency compared with other federal bureaus such as the Bureau of Land Management or the Federal Bureau of Investigation. Despite its newness as a bureau, many of ATF's functions and responsibilities can be traced back to the Prohibition Unit of the IRS created in response to the Volstead Prohibition Enforcement Act of 1919. This act, which prompted ratification of the 18th Amendment to the U.S. Constitution, gave the IRS enforcement authority relating to the illegal manufacture, sale, and transportation of alcoholic beverages.[4]

A close examination of ATF's history indicates that the agency adapted quite well for most of its existence despite assuming responsibility for a variety of diverse functions. Although ATF was delegated more responsibility for administering a multitude of diverse functions, many activities associated with such functions required a similar orientation. Functions assigned to ATF tended to fall within two distinct categories: (a) the collection of taxes and

(b) the regulation of specific industries through registration, licensing, and permit requirements. Underpinning the agency's functions and processes in each area is the policy of *voluntary compliance*. Consequently, ATF emphasized those aspects of its mission related to tax and regulatory compliance in the alcohol, tobacco, and firearms industries.

Although ATF was given law enforcement responsibilities, much of the criminal enforcement activities revolved around the compliance value. The agency's emphasis on voluntary compliance is not surprising, especially because the agency was a division of the IRS for most of its existence. Prior to the late 1970s and early 1980s, ATF special agents devoted a substantial portion of their time to the investigation of illicit manufacture of alcohol and firearms licensing violations.

The emphasis on voluntary compliance served the agency well. Nevertheless, the 1980s marked a turning point. ATF's emphasis on compliance in light of changing priorities on stricter criminal enforcement of firearms violations jeopardized the agency's existence. In 1982, the Reagan administration recommended the abolishment of ATF and the transfer of its firearms, explosive, and arson functions to the Secret Service.[5] The alcohol and tobacco functions were to be turned over to the Customs Service. The administration's recommendation was based on the premise that the transfer of ATF functions to other agencies would reduce cost, enhance efficiency in government operations, and result in a more effective enforcement of firearms, explosive, and arson statutes. The Reagan administration argued that ATF functions relating to alcohol were incompatible with the agency's law enforcement responsibilities. In building its case, the administration argued that ATF had been unsuccessful in reconciling the differences between these two diverse functions. John Walker, assistant secretary of Enforcement and Operations, Department of Treasury, argued this point at the Senate hearing on the proposed abolishment of ATF:

> The proposal to reassign ATF functions to other bureaus was based on the fact that the functions of alcohol and tobacco have no commonality of interest with the criminal enforcement function of

firearms, explosives and arson. There are no identifiable reasons for the diverse functions to be performed in a single agency. I would stress no identifiable reason for the diverse functions to be performed in a single agency. This fact has been previously recognized within the Department. The diversity of function has led to an inefficient organizational structure and to unhealthy competition for resources between criminal enforcement activities and revenue protection and regulation in a declining budget picture. (U.S. Senate Subcommittee of the Committee on Appropriations, 1982, p. 265)

It was no secret among agency personnel and other attentive observers that ATF's senior administrative staff was torn by dissension and strife because of conflict between supporters of tax compliance (revenue protection) and proponents of criminal enforcement. In fact, when the proposal was made to abolish the agency, there was speculation that some of ATF's career officials (those supposedly unhappy with law enforcement's status within the agency) covertly supported the reassignment of the firearms and explosive functions to the Secret Service. From the perspective of those who favored a more vigorous law enforcement role for the agency, such actions seemed to make sense because the reassignment of the law enforcement function also meant the reassignment of personnel to what many in the law enforcement community considered a prestigious organization.

The competition and dissension within the executive cadre between members who advocated tax compliance and those who supported law enforcement were not healthy. In addition to public statements made by Assistant Secretary Walker, the dissension between the two factions is also noted in an ATF (1988) document titled *Long Term Management Change*, which describes changes made in the agency since its proposed abolishment:

For the previous 10 years, since being broke off from the IRS, ATF had tried to find its direction, its focus. Yet management could never resolve the dilemma of having two separate functions, tax compliance and law enforcement. Because a relatively *destructive relationship* [italics added] existed between the two functions responsible for the mission of the bureau, the administrative function often filled the power vacuum that was created. This only caused more acrimony. Existing problems were further exacerbated by the

sensitivity of the Bureau's mission and its being the target of special
interest groups. (p. 7)

The ATF illustration points out the dangers of unhealthy competition and how such competition can weaken the commitment
of a leadership cadre to organizational values. The ongoing dissension within the executive cadre regarding the agency's mission and
the allegation that some members of the administrative staff worked
behind the scene to support the reassignment of the law enforcement function to the Secret Service raise serious questions about
how strongly ATF's executive cadre was committed to core agency
values.

In thinking about the ATF example, the question arises: How
can the administrative conservator prevent or minimize unhealthy
competition among members of the executive cadre? Several strategies can be used to accomplish this purpose. First, the administrative conservator can cultivate a sense of pride in the agency and in
its larger aims and aspirations. This strategy can be put into
practice through one-on-one conversations with members of the
executive cadre, pep talks at executive meetings and team-building
retreats, and, on unusual occasions such as an agency crisis,
appeals for greater cooperation through formal internal correspon-
dence. Another strategy is to give public recognition to those who
exhibit cooperative behaviors. Public pronouncements made at
executive staff meetings, at formal ceremonies, and in internal
communication organs such as agency newsletters are several
useful ways to reward cooperative behaviors. For example, Harry
Wiggins, director of the Virginia Division of Child Support Enforcement, often uses the agency's statewide conference, management
team retreats, and the agency newsletter, *The Support Reporter*, to
reward members of the management team for demonstrating cooperative behaviors.[6]

The administrative conservator can also withhold praise as a
way of expressing dissatisfaction when members of the executive
cadre do not exhibit cooperative behaviors. Stanley E. Morris
(personal communication, 1987), director of the USMS, said it
best: "Sometimes silence or what you don't say is more effective
than chewing someone's . . . out for not playing by the rules. What

you need to understand is that people who get to this level are smart. They are good at reading cues."

Another source of dissension concerns the executive cadre's loss of faith in the agency's capacity to perform its mandated function. When cadre members lose faith in their agency's abilities, the motivation to cooperate is greatly diminished. Without a sufficient level of cooperation, the chances of building or maintaining commitment among the executive cadre are slim (see Wilkins, 1989). Of several factors that can destroy the executive cadre's faith in the agency's abilities, a critical one is "administrative disinvestment" (Wolf, 1987, p. 209). Administrative disinvestment occurs when an agency's administrative capacity to act is severely weakened as a result of deliberate or unconscious actions. According to Larry M. Lane and James F. Wolf (1990), the primary causes of weakened capacity are "continuous resource cutbacks; constant manipulation of administrative structure through reorganization; the failure to maintain key administrative processes such as budgeting, personnel, and policy making; and the loss in the strength of relationships among critical actors in administrative agencies" (p. 4).

Administrative disinvestment presents a challenge for the conservator because it is much easier to cultivate harmonious relationships among cadre members and, in turn, maintain their commitment to core organizational values under favorable conditions. But conditions are not favorable during periods of administrative disinvestment. The uncertainty and agencywide disruptions created by administrative disinvestment raises the stress and frustration level of cadre members, increasing the potential for dysfunctional conflict and dissension. In extreme cases of administrative disinvestment, cadre members are likely to give up and to disinvest themselves because of a feeling of helplessness. As Lane and Wolf (1990) point out,

> the vagaries of political leadership at the agency level create insecurities, uncertainties, and arbitrary program changes which disrupt the stable and continuing processes and relationships of public organizations. . . . The effects of continuing budgetary restrictions, anti-bureaucratic rhetoric, reorganizations, reductions in force,

and various administrative retrenchments have adversely affected the quality of work life and sent the message that a public agency is the wrong place to invest personal energy and identity. As a result, organization and program capacity is being lost daily as workers invest less of themselves in their work, make fewer commitments, and seek ways out of the system. (p. 3)

What should the administrative conservator do to maintain the executive cadre's faith in the agency's abilities during periods of administrative disinvestment? The answer to this question is by no means simple. The ideal strategy would be to stop administrative disinvestment before it begins. But this is not always possible, especially given the political and economic realities of late 20th-century America. Nevertheless, the conservator is not at the total mercy of political and economic forces. For example, in addressing proposed resource cutbacks in a declining budget environment, the administrative conservator could formulate strategies to protect the agency's budget. Many of the strategies identified by Aaron Wildavsky (1990) are relevant here. These include, among others, padding the budget in anticipation of cuts, restructuring budget categories from the previous year to disguise differences in spending, protesting budget cuts by arguing that the program needs all the money or should not be funded at all, and reacting to requests for cuts by suggesting that cuts be taken on programs that enjoy a great deal of political support.

These and other tactics are not 100% successful, however. The administrative conservator must formulate strategies to cope with the adverse effects of administrative disinvestment when it does occur. These strategies should take into consideration the causes of administrative disinvestment and their potential influence on the agency's integrity.

Returning to the previous example of resource cutbacks, assume, for example, that strategies to protect the agency from budget cuts were unsuccessful because of fiscal crisis and that the administrative conservator is forced to make cuts in agency programs and services. What strategies should the conservator use? The extensive literature on cutback management offers a smorgasbord of possibilities ranging from even percentage cuts across-the-board to cutting low-prestige programs or those programs with politically weak clients (Levine, 1978). In selecting strategies to cope with this hypothetical situation, the administrative conservator should be apprised of the trade-offs between two central values governing the allocative decision-making process—*equity* and *efficiency*. In describing the difference between these two values, Charles Levine writes that equity refers to the "distribution of cuts across the organization with an equal probability of hurting all units and employees irrespective of impacts on the long-term capacity of the organization" (p. 320). In contrast, efficiency means the "sorting, sifting, and assignment of cuts to those people and units in the organization so that for a given budget decrement, cuts are allocated to minimize the long-term loss in the total benefit to the organization as a whole, irrespective of their distribution" (p. 320).

Because there are trade-offs in using either equity- or efficiency-driven strategies, the administrative conservator should not only know *what* strategies to use, he or she should also know *when* to use them. This suggests that the conservator should use prudence in selecting strategies; the blind application of strategies governed by either value can undermine the integrity of public bureaucracies and thus destroy the executive cadre's faith in the agency's abilities. For example, strategies governed solely by equity, such as across-the-board cuts, may do more harm than good when an agency's capacity to act has already been severely weakened. Despite the appeal of equity-based strategies, programs and services central to the agency mission should not be required to "share the suffering" with other units. Not all programs and units are created equal; nor should they be treated as such when it comes to protecting an agency's integrity. Should academic departments within a university be required to share an equal burden of budget cuts with the athletic department when they have reached a threshold level whereby their teaching and research capacity is severely weakened? Should the establishment of paternity and enforcement units of a state child support agency, having already endured significant reduction in staff despite a rapidly increasing caseload, share an equal burden of budget cuts with administrative support units? Most would agree that the answer to these questions is no.

Strategies governed by the efficiency value can also do more harm than good if applied inappropriately. If the process of sorting, sifting, and targeting of programs for cuts is mismanaged or driven purely by short-term considerations, the executive cadre is likely to lose faith in the agency's abilities. Examples of mismanagement include failure to communicate the reasons for budget cutbacks; random, ad hoc, or arbitrary decision making; failure to develop support among controlling coalitions within the organization; poor planning and the absence of a cutback strategy; creating winners and losers by pitting units against each other; and establishing a committee to recommend budget cuts and then totally ignoring the committee's recommendations.

I have focused on only one source of administrative disinvestment and its potential adverse affects on the executive cadre. The administrative conservator should also give the same thoughtful consideration to other sources of administrative disinvestment as well.

Strategy: Building and Maintaining Trust

The third strategy for maintaining the executive cadre's commitment to larger institutional goals relates to trust. The administrative conservator should constantly work to foster and maintain a trusting relationship with members of the executive cadre. The term *trust* in this context refers to "faith or confidence in the intentions or actions of a person or group, the expectation of ethical, fair and non-threatening behavior, and concern for the rights of others in exchange relationships" (Carnevale & Wechsler, 1992, p. 473). A trusting relationship is absolutely necessary if the conservator and executive cadre are to work cooperatively in preserving the values of public bureaucracies. This is because trust is an "integrative mechanism that creates and sustains solidarity in social systems"; it also provides the "lubrication that makes it possible for the organization to work" (p. 471).

High levels of distrust between the conservator and executive cadre spell trouble. This is an explosive situation that can set into motion a range of dysfunctional behavioral dynamics that threaten institutional integrity. Samuel Culbert and John McDonough (1985), two authors who have written extensively about trust in organizations, warn of this possibility. According to Culbert and McDonough, "without trust, individuals over-personalize criticism and seek to hide weak spots in their performance. . . . Communication becomes wordy and defensive as individuals fight over issues that need to be open-mindedly discussed" (pp. 17-18).

The administrative conservator can and should use a variety of strategies to cultivate and maintain a trusting relationship with members of the executive cadre. The following strategies are worthy of serious consideration. (For discussion of additional strategies for developing trust, see Britton & Stallings, 1986; Culbert & McDonough, 1985; Fairholm, 1994.)

The conservator should honor both formal and informal commitments made with cadre members. The executive cadre must have confidence that the conservator will keep his or her word. There is certainly nothing novel about this strategy, and one wonders why it is worth mentioning. But keeping one's word is basic to any discussion of trust. Most people need not think too hard to recall a situation in which a person in a position of authority did not keep (or appeared not to have kept) his or her word.

Another strategy is to take up causes that are important to cadre members. There are times when the administrative conservators should spend some of their political capital to obtain resources cadre members want, even though it is not a top priority. Kaufman (1981a, chap. 2) suggests the value of this strategy in his study of federal bureau chiefs. Kaufman recounts a situation in which IRS Commissioner Jerome Kurtz persuaded an assistant secretary of the Treasury (a political appointee) to abandon plans to exercise direct authority over revenue agents. Members of Kurtz's executive cadre were afraid that changing the reporting relationship would set a precedent and eventually change the nature and scope of the revenue agents' role. Although this was not a burning issue for Kurtz, Kaufman suggests that the commissioner's willingness to fight for something the executive cadre valued was an important symbolic act; it demonstrated unity with the executive cadre and instilled a sense of confidence in the commissioner.

The next strategy involves supporting the decisions and actions of cadre members when called on to do so. There are at least two instances in which the conservator's support is essential: (a) when the decision of a cadre member is called into question by individuals or groups adversely affected by the decision and (b) during an organizational crisis. With regard to the first instance, it is not uncommon for a dissatisfied party to maneuver to have a particular decision overturned by appealing to higher authority. This tactic, sometimes described as "going over the head" of the administrative official who made the decision, is and should be available to parties both inside and outside public bureaucracies. Although overturning a decision of a cadre member may be necessary in some instances, such action should be the exception rather than the rule. If the decisions of cadre members are consistently overruled because of stylistic (i.e., difference in how one approaches a decision) rather than substantive concerns (i.e., violation of policy and key process values), they are likely to feel undermined. Such feelings can breed resentment and, in turn, create an environment of distrust. Executive cadre members should feel that they have the responsibility as well as the authority to make decisions without interference from the administrative conservator. They should not feel as if "the rug will be pulled from underneath them" once they make a decision.

The second instance, an organizational crisis, is a crucial period that tests the level of trust between the conservator and the executive cadre. The term *crisis* is used in a narrow sense and refers to a period of difficulty experienced by an agency. For example, the explosion of the space shuttle *Challenger* created an organizational crisis for NASA. The administrative conservator should provide public and private support for cadre members (and their staff) during an organizational crisis when it is determined that they have faithfully fulfilled their duties and responsibilities according to the spirit and letter of the law and to other acceptable standards of conduct. If a search begins for a scapegoat before all the facts are in or if the conservator is perceived as engaging in career-saving actions (e.g., creating distance or disassociating from particular cadre members), the conservator stands a chance of losing the executive cadre's faith and confidence. During an organizational crisis, the conservator should give cadre members the benefit of the doubt that they have acted appropriately. It is during such times that the trust between the conservator and executive cadre is put on the line, as shown in the following example of an organizational crisis involving the Cuyahoga County (Ohio) Department of Children and Family Services (DCFS).

The Cuyahoga County DCFS is responsible for investigating and providing services related to child abuse and neglect (the city of Cleveland and several adjacent municipalities are located in Cuyahoga County).[7] In 1993, DCFS employed approximately 939 people. Of the agency's employees, 240 were social workers who handled about 180 cases on an ongoing basis. Caseworkers provide a variety of services for children and their families. These services include but are not limited to assisting families locate food, clothing, shelter, and medical care; linking parents with professional counseling services and support groups to cope with domestic violence and substance abuse; and locating adoptive homes for children who had been removed from their families.

In 1992, Judith Goodhand, a veteran social service administrator, became DCFS's executive director. When Goodhand assumed the directorship, she immediately began to institute a different philosophy for handling cases of child abuse and neglect. Instead of embracing the widely held philosophy that the best way to assist abused or neglected children is to remove them from their homes, Goodhand adopted the position that children should be removed from their homes only as a last resort. She advocated a family preservation approach that focused on making dysfunctional families work. In a newspaper article outlining this philosophy, Goodhand (1993) states:

- We believe that most families love their children and want to do the best for them;
- We believe that children have the right to live with their own families and should be deprived of that right only when their safety demands it;
- We believe that children and families are harmed when they are separated, and we feel we must exercise our legal authority with great caution and with full knowledge of its potential for damage;

- We believe that families need and deserve the support and the resources of the community to help them raise their children;
- We believe that no child should be separated from the family for reasons of poverty;
- Most of all, we believe that families do a much better job of raising children than agencies do, so our commitment—our vision—is to ensure that all children have families. (p. B7)[8]

Goodhand was well aware of the risks associated with the family preservation philosophy. Although the agency developed a detailed system of policies and procedures to assist caseworkers in determining when a child should be removed from the home, the system was not foolproof. Because of the nature of DCFS's business, the possibility exists that a caseworker could, after having faithfully followed agency procedures and other appropriate guides for action (e.g., experience and intuition), make a decision that jeopardizes a child's safety. This possibility was real and firmly imprinted on the mind of many of the agency's social workers. Prior to Goodhand's arrival, a 10-year-old boy committed suicide after DCFS caseworkers failed to remove him from the home after numerous reports of abuse.

In August 1993, Goodhand's worst nightmare became a reality. A 21-month-old Cleveland girl died of internal bleeding caused by an injury to the abdomen. Her mother was charged with the crime. During the same month the toddler was born, DCFS took custody of the child after the agency received complaints that the mother, an alcoholic and crack cocaine addict at the time, was neglecting the child. After a court hearing in July 1993, DCFS returned the child to her mother. The agency did so because caseworkers determined that the mother had addressed the issues that prompted removal of the child from the home. The mother had been drug-free for 18 months and attended Alcoholics Anonymous meetings on a regular basis. She was described by an agency official as a model patient. The Cuyahoga County Juvenile Court judge called for an investigation to determine why the child had been returned to her mother.

During this organizational crisis, Goodhand publicly supported the actions of her staff. For example, she held a news conference to defend the agency, members of the executive cadre, and the caseworkers directly involved in the case. In responding to questions about the agency's decision to return the child to her mother, Goodhand confidently replied: "My feeling is that at this point, we have indeed followed good practice in not taking custody of the girl. There had never been an indication of abuse in the family" (Dubail & Gillispie, 1993, p. A1).[9] Goodhand also insulated agency caseworkers from the press, which had begun a search for a villain to blame for the child's death. She prohibited agency personnel from revealing the names of those intimately involved with the case. According to a caseworker (personal communication, November 25, 1993) who supported the decision to return the child to the mother, Goodhand was very supportive in public and private discussions. He commented that Goodhand "always made herself available. . . . She always made the time to talk during these difficult times." The caseworker also stated that his coworkers were "pleased to see that Judith Goodhand supported him because this had not been the agency's practice in the past." He explained that "in the past, the practice was to blame the worker for everything. . . . We were hung out to dry." He also stated that Goodhand's actions "lifted the morale and reduced the amount of fear they [the caseworkers] had in performing their jobs."

Goodhand's actions illustrate the positive benefits of supporting cadre members and their staff during an organizational crisis. From the perspective of administrative conservatorship, Goodhand's actions provide a textbook example of what should be done. But supporting the decisions of cadre members is not without risk, especially during the midst or immediate aftermath of a crisis, when all of the facts are not in. Consider the case of Stephen Higgins, former director of the Bureau of Alcohol, Tobacco and Firearms.

On February 28, 1993, ATF agents raided the 77-acre Branch Davidian compound located near Waco, Texas. ATF conducted the raid because it had accumulated firm evidence that the religious cult had committed numerous federal weapons violations and that the cult's charismatic leader, David Koresh, had made statements encouraging cult members to kill citizens in nearby Waco (Department of the Treasury, 1993). Because members of the cult were heavily armed, AFT officials responsible for planning and executing the commando operation were given explicit instructions not to proceed with the raid if they lost the element of surprise.

The operation was a disaster, and, from all accounts, it will go down in history as one of the worst chapters in U.S. law enforcement history.[10] Four ATF agents and six members of the religious sect were killed and 15 others wounded during the initial shootout. In the immediate aftermath of the botched raid, ATF Director Higgins publicly assumed total responsibility for his agency's actions. He also made public statements supporting the decision of certain cadre members and their staff.

The Department of the Treasury investigation (1993) into the raid revealed that three members of the ATF's executive cadre (Daniel Hartnett, associate director of law enforcement; Edward Conroy, deputy associate director of law enforcement; and David Troy, intelligence chief) and the raid commanders (Phillip Chojnacki and Charles Sarabyn) made misleading or deliberately deceptive statements. The report stated that Chojnacki and Sarabyn "appear to have engaged in a concerted effort to conceal their errors in judgement" (p. 193). They lied to their superiors and investigators. Both had been informed by an undercover agent inside the compound that the element of surprise was lost, but they ignored this information and decided to proceed with the raid. To make matters worse, Chojnacki and Sarabyn then tried to cover up their errors in judgment by making significant revisions in the document outlining the operation's plans and by reconstructing events to give the impression that the raid failed because of a surprise ambush. Higgins, apparently giving those in charge of the operation the benefit of the doubt, unknowingly perpetuated this misleading version of events and steadfastly supported the actions of ATF administrators and agents. On two different appearances on network television, Higgins publicly defended the actions of ATF executives and agents. Higgins's exchange with reporters on CBS's *Face the Nation*, a weekly news program, is illustrative:

Q. *[reporter]* There has been some suggestion that perhaps your agents knew beforehand that the security had been compromised, that they were aware that Mr. Koresh had received some sort of phone call. Can you just give us your side of that?

A. *[Higgins]* Without being too specific, let me say as I did earlier, this plan was based on the element of surprise. It had to be done quickly, and it had to be a surprise. We would not send our agents into a situation where we didn't think we had the element of surprise.

Q. *[reporter]* But your bottom line is that you absolutely did not believe the security had been compromised when the agents went into the compound?

A. *[Higgins]* Absolutely not, because as you can see, we walked into an ambush, and there's no way that our people, from the team members to the leadership, would have allowed that to happen had they had known it. (quoted in Department of the Treasury, 1993, p. 199)

On March 29, 1993, Higgins made similar statements on NBC's *Today Show*, a morning news and talk show:

Q. *[talk show host]* Let's talk about one of the other charges, and that is that you have, in fact, said that cult members were tipped off, and now there are reports that bureau supervisors knew that the element of surprise had been lost and yet decided to go ahead with the raid anyway. Is that correct?

A. *[Higgins]* This was a plan which depended on the element of surprise. We could not have executed the plan if our supervisors felt like we had lost that element. So my position has been and continues to be we did not believe that we had lost that element of surprise. (quoted in Department of the Treasury, 1993, p. 205)

In addition to the statements above, the Treasury Department's report speculates that Higgins, Hartnett, and other ATF officials may have perpetuated the misleading version of the raid in testimony before a congressional subcommittee reviewing the agency's actions.

It is clear from all accounts that Higgins did not know he was being deceived by members of his executive cadre. He trusted ATF executives and assumed that they had acted responsibly. Higgins's loyalty and unwavering support of ATF executives eventually cost him the directorship of ATF. After 32 years of service, this highly respected and dedicated administrative executive left the government under a dark cloud. Higgins was removed from his post along with several ATF officials. The Department of the Treasury (1993) report was critical of Higgins and stated that he "must accept responsibility for continuing to take public positions on the issue when repeated questions from the media and information readily available to him should have made it clear that he was on shaky ground" (p. 205). The reported also stated that "Higgins never questioned his subordinates to determine the facts until early April" (p. 205).

An Appropriately Composed Executive Cadre

The executive cadre's capacity to protect core organizational values is also strengthened when the group is appropriately composed in terms of skills and perspectives. The phrase "appropriately composed" refers to the suitability of the cadre's structure as measured by the commonality and complementary character of skills, attitudes, and behaviors required to preserve the integrity of public bureaucracies. Many who write about organizational demography suggest that attributes of organizational members such as age, gender, educational background, race, experience, and time of entry into the organization have an influence on the willingness of individuals to voluntarily cooperate. (See McNeil & Thompson, 1971; Pfeffer, 1985; Pfeffer & O'Reilly, 1987.) The concept of organizational demography provides important insights into maintaining the executive cadre's capacity to protect core organizational values. The demographic composition of the executive cadre is an area worthy of the administrative conservator's time and energy. Common demographic characteristics cultivate particular habits, dispositions, and attitudes necessary for achieving social integration, cohesion and, thereby, cooperation among cadre members (Wamsley & Zald, 1976).

The maintenance of functions and processes that determine the executive cadre's demographic composition should be of utmost importance to the administrative conservator. The cadre's composition assists in the cultivation of a distinctive orientation that is vital to sustaining a shared perspective. Agency functions and processes relating to recruitment, selection, and socialization of cadre members are cases in point. These functions and processes are designed to promote a shared perspective of the nature of the enterprise. Their effectiveness is measured by the extent to which they produce conformity in particular habits, attitudes, and dispositions of cadre members. In other words, the effectiveness of socialization processes is shown by the degree to which cadre members fit in. Socialization failures can have far-reaching implications for the organization because such failures may prompt desirable employees to leave the organization or encourage those who stay to engage in sabotage (see Schein, 1985).

The maintenance of a shared perspective through conformity is not an end in itself; rather, it is a means of sustaining conditions necessary for cooperation. Although excessive conformity has a restrictive effect on the executive cadre's capacity to adapt to evolutionary changes, too little conformity may make social integration, compatibility, and the development of a shared perspective difficult. The net result may be the creation of conditions that hinder cooperation (see Barnard, 1938).

The administrative conservator should maintain the suitability of the executive cadre's demographic composition with respect to the agency's field of action, its core technology, its stage of historical development, and the level of administrative action. The demographic composition of the executive cadre must reflect the agency's values and field of action. The term *field of action* refers to an area or sphere of action. Hence, one can speak of the fields of health, law, education, agriculture, and so forth. The executive cadre's composition should remain consistent with or tailored to fit the agency's field of action. An examination of the executive cadre of most governmental agencies with respect to demographic composition makes it clear that the skill and perspectives of cadre members reflect their respective agency's field of action. For example, Harold Siedman (1980) observes that the executive cadre of Department of Agriculture agencies such as the Soil Conservation Service, Farmers Home Administration, and the Cooperative Extension Service is largely composed of individuals who received their formal education from land grant universities. These individuals also have considerable experience and advanced training in an agriculture-related area. Thus, it is safe to conclude that the executive cadre of Department of Agriculture agencies is largely composed of individuals whose skills and perspectives are tailored to agricultural functions and values. Agriculture-related skills and perspectives would not be well suited for an executive cadre of, for example, the FBI or HUD.

The administrative conservator should also ensure that the cadre's composition remains well suited for the dominant core technology employed by the agency. Governmental agencies employ a variety of different technologies to transform inputs into outputs. According to James D. Thompson (1967, chap. 2), organizational technologies consist of three major varieties: long-linked, mediating, and intensive. Long-linked technologies involve serially interdependent tasks with activities geared to the requirements of the next—for instance, the mass-production assembly line. Mediating technologies embody the linking of clientele who are interdependent with goods and services. For example, state child support enforcement agencies seek to link responsible parents to their children through support payments. Intensive technologies entail the use of multiple techniques to create change in some object (human or nonhuman). The selection and application of techniques are guided by responses received from the object. For example, a state juvenile correctional agency may use a variety of techniques in the treatment and rehabilitation of a youthful offender. The agency may use diagnostic testing, individual counseling, family counseling, or a host of other techniques specifically designed to treat the youth. The order and combination of such techniques is conditioned by the feedback received from the youth.

The type of technology employed by the agency has an influence on the type of skills and perspectives needed within the executive cadre. As noted by Thompson (1967), "differences in the technical function should also make for differences at the managerial and institutional levels of the organization" (p. 12). This suggests that the executive cadre's demographic composition should be appropriate for the specific technologies operated by the agency. For example, the skills and perspectives needed to operate core technologies of the U.S. Army's Radford Army Ammunition Plant are different from those required to operate technologies of the Farmington State Mental Hospital in the Missouri Department of Mental Health. In a general way, the mass production of army ammunition (a long-linked technology) requires skills and perspectives that are mainly oriented toward instrumental efficiency. In contrast, the treatment of a mentally ill patient (intensive technology) requires skills and perspectives that are oriented toward ongoing assessment of problems and the application of multiple techniques.[11]

The executive cadre's demographic composition should also be well suited to cope with developmental problems facing the agency as a result of its stage of historical development.[12] Different skills and orientations are needed within the executive cadre to cope with different types of developmental problems precipitated by the agency's stage of historical development. For example, the nature of some developmental problems may require a highly technical orientation and related skills, whereas others may require a broader generalist orientation. When confronted with developmental problems of a technical nature (or vice versa), a predominate generalist's orientation within the executive cadre can weaken the cadre's capacity to protect shared organizational values.[13] The GAO provides a concrete example of this argument.

For most of its institutional life, the GAO performed the role of fiscal and management auditor for Congress. In performing this oversight function, the GAO concentrated its efforts on examining the extent to which government agencies adhered to legally binding mandates and whether they used the most effective administrative practices to ensure that public funds were wisely spent. The skills and perspectives of GAO personnel reflected a concern with the nitty-gritty aspects of government. The executive cadre and middle- and entry-level staff were composed of individuals who possessed technical expertise and experience in either law or accounting.

During the 15-year tenure of Comptroller General Elmer Staats (1966-1981), the GAO's activities evolved to include program auditing, a euphemism for program evaluation. Expansion into the realm of policy analysis was a significant milestone in the GAO's institutional life, thus marking a transition to a new stage of historical development. Because this new approach required a different orientation among agency personnel, the program evaluation function created developmental problems for the GAO. The skills and perspectives required to perform traditional auditing are distinct from those needed to conduct program evaluations. This difference is reflected by the types of questions involved in the two activities. In traditional auditing, GAO personnel attempt to answer such questions as "Are funds being spent legally?" and "Is it possible to eliminate waste and inefficient use of public funds?" (J. T. Rourke, 1978, p. 454; Walker, 1986). These questions focus on managerial efficiency and the legal expenditure of public funds. Extensive knowledge of an agency's procedures is required to answer such questions. In contrast, GAO personnel conducting program evaluations raise a different set of questions including "Are federal programs achieving their objectives?" and "Are there other ways of accomplishing program objectives at lower costs?" (J. T. Rourke, 1978, p. 454). These questions are not so much concerned about how an agency's program operates in a procedural sense; rather, they concentrate on the extent to which the agency has achieved programmatic goals, which requires a much broader understanding of an agency's functions and operations.

As stated earlier, the program evaluation function posed developmental problems for the GAO because the skills and perspectives of its personnel were not entirely well suited for the agency's new stage of historical development. Numerous institutional changes were needed to ensure that the GAO's executive cadre and other staff had the skills and perspectives to cope with developmental problems confronting the agency. Administrative changes instituted by Comptroller General Staats in the mid-1970s can be interpreted as an attempt to align the agency's skills and orientations with its new stage of historical development. Writing during the GAO's transition, John T. Rourke (1978) noted that Staats restructured the organization along functional lines as opposed to agency lines, changed personnel policies to conform to the new shift in direction, and filled several key executive positions with people from outside the GAO. Rourke concludes that Comptroller General Staats recognized that the skills and perspectives of GAO personnel, especially within the executive cadre, did not mesh well with the agency's stage of historical development.

The administrative conservator should make certain that the executive cadre's demographic composition is appropriate for the institutional level of organizational action. Organization theorists have identified three different levels of organizational action: technical, managerial, and institutional (see Thompson, 1967). The technical level is the locale of the agency's economy or production systems. As such, efficient operation of the technical function is of primary importance. The managerial level performs a service function for the technical level. This typically includes the acquisition of needed resources to ensure the efficient and effective operation of the technical task as well as mediating between users of the agency's products and the technical operation. The third level is the institutional level, which focuses primarily on overall direction and legitimacy of the agency. Administrative actions at this level are "marked by a concern for the evolution of the organization as a whole, including its changing aims and capabilities" (Selznick, 1957, p. 5). Although functions performed at each level are interdependent, they are qualitatively different. This suggests that the skills and perspectives needed to successfully perform the functions at each level are different. For example, specialized expertise is needed at the technical level, whereas a "deeper more comprehensive understanding of social organization" is needed at the institutional level (p. 4). Failure to understand the qualitative differences among levels may result in an inappropriately composed executive cadre that can undermine the integrity of public bureaucracies. Thompson (1967) warns of such consequences:

> If the powerful inner circle is composed solely of individuals with responsibilities in the managerial layer, we would expect problemistic search, not opportunistic surveillance, to prevail. The same result can be obtained when non-managerial members of the inner circle are personally intolerant of ambiguity. Default at the institutional level, however, is more likely to come because of a lack of a sharp distinction, conceptually between managerial and institutional matters. . . . The conversion of administrators from managerial to institutional responsibilities is more than a promotion, for it entails a shift in attention from technical to organizational rationality, from instrumental to social assessments. (p. 153)

In summary, the administrative conservator should maintain an appropriately composed executive cadre as a means of protecting core organizational values. In performing this task, the conservator ensures that the executive cadre's demographic composition is well suited for the agency's field of action, its dominant technological core, its stage of historical development, and the appropriate level of organizational action. The administrative conservator should continually take stock of the executive cadre's demographic composition and make the necessary adjustments to preserve the integrity of public bureaucracies.

Summary

The maintenance of a viable executive cadre is essential for conserving the values of pubic bureaucracies. In this context, a viable executive cadre has the capacity to protect the organization's core values from serious corruption. The maintenance of a viable executive cadre requires that the administrative conservator build and sustain commitment among cadre members to larger agency goals and values. Strategies useful for such purposes include using incentives and persuasion, minimizing dissension among cadre members, and building and maintaining trusting relationships with cadre members. The administrative conservator should also constantly monitor and adjust the executive cadre's demographic composition to ensure that it is well suited for preserving the integrity of public bureaucracies.

Notes

1. I selected this definition because it contains many of the common features associated with the value phenomenon. For a discussion of the concept of values and its intrinsic characteristics, see Robin M. Williams, Jr. (1969).

2. This view of commitment is consistent with the individual-organizational goal congruence perspective. For an extensive review of theoretical and empirical work concerning the concept of organization commitment, see Richard Mowday, Richard Steers, and Lyman Porter (1982). Also see Arnon Reicher (1985).

3. Much of the historical information used in this discussion is drawn from Bureau of Alcohol, Tobacco and Firearms pamphlets *ATF Facts: Mission and Responsibilities* (n.d.-a) and *Bureaucratic Breakdown* (n.d.-b).

4. In 1930, the Prohibition unit was transferred to the Justice Department and was given full bureau status. The move was designed to strengthen the federal government's capacity to combat the illicit manufacture, sale, and transportation of alcoholic beverages by organized crime syndicates. The Bureau of Prohibition's enforcement efforts were popularized in Oscar Fraley's novel *The Untouchables*, which highlighted the exploits of Eliot Ness and the special unit he directed in Chicago. ATF has proudly made Ness one of its organizational heroes.

5. The Clinton administration made a similar proposal as part of Vice President Gore's "reinventing government" initiative. The Clinton administration abandoned the idea when the Brady Bill was passed by both houses of Congress. The bill, named after James Brady, President Reagan's press secretary who was wounded in an attempted assassination of the president, requires a 5-day waiting period prior to the purchase of a handgun. ATF is to assume a major role in enforcing the new law.

6. These observations are based on my personal experiences as a consultant with this agency during a 2-year period.

7. Most of the information used to describe the DCFS case is based on a series of articles printed in the Cleveland (Ohio) newspaper *The Plain Dealer*. See Goodhand's "A County Agency Just for Children" (1993), Dubail and Gillispie's "Removing Children Is the Last Resort" (1993a), Dubail's "Childhood Lost" (1993), "Police Probe Death of 1 Year Old" (1993), Gillispie's "Toddler Died After Mother Punched Her, Police Say" (1993), and Dubail and Gillispie's "Girl's Death Starts Feud Over Custody Action" (1993b). © The Plain Dealer; used with permission.

8. Goodhand, J. (May 27, 1993). A county agency just for our children. *The Plain Dealer*, Cleveland, Ohio, p. B7; reprinted by permission.

9. Dubail, J., and Gillispie, M. (April 11, 1993). Removing children is the last resort. *The Plain Dealer*, Cleveland, Ohio, p. B3; reprinted by permission.

10. The ill-fated raid, siege, and eventual fire on April 19, 1993, which destroyed the compound and killed 85 men, women, and children, including David Koresh, the cult's leader, were prominent news during much of 1993.

11. James Q. Wilson (1989, chap. 9 and 11) offers additional support for the arguments advanced here. In his discussion of executives and agency types, Wilson identifies four types of agencies: coping, craft, procedural, and production. Each requires a specific type of executive.

12. The term *stage of historical development* is used instead of the more common term *life cycle*. These terms are not synonymous. The life-cycle framework is concerned with the proper sequencing of an agency's action in relationship to its age or period of existence. Public bureaucracies are presumed to pass through predictable stages (i.e., childhood, adolescence, maturity, etc.). The difficulty with the life framework is that agencies do not follow predictable stages. The stage of historical development framework focuses on developmental problems, the evolutionary circumstances confronting the agency created by a series of changes. As such, the stage of historical development refers to a portion of time marked by a series of changes that result in the institution evolving to a different state. See Selznick (1957) for a discussion of this point.

13. Selznick (1957) makes this point when he observes, "As new problems emerge, individuals whose way of thinking and responding served the organization well in an early stage may be ill-fitted for the new tasks. Characteristically, this is not so much a matter of technical knowledge as of attitudes and habits. . . . The more firmly set the personal pattern—the less adaptable the individual" (p. 108).

5

Conserving Support

ADMINISTRATIVE CONSERVATORS have little chance of preserving the integrity of public bureaucracies if they fail to build and maintain a sufficient level of support for their programs and activities.[1] Support is a key source of *power*, and, as Norton Long (1949) advises, power is the "lifeblood of administration" (p. 257).[2] This discussion of conserving support concentrates on the administrative conservator's efforts to build and sustain support among an agency or program's key external constituencies as well as among internal interest groups. First, I examine conserving external support within the context of sustaining a favorable organizational image and maintaining strength with key external constituencies. Second, with respect to internal support, I briefly discuss the maintenance of commitment among internal interest groups by using the strategy of co-optation.

Conserving External Support

A Favorable Public Image

The notion that organizations depend on the external environment for their existence is a dominant and well-established perspective in the field of organization theory. In this view, the external environment is a constraint that interferes with the attainment of organizational goals. Interest in the external environment and its relationships to organizational performance has prompted theorists to investigate a multitude of topics that relate to the management of environmental dependency. To avoid straying from the task at hand, in this chapter I do not review this voluminous literature or engage in an extended discussion of the topic. Here it is enough to say that organizations, both public and private, are not self-sufficient and, therefore, are dependent on their external environment for support. This support ranges from financial and human resources to social legitimacy (see Pfeffer & Salancik, 1978).

For public bureaucracies, creating and sustaining a favorable public image are especially crucial for success. Charles Perrow (1961) suggests that a "predominately favorable public" image translates into "prestige," which, in turn, increases the likelihood that administrative agencies will continue to secure vital resources from the external environment (p. 335). The extent to which an agency successfully acquires necessary resources is an indicator of external support. A review of Perrow's work on organizational prestige is useful for advancing this discussion.

Perrow (1961) asserts that organizational prestige may be based on intrinsic and/or extrinsic characteristics of the product or service. Intrinsic characteristics pertain to the quality of the product or service as determined by those capable of evaluating it. The extrinsic quality of an organization's product or service is measured against established standards highly prized in a particular field of action. Extrinsic characteristics have little to do with the quality of the product per se. Instead, prestige may be based on association with "value laden symbols" (p. 336) or characteristics of the organization that are not directly related to the quality of the product or service itself. Examples of extrinsic characteristics include the physical quality of the building in which the organization is located and the type of publicity generated by the organization.

Perrow (1961) suggests that prestige based on the intrinsic quality of a product or service is most desirable if it can withstand scrutiny and is easy to evaluate by those who use it. There are, however, circumstances that make external evaluation difficult. The highly technical nature of the product or service is a case in point. Outside validating groups may be used to "certify" the intrinsic quality of the product or service. As Perrow observes, "the more difficult it is to establish the intrinsic quality, the more the organization needs other groups for validation" (p. 337). Reputable accrediting bodies or professional associations are established for such purposes. Outside groups used to validate intrinsic characteristics either must be users of the product or must have sufficient expertise to evaluate it.

In addition to validating groups, Perrow (1961) contends that organizations may use *indirect indexes* to cultivate and maintain a favorable public image.[3] The use of indirect indexes involves "publicizing of characteristics of the organization which are thought to insure quality" (p. 337). For example, an academic department within a university might use as indirect indexes the number of articles published by faculty members in scholarly journals, the number and amount of research grants funded, and the placement of graduate students at nationally recognized institutions. Indirect indexes of quality are often included in official documents prepared for public consumption, such as annual reports and other publicity-generating documents.

Perrow warns that an overemphasis on indirect indexes or extrinsic characteristics of the organization can result in unintended consequences. Preoccupation with stressing extrinsic characteristics or flaunting indirect indexes of quality may take precedence over maintaining the quality of products and services. Such actions may ultimately have an adverse affect on an organization's favorable public image.

Perrow's analytical construct of prestige on the basis of intrinsic and extrinsic characteristics provides important insights into how the administrative conservator might maintain an agency's favorable public image. Such maintenance requires that the administrative conservator (a) protect the agency's reputation for consistent compliance with standards used to measure the intrinsic quality of its products and services and (b) ensure that indirect indexes of quality included in official documents remain accurate and meaningful.

Strategy: Complying With Established Standards

The agency's reputation for consistently receiving favorable evaluations on the intrinsic quality of its products and services is an essential requirement for maintaining its favorable public image. The concept *reputation* has special significance and is defined as a "general estimation in which a person or a thing is held by the public" (*American Heritage Dictionary*, 1982, p. 1050). The key word in this definition is *estimation*, which implies judgment or opinion. The judgment and opinions of an agency's key constituents are influenced by the consistent quality of its products or services over time.

The administrative conservator should ensure that the agency consistently receives favorable evaluations on the intrinsic quality of products and services. It is this perception of consistency, or lack thereof, that determines an agency's reputation and thus contributes to its public image. The failure of an agency to receive consistently favorable evaluations can lead to a lack of public trust and, consequently, a "bad reputation." Such a perception, especially if it becomes widespread, can create an unfavorable public image and ultimately result in withdrawal of support by the agency's key constituents.

The administrative conservator should constantly monitor, inspect, and update agency operations to maintain a reputation for uniform compliance with established standards. Professional associations often play an important role in developing and institutionalizing standards. These standards vary according to the nature of the agency's business as well as its field or realm of action. For example, the standards used to measure the intrinsic quality of dams and bridges built by the U.S. Army Corps of Engineers are different from those used to measure the intrinsic quality of the services provided by the U.S. Postal Service or the National Institutes of Health Centers for Disease Control. As far as professional associations are concerned, the American Society of Civil Engineers has a great deal of influence on standards used to measure the intrinsic quality of dams and bridges built by the Army Corps of Engineers.

To ensure consistent compliance with established standards, the administrative conservator could use several strategies ranging from periodic detailed inspections to strict regulation of agency activities. Although these strategies are useful, I am especially interested in maintaining compliance with established standards through the adoption of innovations.

The administrative conservator should be prepared to update the agency's operation through the adoption of innovations when the need arises. Such decisions, however, should be implemented at the appropriate pace. The phrase "appropriate pace" refers to a regulated speed at which agency operations are updated. The administrative conservator should know when to update agency operations as a means of preserving its integrity. In other words, *timing* is an important consideration in the adoption of innovations.

The question of timing is multifaceted in nature in that the administrative conservator should (a) minimize the premature adoption of innovations and (b) avoid the perception (real or imagined) of lagging in making changes. The premature adoption of innovations can result in the incorporation of programs, policies, and technologies that may not add much to an agency's performance or reputation. In fact, they can have just the opposite effect. Once innovations are adopted and incorporated as part of the formal structure, they constrain the agency in terms of pursuing future courses of action. (See Dimaggio & Powell, 1983; Hannan & Freeman, 1984.) The premature adoption of some innovations is also a problem because the shakeout period may result in the elimination of some innovations and the institutionalization of others. For example, an agency may be saddled with an innovation it adopted, although its value is eventually depreciated during the shakeout period. The early adoption of computer systems as a strategy for making organizations more efficient and modern is such a case.

Many organizations were early adopters of computers. This technology was incorporated into the formal structure of organizations to improve efficiency and to convey the message of being rational and modern. Organizations invested substantial sums of money into computer systems that became obsolete because of rapid technological developments. Because of the huge sunk costs tied up in these investments, many organizations are now stuck with antiquated equipment. The very use of these systems conveys the image that the organization is outdated, the perception it ironically attempted to avoid by incorporating the system in the first place. The IRS and the FAA have been caught in this predicament. For at least 25 years, the IRS tax-processing system has been criticized as old-fashioned, unwieldy, and indifferent to the needs of taxpayers as well as the agency itself (GAO, 1991c; see also GAO, 1991b). After numerous failures to modify the system, the IRS has initiated an $8 billion computer modernization project called the Tax System Modernization Program designed to update its information system.

The FAA has also been criticized for failing to modernize its computer operations at an appropriate pace. FAA officials have been accused of negligence for not upgrading the agency's computer system:

> To ensure safe air travel, establish regulatory standards, maintain security, and promote air commerce, the Federal Aviation Administration (FAA) requires vast amounts of information technology. Computers are especially critical in controlling over 200,000 flights across the nation daily. Although FAA has recently made some limited improvements, it has not implemented a comprehensive management program for its major automated systems because such a program is not a priority. As a result, FAA lacks adequate computer capacity policies, procedures, expertise, and tools. Without a comprehensive program, FAA does not know how long current systems, such as those air traffic controllers use to separate aircraft, will continue to meet capacity requirements, nor does it know its future capacity needs. (GAO, 1991b, p. 16; see also GAO, 1991a)

The other aspect of the timing issue relates to a perception of delaying the implementation of innovations. The image as a laggard may adversely affect an agency's favorable public image (see Rogers & Shoemaker, 1971). Innovations should be adopted in a timely manner to avoid claims of irresponsibility, which is what happened to the Department of Labor's Wage and Hour Division. The Department of Labor is mandated to determine the market rate and wages and benefits for service employees working under government contracts of $2,500 or more. The Department's Wage and Hour Division (WHD) is delegated responsibility for wage rate calculations.

The accurate calculation of wage and benefit rates is important for two reasons. First, accurate determinations of the market rate ensure that service employees are fairly compensated for the labor. Second, accurate determinations ensure that tax dollars are wisely saved by eliminating overpayment to service employees. In a report issued by the GAO (1987), the WHD was cited for inaccurate assessment of wage rates:

> A potential problem may exist with the accuracy of wage rate calculations in SCA [Service Contract Act] determinations. Inaccuracies in the Department of Labor's Wage and Hour Division both overstate and understate wage rates. The inaccuracies were due to incorrect copying of rates from source documents, incorrect use of source data in calculations, and mathematical errors. WHD is taking steps to correct the record keeping problems, including designing a computerized system for preparing and tracking SCA determinations. (p. 19)

The GAO evaluation revealed that the WHD's use of manual record-keeping procedures resulted in inefficiencies in the agency's operations. Administrative executives of the agency were accused of being laggards because they did not adopt computerized record-keeping systems in a timely manner.

Two major factors can trigger the need to update the agency's operations: recognition of emerging trends and reaction to major events. The administrative conservator should establish functions and processes to identify and monitor trends that may ultimately have an impact on the agency's operation. For example, Stanley Morris of the U.S. Marshals Service established a threat analysis unit to identify and monitor trends. The administrative conservator should also be sensitive to major events that could affect the agency's operations. Examples of major events include changes in mandating statutes, critical evaluation of a companion agency's operations by an oversight body or the press, a widely publicized scandal within the agency's field of action resulting from the inefficient operation of technologies, and disaster or tragedy. There is little novel about the notion that administrative executives seek to update their agency's operations in response to emerging trends or major events. In fact, executives of private sector firms engage in similar actions. The modernization of a governmental agency's operation through the adoption of innovations is a more complex process, however, because these agencies depend on legislative appropriations. Adequate knowledge of when to modernize an agency's operation is only one part of the equation; securing sufficient support to do so is another. The administrative conservator must convince legislative appropriations committees of the need to revise the agency's operations to secure funding. The political process can make this a difficult task at times (see Schick, 1980; Wildavsky, 1990).

The failure of administrative executives to secure adequate funding for updating operations in a timely manner can negatively affect their agency's favorable public image. The Department of Justice's defense procurement fraud unit is a case in point. The unit was established in 1982 to investigate fraud in the procurement of defense contracts. The criminal division of the Justice Department is delegated responsibility for prosecuting fraud cases. In the wake of the defense procurement scandal, the GAO was called in to investigate the Justice Department's handling of defense procurement fraud cases. The GAO (1988a) was extremely critical of the department's operations in the investigation and prosecution of fraud cases. Justice Department officials argued that they had requested an increase in appropriations from Congress to address many of the problems identified by the GAO. But Congress rejected Justice's request and substantially cut the department's budget. Although department officials recognized the need to enhance the capacity of the defense procurement fraud unit, their inability to secure adequate funding to do so had an adverse effect on the department's public image.

Strategy: Maintaining Accuracy of Indirect Indexes of Quality

In addition to maintaining the agency's reputation for compliance with established standards, the administrative conservator may also use indirect indexes of quality to sustain the agency's favorable public image. As previously discussed, this strategy involves publicizing in official documents characteristics of the agency that symbolize quality. Although the use of indirect indexes is an effective means of marketing the quality of an agency's products or services, the administrative conservator should ensure that such indexes remain accurate and meaningful once they are included in official documents for public consumption. The accuracy of an indirect index is measured by the degree to which it conforms to the truth, that is, a close approximation of the reality that exists within the agency. An indirect index is considered meaningful when it has significance and importance in a specific institutional context.

Governmental agencies commonly include indirect indexes in official documents (especially annual reports) to publicize the quality of their programs and services. In fact, indirect indexes are integral components of many agencies' "propaganda" efforts. (For a discussion of agency propaganda, see Altheide & Johnson, 1980.) In its 14-page official document *Outline of U.S. Marshal Activities*, the USMS (n.d.) skillfully uses several indirect indexes to promote its activities. The document devotes, on the average, half a page to describing each of the USMS's major duties and responsibilities. These include, among others, court security, the receipt and processing of federal prisoners, fugitive investigations, transportation and movement of prisoners, and the management of assets seized as a result of law enforcement actions by other federal agencies. In describing each of its major duties and responsibilities, the USMS uses a variety of indirect indexes of quality. For example, the "number of weapons confiscated from individuals prior to entering Federal courthouses" is used as an indirect index to publicize the quality of the USMS court security program. The document states, "each year, court security officers discover more and more dangerous weapons during routine security screening at Federal courthouses. In FY 1987, they *prevented 14,000 illegal and 53,000 legal weapons from being carried into Federal courthouses*" (p. 4; italics added).

The "number of court appearances made by prisoners transported" is another indirect index that markets the quality of the USMS prisoner transportation program. In a section of the document describing the transportation and movement of prisoners, the USMS (n.d.) states:

> The U.S. Marshals [Service] is responsible for: (1) the timely production of federal prisoners for legal hearings or meetings with counsel; (2) the production of prisoners at trial (*in FY 1987, the Service produced prisoners for 290,000 court appearances*) [italics added]; (3) the movement of sentenced prisoners to institutions for service of sentence and transfer of sentenced prisoners between institutions; and (4) ensuring the rights, safety, and security of pretrial detainee and sentenced prisoners in custody. (p. 6)

The document includes a host of other indirect indexes of quality, such as the number of federal arrest warrants received in a given year, the number of prisoners received and processed, the number of protective service details established because of judicial threats, the number of witnesses protected, and the dollar amount of assets managed as a result of seized and forfeited property.

The administrative conservator should encourage and, indeed, support the inclusion of indirect indexes in official documents to publicize the quality of an agency's programs and services. These indexes, however, must be accurate and meaningful if they are to contribute to the maintenance of the agency's favorable public image. In the previous examples, it is fair to say that the indirect indexes of quality used by the USMS are presumed to be accurate. If, however, the GAO discovered that the number of prisoners produced for court appearances was grossly inaccurate, for example, the agency's public image would be adversely affected. Or, if the USMS used a meaningless indirect index such as the "average height and weight of individuals searched during routine security screening at Federal courthouses," questions concerning the quality of its operation would emerge. Such questions may be prompted by the perception that overemphasis on meaningless indirect indexes signals a lack of confidence in the quality of the agency's operation. The agency may be perceived as merely reaching for straws to justify its existence. Perceptions of this nature would no doubt tarnish the agency's favorable public image.[4]

The administrative conservator should constantly monitor and inspect information prepared for public consumption to ensure that indirect indexes of quality are meaningful and accurate. Failure to do so can result in a credibility gap that could severely damage the agency's favorable public image.

The Maintenance of External Alliances

The preceding discussion suggests that the maintenance of a favorable public image is an effective strategy for sustaining support for an agency's programs and services. Although effective, this strategy alone is insufficient to sustain external support over time. It is possible for an agency to enjoy a favorable public image and yet lack sufficient support among legislative bodies to secure funding for its programs. In addition to building and maintaining a favorable public image, the administrative conservator should *sustain strength with key constituents to ensure support* (see F. E. Rourke, 1969, chap. 2). Sustaining strength refers to the ongoing efforts of the administrative conservator to cultivate and maintain supportive relationships among an alliance of individuals, groups, and organizations who are willing to take action on behalf of the agency. This alliance consists of a multitude of actors, both inside and outside of government, who are affected by or have an interest in the agency's activities.

The maintenance of a strong alliance of external supporters requires that the administrative conservator provide, on an ongoing basis, inducements and related rewards in exchange for support. This exchange relationship is governed by a set of explicit and/or implicit understandings that establish expectations for the parties involved. These expectations define in a broad sense the behaviors needed from supporters to advance agency aims as well as the rewards pledged by the conservator for support. Inducements and related rewards available to the administrative conservator include agency services, benefits, and favors. The conservator's capacity to dispense agency services and benefits valued by supporters is vital to the maintenance of agency support. According to Francis E. Rourke (1969), "Agencies that are not in a position to dispense important benefits or favors to any segment of the community are in a disadvantageous position with respect to their ability to attract organized support" (pp. 14-15).

Agency services, benefits, and favors provided by the conservator in exchange for support should be appropriate. In other words, such services and benefits should be within the legitimate and legal realm of the agency's activities. For example, the director of the Higher Education Management Services, U.S. Department of Education, should not provide special favors to a congresswoman that give an unfair advantage to a university within her district in competing for research grants awarded by the agency. If the director, for example, disregarded internal procedures (in exchange for support on favorable agency legislation) and awarded a multimillion-dollar grant to the university in the congresswoman's district, such action would be inappropriate, if not illegal. The director could, as a way of rendering an appropriate service to the congressional supporter, instruct the staff to provide technical assistance to the university in proposal development. This service is within the legitimate and legal scope of the agency's activities.

The administrative conservator should exercise discretion when dispensing agency benefits in exchange for support. Agency benefits rendered should be enough to secure and maintain support but not too much to earn the disrespect and envy from others. In the previous illustration concerning the Higher Education Management Services, the director should ensure that the staff is not perceived as providing excessive technical assistance to the university in the congresswoman's district. The failure to do so may lead to accusations by others that the agency is giving preferential treatment and therefore is engaged in inequitable decision making in the awarding of research grants.

The administrative conservator has at his or her disposal a variety of appropriate services, benefits, and favors that can be rendered to supporters. These include, among others, sharing agency expertise and resources with supporters, responding quickly to requests for information, giving public recognition to supporters as a means of generating positive publicity for them, and publicly endorsing supporters' activities. Agency expertise can be shared through formal training programs or by providing direct technical assistance. For example, the USMS often conducts seminars for sheriffs to improve their court security operations. The USMS also provides direct financial support to sheriff departments through its Cooperative Agreement Program, which provides financial assistance to upgrade jail facilities and expand jail capacity. In exchange for such assistance, the USMS is guaranteed jail space for federal prisoners. As noted in Chapter 3, the USMS uses both of its Boeing 727 aircraft as part of the National Prison Transportation System to assist other agencies in the long-distance movement of prisoners. The USMS coordinates and schedules the majority of long-distance transfers between institutions operated by the Federal Bureau of Prisons. The agency also transports prisoners for the Immigration and Naturalization Service and for a variety of state and local agencies (USMS, n.d.).

Quick response to requests for information is another service that can be rendered by the administrative conservator to supporters. Administrative agencies are inundated daily with inquiries from the executive and legislative branches, interest groups, other agencies, clients, and the general public. A timely and reasonable response to such inquiries is important to avoid giving the impression that the conservator or the agency is unresponsive. The appearance of unresponsiveness is a formula for disaster. In the words of W. Michael Blumenthal (1979), former Treasury secretary and former chairman of the Bendix Corporation, "Appearance is as important as reality" (p. 37). What constitutes a timely and reasonable response is influenced by the type of information sought and who requested it. For example, if a request for an agency publication routinely takes 3 weeks to process once received, the response time for a supporter could be reduced by as much as 2 weeks or less depending on the urgency of the request. Although a quick response is a desirable goal for handling requests from supporters, there are times when circumstances prevent significant reduction in the normal response time. In such instances, the administrative conservator should keep supporters informed by providing information on the process involved in handling the request, on when action on the request is most likely to occur, and on when supporters can expect a partial or complete response on the matter. In addition, periodic updates are useful to let supporters know that their request is getting attention.

Another service is giving credit and recognition to supporters to generate positive publicity for them. One finds little disagreement with the assertion that political elites, interest groups, and governmental agencies seek to exploit opportunities that publicize their activities and accomplishments. This behavior is easy to understand, especially because positive publicity can enhance an individual or organization's public image. I have already discussed the symbiotic relationship between a favorable public image and the maintenance of external agency support. Although receiving public credit and recognition is a service highly valued by political elites and interest groups alike, this service has special significance for governmental agencies. This is because such agencies are restricted from engaging in public relations activities that promote their interest. Consequently, governmental agencies seek alternative means of publicizing their activities. As mentioned earlier, governmental agencies skillfully use official documents to publicize their accomplishments. Although such use can be effective, there are limitations to this approach, especially because a thin line exists between public information and public relations activities.[5] Governmental agencies assiduously attempt to avoid giving the impression that they are actively involved in propagandizing the public or lobbying the legislature as a means of gaining support for their activities.

Public credit and recognition can be rendered as a service in several ways. One way is for the administrative conservator to give supporters prestigious awards at highly publicized formal ceremonies and large public gatherings such as conferences and conventions. For example, at its annual conference and exhibition, the National Sheriffs' Association (NSA) presents a president's award in recognition of professional efforts taken by an individual to improve the cooperation between sheriff departments and other criminal justice organizations. At the NSA's 48th Annual Convention and Exhibition held in 1988, the director of the USMS received the president's award in recognition of his agency's assistance to sheriff departments in improving courtroom security. The award

was presented at a formal ceremony by the NSA president and George Bush, then vice president of the United States and the Republican party presidential candidate. Of course, the national press coverage of this event generated a great deal of positive publicity for the USMS.

The administrative conservator may also give supporters public credit in interviews with journalists and others seeking information on the agency's activities. These interviews may be either public or private. Public interviews often take place at press conferences called by agency officials to publicize significant events, whereas private interviews usually occur on a one-on-one basis. Federal law enforcement agencies involved in preventing the illegal sale and distribution of narcotics and other controlled substances often use this method. For example, in an article published by *The Odessa American* (a Texas newspaper) concerning the seizure of property that federal officials suspected was used for drug trafficking, a USMS official gives public credit and recognition to several of the agency's supporters:

> La Morenita—a grocery, laundromat, gift shop, and pool hall—has been closed by federal officials enforcing a statute that allows them to seize property suspected of being used for drug trafficking, reports said. Deputy U.S. Marshall Edward DeCoste said today that a *joint investigation by the Midland County Sheriff's Department, Midland Police Department, and the U.S. Drug Enforcement Administration* [italics added] led to the closure of the business through federal court action. ("Officials Seize Midland Store," 1988, p. 13A)[6]

The preceding discussion suggests that sheriff departments are important supporters of the USMS. The U.S. Drug Enforcement Administration is also recognized in law enforcement circles as one of the agency's allies. Statements appearing in the *Drug Enforcement Report*, a Washington newsletter devoted to drug enforcement activities, provide evidence of this supportive relationship. In an article devoted to a dispute between the USMS and the FBI concerning federal fugitive investigation, the newsletter states:

> The U.S. Marshals Service and its frequent ally in the capture of drug fugitives, the *Drug Enforcement Administration,* apparently

have withstood a major challenge by the Federal Bureau of Investigation to keep their key role in pursuing fugitives. . . . The DEA
has been somewhat caught in the middle in the internal dispute,
because it is subordinate to the FBI within the Justice Department
hierarchy, yet it also *teams up often and successfully with the
Marshals Service* in the pursuit of key narcotic fugitives. . . . The
Marshals Service has grown increasingly aggressive and more creative, in finding ways to locate fugitives and bring them home for
prosecution. When the investigation involves a drug fugitive, the
Service often has the DEA as a *prime ally*. Indeed, DEA itself
sometimes takes the lead in a fugitive pursuit, as it did when U.S.
authorities arranged the capture in Colombia of Medellin Cartel
drug-lord Carlos Lehder Rivas. Once the DEA brought Lehder back
to the U.S., however, he was immediately handed over to the
Marshals Service [italics added]. ("U.S. Marshals Preserve Role,"
1988, p. 1)

The administrative conservator can also publicly endorse supporters' activities as a way of providing an appropriate service. These
endorsements consist of two types, broadly categorized as direct and
indirect expressions of approval. Direct expressions of approval
involve favorable public pronouncements made on behalf of a supporter. Public pronouncements can be made before a public audience
that typically includes, among others, journalists, members of legislative committees, agency personnel, and members of professional
associations. Written statements of support are expressed in official
letters and in resolutions passed by formally recognized bodies. For
example, officials representing several state agencies submitted official letters in support of the ATF when the agency was targeted for
abolishment in 1982. A letter prepared by L. Joyce Hampers, commissioner of the Massachusetts Department of Revenue is illustrative.[7]
The commissioner states in a February 2, 1982, letter to the Subcommittee on Treasury, Postal Service, and General Government:

> As I did previously in a November 2, 1981 letter to Treasury Secretary
> Regan, I would like to express my concern over plans to curtail the
> Tobacco Enforcement Program of the Bureau of Alcohol, Tobacco
> and Firearms (ATF) and enforcement of the Federal Contraband
> Cigarette Act (P.L. 95-575).
>   While statistical research on Massachusetts tax losses due to
> cigarette bootlegging vary from the 1975 ACIR (Advisory Commis-

sion on Intergovernmental Relations Study) projection of $12.5 million annually, to a 1980 Massachusetts Legislative Research Bureau Study that projects annual losses at $17 million, our cigarette excise tax revenue has increased in both fiscal years 1980 and 1981, $2.7 million and $4.1 million, respectively. We attribute these increases, in part, to ATF and Massachusetts combined enforcement efforts.

Having awareness that the National Tobacco Tax Association (NTTA) plans to submit a statement, reflecting Association resolutions expressing support of ATF activity against cigarette smuggling, I only wish to emphasize local concerns over this national problem.

I wish to strongly suggest appropriations for contraband cigarette enforcement in the ATF and enforcement of P.L. 95-575.

I remain concerned that the withdrawal of ATF from its Tobacco Enforcement Program will result in a revival of the cigarette bootlegging problem.

Thank you for your consideration of my statement. (U.S. Senate Subcommittee of the Committee on Appropriations, 1982, p. 126)

Several resolutions were also presented as written statements of support on behalf of ATF activities. For example, the National Association of State Liquor Administrators passed this resolution:

Whereas proposals have been advanced to dismember the Treasury Department's Bureau of Alcohol, Tobacco and Firearms, drastically reduce the staffing, and reassigning its regulatory functions to other agencies of the Federal Government; and;

Whereas coinciding with such dismemberment of the Bureau of Alcohol, Tobacco and Firearms is a proposal to amend the Federal Alcohol Administration Act to such an extent that many of the regulatory principles embraced by the National Conference of Liquor Administrators will no longer be adhered to by the federal agencies ultimately charged with regulation of the various aspects of beverage alcohol traffic; and . . .

Whereas it is recognized that the occurrence of either one or both federal proposals, that is, the revision of the Federal Alcohol Administration Act or the dismemberment of the Bureau of Alcohol, Tobacco and Firearms, could be disastrous in terms of the "spinoff" issue and problems which could be faced by the individual states: now, therefore be it *Resolved,* That the Executive Committee of the National Conference of State Liquor Administrators meeting in Scottsdale, Arizona, on November 13, 1981:

1. Oppose any plan to dismember the activities, reduce the funding, reassign responsibilities, or in any way lessen or alter the ability of the Bureau of Alcohol, Tobacco and Firearms to conduct its duties and responsibilities as currently defined and conducted; and

2. Oppose any effort to amend the Federal Alcohol Administration Act in such a manner as to alter the existing substantive law that presently provides protection against the abuses and problems which occurred early in this century and led to the institution of national prohibition, the repeal of which was brought about wholly or partially on the basis that the federal government would operate a strong program of enforcement and regulation.

Done in Scottsdale, Arizona, this 13th day of November, 1981. (U.S. Senate Subcommittee of the Committee on Appropriations, 1982, p. 13)

The next type of endorsement, indirect expressions of approval, involves tacit acts of support. Such endorsements are implied without being directly stated. For example, when the administrative conservator agrees to serve on the board of directors of a supporter's organization, he or she is indirectly expressing approval of its activities.

Another example of an indirect expression of approval is the sanctioning of participation by agency personnel in events sponsored by supporters, such as conferences, special ceremonies, educational programs, and other public gatherings.[8] Again, the USMS provides an illustration. As previously indicated, the NSA is an important supporter of the USMS. The USMS director, as a means of endorsing the NSA's activities, sanctioned the participation of agency personnel at the association's annual conference and exhibition, as reflected by statements appearing in an internal USMS newsletter. On the first page of the newsletter, under the heading "National Sheriffs' Association Conference" (1988), the director states:

The National Sheriffs' Association (NSA) held its 48th Annual Conference and Exhibition last week in Louisville, Kentucky. Marshals Service representatives attended and participated in numerous sessions, including a Court Security Seminar. . . . The USMS exhibit occupied a prime position with the exhibition from other law enforcement agencies and various vendors of police and security products. (p. 1)

Although the director did not explicitly state in the newsletter that agency personnel had his blessings to participate in the event, it is implied that he sanctioned such actions. By noting the participation of agency personnel in the conference, the director in fact communicated his approval. As Edgar Schein (1985) observes, "what leaders pay attention to, measure, and control" is a powerful method of communicating what is important to them (p. 225).

A last example of an indirect expression of approval is the acceptance of invitations to deliver keynote addresses at events sponsored by supporters. It is generally well known that ranking government officials receive numerous requests to provide this service. The administrative conservator should be selective in accepting public speaking engagements. Requests made by supporters should be given priority. In accepting such requests, the administrative conservator is indirectly endorsing the supporters' activities. For example, it is inconceivable to think that a ranking government official would accept an invitation to address a formal gathering of the Ku Klux Klan. Doing so would convey the message that the official endorses the activities of this organization.

The Binding of Parochial Group Egotism

For some time now, organization theorists have argued that organizations are composed of a multitude of formal and informal groups that seek to promote their own vested interests. These entities have been described by such names as internal interest groups, coalitions, constituencies, and stakeholders. Despite the diversity of terminology, writers agree that it is the task of administrative leadership to "bind parochial group egotism to larger loyalties and aspirations" (Selznick, 1957, pp. 93-94). Stated another way, it is the responsibility of administrative leaders to build and sustain commitment among internal interest groups to core agency values. This is not always an easy task, especially because organizational members experience multiple commitments (see Reicher, 1985).

There are several useful strategies for building and sustaining commitment among internal interest groups. Many of these strategies have already been mentioned in the previous discussion of the executive cadre. These include selectively recruiting and choosing organization members, offering incentives, using persuasion, minimizing dissension, and building and maintaining high levels of trust. Rather than commenting further on these strategies, I will discuss the use of co-optation as a strategy.

The term *co-optation* is defined as the "process of absorbing new elements into the leadership or policy determining structure as a means of averting threats to its stability or existence" (Selznick, 1948, p. 34). From this perspective, co-optation is an adaptive or adjustment strategy used by administrative executives to cope with perceived threatening organizational circumstance. There are two different forms of co-optation: formal and informal. Formal co-optation involves absorbing new elements into leadership or policy-determining structure to lend legitimacy and respectability to formal authority. This form of co-optation is used when the confidence in formal authority is questioned. For example, to increase their legitimacy, urban police departments frequently may appoint leaders from minority communities to advisory boards. In many minority communities, police departments are held in low esteem because of the perception of racism, which results in a lack of trust and confidence. As a result, the legitimacy and authority of these police departments as advocates of law and order are called into question.[9]

Informal co-optation has little to do with legitimacy per se; rather, this form of co-optation is undertaken in response to demands for the sharing of power. Selznick (1948) describes informal co-optation this way:

> Cooptation [sic] may be a response to specific centers of power. This is not a matter of legitimacy or of a general and diffuse lack of confidence. They may be well established; and yet organized forces which are able to threaten the formal authority may effectively

shape its structure and policy. The organization in respect to its institutional environment—or the leadership in respect to its rank— must take these forces into account. . . . This form of cooptation is expressed in informal terms, for the problem is not one of responding to a state of imbalance with respect to "people as a whole" but one of meeting the pressure of specific individuals or interest groups which are in a position to enforce demands. (pp. 34-35)

Co-optation is considered informal when formal authority never publicly acknowledges that concessions have been made to share power in response to pressure. To make such concessions would "undermine the sense of legitimacy of the formal authority within the community" (p. 35). An example of informal co-optation is the incorporation of more women into the leadership or policy-determining structure of an organization in response to pressure from organized women's groups.

Although administrative conservators may use both forms of co-optation as a response to external and internal pressures, organization theorists tend to focus primarily on the co-optation of elements in the external environment. Little attention is devoted to co-optation within the organization.[10] Moreover, co-optation seems to carry a negative connotation and is seen as merely an exercise in elite manipulation. This is unfortunate because co-optation is a viable strategy for securing cooperation from internal interest groups. Let us consider informal co-optation within public bureaucracies, specifically designed to maintain support among internal interest groups.

Co-optation is a useful strategy for securing commitment and, thereby, maintaining support among internal interest groups. But the intended consequences of informal co-optation (internal security, stability, and broader administrative discretion) are not permanent or guaranteed. The effectiveness of informal co-optation is contingent, in part, on the successful integration of co-opted groups into the decision-making structure. Successful integration refers to the degree to which co-opted groups perceive (in a real or imagined way) that they legitimately share the power with those in authority. This perception is cultivated and sustained by the "accumulating history of power outcomes" (Olson & Cromwell,

1975, p. 6). The term *power outcome* refers to the consequences of negotiations that determine the allocation and control of scarce organizational resources. In other words, co-opted groups must perceive that they are periodic recipients of *benefits* allocated through the decision-making structure. I will substitute the term *benefits* for *power outcomes* because it is better suited for this discussion.

The administrative conservator should ensure that co-opted groups receive an equitable share of benefits allocated through the policy-making structure. *Equitable share* refers not to the distribution of resources on a one-to-one basis but rather to the quantity and quality of benefits accumulated over time. Quantity suggests the number of benefits accumulated during a period, whereas the quality of benefits stems from the degree of "organizational slack" (March & Simon, 1958, p. 126). The term *organizational slack* refers to the extent to which the agency has an abundance or excess of resources to achieve a minimal level of effectiveness. For example, a large degree of slack increases opportunities for the acquisition of resources, making their acquisition less valuable to the recipient. In contrast, a limited degree of slack results in tighter restrictions on the allocation of scarce organizational resources, thus making benefits acquired via co-optation seem more valued to the co-opted. The quality of a benefit is, thus, measured by the scarcity of critical resources. The ability of administrative executives to acquire several new positions during periods of retrenchment is an example of a quality benefit.

To reiterate, the administrative conservator should ensure that co-opted interest groups receive, on an ongoing basis, an equitable share of benefits allocated through the decision-making structure. Failure to do so may undermine the usefulness of co-optation as a strategy for maintaining support. This assertion is based on the premise that co-opted groups are more likely to perceive a breach of contract if formal agreements made in exchange for internal security and stability are not honored. If this occurs, co-opted groups may withdraw support and become antagonistic toward those within the policy-determining structure. This poses a threat to the agency's integrity because co-opted groups are in a strategic position to restrict the available mode of administrative action if they so desire (Thompson, 1967). The erosion of internal support, especially if it becomes widespread, is dangerous.

How should the administrative conservator ensure that co-opted groups are periodic recipients of valued benefits allocated through the policy-making structure? The answer to this question is twofold. First, the administrative conservator should be fully aware of *who* is getting *what* in the allocation of scarce organizational resources. In other words, the administrative conservator should keep score on the quantity and quality of benefits received by the various internal interest groups over time. Second, the administrative conservator should at times exercise control over the decision-making process to prevent or minimize the inequities in the allocation of benefits. In reference to the first point, the comments of Stephen F. Higgins (personal communication, 1987), former ATF director, revealed the importance of keeping score on who is receiving what type of benefit. When recounting a situation in which he created a deputy director position in response to internal criticism that law enforcement interests were not sufficiently represented at the national headquarters level, Higgins commented that he wanted law enforcement personnel to "feel like part of the game" so that they could help "sell the agency's programs." He went on to say: "You must strike a balance when making decisions. You must first do what is right. You must also make sure that the goodies are spread around."

By creating a deputy director of law enforcement, Higgins responded to demands for the sharing of power as a means of securing support from those who advocated a stronger role for law enforcement within the agency. If this is indeed the case, Higgins used informal co-optation as a strategy for building and maintaining support among the law enforcement faction. Higgins's comments are also interesting in that they reflect an explicit concern for how the agency's benefits are allocated. The phrases "strike a balance" and "spread the goodies around" can be interpreted to mean that Higgins was interested in ensuring that supporters of the law enforcement function received an equitable share of benefits allocated through the policy-making structure.

Norman Carlson (personal communication, October 3, 1986), former director of the Federal Bureau of Prisons, made a similar point when discussing the agency's annual awards program. Carlson mentioned the importance of what he termed the "equitable distribution of awards." He indicated that although the equitable distribution of awards was not an explicitly stated criterion for selecting award recipients, the awards committee was encouraged to consider gender, race, geographical region, tenure, occupational group (line vs. staff), and so forth.

The conservator can exercise control over the decision-making process as a means of ensuring that co-opted groups receive an equitable share of benefits. For example, control may be instituted by influencing the criteria on which decisions are based (see Pfeffer, 1981). In the above discussion concerning the selection of award recipients, Carlson exercised control over the decision-making process by influencing the criteria on which awards were made; he encouraged the selection committee to consider gender, race, geographical region, tenure, and occupational group when making award selections.

Summary

Building and maintaining support for an agency's programs and activities are critical leadership functions that warrant the administrative conservator's undivided focus. The administrative conservator should give special attention to preserving both external and internal support. In conserving external support, the administrative conservator should concentrate on maintaining a favorable public image as well as sustaining strength with key constituents. The maintenance of a favorable public image requires that the administrative conservator ensure that the agency sustains a reputation for consistent compliance with standards used to measure the intrinsic quality of its product, services, and activities. The conservator should also ensure that indirect indexes of quality included in official documents remain accurate and meaningful. As a mean of sustaining strength with the agency's key constituents, the administrative conservator should provide inducements and related rewards in exchange for support. These inducements and rewards should be appropriate agency benefits, services, and favors.

In an effort to build and maintain internal support, the administrative conservator should "bind parochial group egotism to larger loyalties and aspirations" (Selznick, 1957, pp. 93-94). This essentially means that the conservator should sustain commitment among internal interest groups to core agency values. Co-optation is an effective strategy for this purpose. The effectiveness of co-optation, however, is contingent on the successful integration of co-opted groups into the policy-determining structure. Successful integration is measured by the degree to which adopted groups perceive that they are periodic recipients of benefits allocated through the policy-determining structure. The administrative conservator should ensure that co-opted groups receive an equitable share of benefits. This is achieved, in part, by keeping score on the quantity and quality of benefits received by the various internal interest groups as well as exercising control over the decision-making process.

Notes

1. The term *support* is used in the manner advocated by David Easton (1965). Easton suggests that support consists of two forms: overt and covert. Overt support is defined as favorable actions taken on behalf of a person, group, or institution. Overt support consists of externally observable behaviors. In contrast, covert support involves favorable attitudes or sentiments toward a person, group, or institution. Easton says that covert support is a "frame of mind" that involves a "readiness to act on behalf of someone or something." Such support is an "internal form of behavior" (pp. 159-160).

2. Francis E. Rourke (1969, chap. 2) also notes the symbiotic relationship between support generated by administrative agencies and power.

3. Perrow (1961) uses the term *indexes* as opposed to *indices*. To avoid confusion, I use Perrow's term.

4. The Radford Army Ammunition Plant case discussed in Chapter 3 provides a textbook example. The number of work-hours without lost-time injury proved to be an inaccurate indirect index, thereby adversely affecting the plant's public image.

5. Theoretically speaking, public information activities are designed to inform salient publics about an agency's activities. In contrast, public relations activities are initiated solely to sell and promote an agency's programs. For a discussion of this point, see F. E. Rourke (1961, chap. 8).

6. From "Officials Seize Midland Store," April 13, 1988, *The Odessa American*, p. 13A. Reprinted by permission of *The Odessa American*.

7. Other governmental agencies that submitted official letters of support on behalf of ATF include the Arizona State Department of Liquor, Licenses, and

Control; Florida State Department of Business Regulation; New Jersey Division of Taxation; New York Office of Taxation and Finance; Comptroller of the State Treasury, State of Maryland; and the Texas Alcohol Beverage Commission.

   8. The term *sanctioning* as used here refers to authoritative approval and should not be confused with coercive measures employed to punish a party, as in international law.

   9. The videotaped beating of motorist Rodney King, an African American, by Los Angeles police officers in 1991 merely reinforces this perception. The trial, subsequent acquittal, and rioting in Los Angeles received major news coverage during 1992.

   10. The work of Pfeffer (1981) is a notable exception. There are at least two reasons why organization theorists have not paid much attention to co-optation within the organization. First, Selznick (1949), the person perhaps most responsible for popularizing the term *co-optation*, places an emphasis on the external environment. Although Selznick was concerned with the external environment, he does recognize the value of co-optation *within* the organization as indicated by this passage from his previously cited article, "Foundations of the Theory of Organization" (1948): "The representation of interest through administrative constituencies is a typical example of this process. Or, within an organization individuals upon which the group is dependent for funds or other resources may insist upon and receive a share in the determination of policy" (p. 35). Second, the influential work of Thompson (1967) has deflected attention from co-optation within the organization. Thompson discusses co-optation exclusively from an external environment perspective. He contends that co-optation is a cooperative strategy for managing dependency in the task environment. Many organization theorists have not deviated from this tradition.

6

The Administrator as Conservator

◆ THE FEAR OF A POWERFUL BUREAUCRACY controlled by a cadre of nonelected and unresponsive civil servants is a matter that should concern all who embrace democratic values. The unfortunate legacy of J. Edgar Hoover and Robert Moses, among others, provides a constant reminder of what can happen when bureaucratic leaders accumulate enormous power and then use such power to dominate those inside and outside their respective organizations (see Lewis, 1980). But the actions of a small handful of powerful executives should not preclude an appreciation of the importance and value of bureaucratic leaders. Contrary to the views held by many scholars, bureaucratic leaders do not pose a threat to democracy. When guided by constitutional principles, they help maintain stability of the American regime by preserving the integrity of public bureaucracies and, in turn, constitutional processes, values, and beliefs. Viewed from this perspective, bureaucratic leaders are administrative conservators, and they are actively engaged in a special type of leadership called *administrative conservatorship.*

Throughout this book, I have emphasized that administrative conservatorship is a form of statesmanship. It requires professional expertise, political skill, and a sophisticated understanding of what it means to be an active participant in governance. The conservator not only should be responsive to the various constitutional masters but also must preserve the executive and nonexecutive authority invested in public bureaucracies, maintain commitment among the executive cadre to core agency values, and sustain support among key external constituents and internal interest groups. Given the complexity and scope of these requirements, more intellectual resources should be devoted to trying to understand bureaucratic leadership instead of pretending that it does not or should not exist. We as a nation can no longer afford to remain complacent about the role and function of bureaucratic leaders in our democratic government.

The Janus-Faced Nature of Conservatorship

Nothing would be more gratifying than to authoritatively state that the ideas and concepts discussed here are immune from distortion. Unfortunately, I cannot make this claim. The potential exists that some individuals, in the name of maintaining stability of the American regime, will use the power, authority, and resources of public bureaucracies for purposes other than the common good. At one extreme, administrative conservatorship may be reduced to merely administrative *conservership,* as bureaucratic leaders ignore the expressed desires of the citizenry and other democratic institutions and processes to maximize their personal power and position. At the other extreme, stability of the regime may be used by public entrepreneurs to justify the dismantling of public bureaucracies in their misconceived quest to "reinvent government" (see Osborne & Graebler, 1991; see also critique by Goodsell, 1993). Although both the conserver and the entrepreneur pose a serious threat to democratic government, they are not the primary concern. Of special concern are the potential abuses of those who march under the banner of administrative conservatorship.

Similar to other models of administrative leadership, administrative conservatorship is Janus-faced.[1] One face reflects a virtuous civil servant who is a friend of the Republic and a guardian of the public good. The other face is frightening. It reflects a civil servant who is a notoriously dangerous individual whose intentions and actions are antithetical to democracy. This side of conservatorship emerges when prescriptions outlined in preceding chapters are distorted and abused. Although it is virtually impossible to anticipate or predict all the potential abuses, I can, however, speculate on a few.

The Abuse of Executive and Nonexecutive Authority

In Chapter 3, I noted that the administrative conservator is responsible for preserving both the executive and the nonexecutive authority vested in public bureaucracies to conserve the mission. Executive authority involves the right and power to issue commands and to perform certain acts in a specified realm, whereas nonexecutive authority "does not involve any right to command or to act on or for another" (DeGeorge, 1985, p. 22). Nonexecutive authority is derived from superior knowledge and competence in a particular field or realm.

With respect to executive authority, I suggested that the administrative conservator should be sensitive to the limits placed on such authority because flagrant violations of these limits could undermine the agency's authority. Two violations in particular merit attention: violations of the spirit of the law and violations of the letter of the law. Violations of the spirit of the law occur when an agency's activities are unacceptable to its employees and other external stakeholders because they are perceived as inconsistent with its reason for existence; when administrative executives and other agency officials are overly zealous in carrying out statutory provisions; and when officials are unenergetic, inattentive, or negligent in carrying out legally mandated responsibilities. Violations of the letter of the law arise when officials of public bureaucracies disregard the primary, ordinary, and plain meaning of the language used in statutory mandates and in other legally binding acts that specify an agency's field of action, the purpose of its activity, and the type of tasks it is designated to perform.

Because coercive power often accompanies executive authority, one need not be very creative to envision how bureaucratic leaders might abuse such authority. Indeed, the potential or actual misuse of an agency's executive authority partially explains the ambivalence many Americans feel toward bureaucratic power. The disgraceful and gestapolike actions of the U.S. Postal Inspection Service, for example, have done little to allay such fears. The U.S. Postal Inspection Service became the focus of a congressional investigation when it was disclosed that the agency had botched a drug sting operation.[2] Inspectors Tim Marshall and Daniel Kuack directed a yearlong investigation that was supposed to identify and prosecute Postal Service employees in the Cleveland (Ohio) area involved in the illegal distribution of controlled substances. Marshall and Kuack used five informants (most of whom had criminal records) to purchase drugs primarily from Postal Service employees. The sting operation backfired when it was discovered that the Postal Inspection Service itself had become the victim of a scam orchestrated by its own informants. The informants organized phony drug deals, fabricated audio recordings of drug transactions, and pocketed over $200,000 in wages and funds used to purchase narcotics. By the completion of the operation, the Postal Inspection Service had ruined the lives of more than 30 innocent Postal Service employees, all of whom were African American. The falsely accused postal employees lost their jobs and faced criminal drug trafficking charges.[3]

The Postal Inspector Service case illustrates an egregious abuse of an agency's executive authority. Some forms of abuse are much more subtle. Intimidation, for example, refers to unjustifiable actions taken by bureaucratic leaders for the sole purpose of creating fear among those affected by an agency's activities. Fear is created by implicit or explicit threats to use an agency's coercive powers (see Buzan, 1983, chap. 1-3). For example, officials of the IRS can engage in intimidation by ordering an audit of an individual's or a company's tax records without sufficient justification.

The threat of fines or imprisonment is enough to create fear in most persons, even when we have faithfully complied with federal tax laws. Administrative officials of a local or state health department can engage in intimidation by consistently ordering unannounced inspections of a particular eating establishment for reasons other than those related to public health and safety. The threat of closing the establishment, with the resulting loss of revenue, creates fear in any business owner. Administrative officials of the Securities and Exchange Commission can intimidate investment firms by frequently ordering a review of transactions by stockbrokers (without ample justification) under the pretext of ensuring compliance with federal laws that prevent fraudulent sales practices.

The potential abuse of an agency's nonexecutive authority also deserves serious consideration. The discussion of nonexecutive authority focused on epistemic authority. Epistemic authority (a specific form of nonexecutive authority) is legitimate if what an administrative executive says is believed and, therefore, accepted by those for whom he or she is an authority. The statements of bureaucratic leaders are believed and accepted because it is assumed that they have superior knowledge and competence in a particular field and that they are telling the truth. As with all types of authority, epistemic authority is limited. Violation of these limits can undermine an official's epistemic authority and adversely affect the agency's credibility. Violations are readily apparent when there are sufficient reasons *not to believe* what is said by bureaucratic leaders because of a loss of confidence and trust. Thus, violations of an agency's epistemic authority consist of those infractions that undermine the public's trust in the agency's capacity to serve the common good. Two types of violations are deliberate deception and the use of epistemic authority for personal benefit. Deliberate deception involves conscious actions taken by administrative officials to mislead legislative, executive, and judicial bodies, as well as the general public. For example, Lieutenant Colonel Oliver L. North engaged in deliberate deception when he misled Congress about the Reagan administration's secret arms transactions with the government of Iran. David M. Hartnett, Edward D. Conroy, Phillip Chojnacki, and Charles Sarabyn, ATF officials responsible for the ill-fated raid on the Branch Davidian compound, deliberately deceived Stephen Higgins (the agency's director), investigators, and the American public (Department of the Treasury, 1988).

The other improper use of epistemic authority involves a bureaucratic leader's abuse of specialized knowledge and competence (acquired largely as a result of or directly related to his or her formal position) for personal gain. As the case involving Lance Wilson (the HUD official accused of questionable conduct) illustrates, abuses of epistemic authority can create a credibility problem for public bureaucracies in general (Kuntz, 1989).

Although the bureaucratic leader's abuse of epistemic authority does not involve the exercise of an agency's coercive powers, the damage of such abuse to the public good should not be underestimated. For example, if an official of the FDA deliberately deceived the public by fabricating, falsifying, or disregarding test results concerning the safety of a drug to ensure its approval, the public's health and safety are placed in jeopardy. If it were discovered that the same administrative official had financial interests in the pharmaceutical company authorized to distribute the drug once approved, the public trust and confidence in the agency would be severely shaken. This would no doubt undermine the FDA's integrity and, thereby, adversely affect the agency's capacity to act.

Misplaced Priorities: Personal Loyalty
Versus Institutional Fidelity

In Chapter 4, I argued that the executive cadre performs an important role in conserving the core values of public bureaucracies. Because of its value protection role, I suggested that the administrative conservator should concentrate on building and maintaining a viable executive cadre. This entails sustaining commitment among the executive cadre to core agency values as well as ensuring that the cadre is appropriately composed in terms of skills and perspectives. To maintain commitment among the executive cadre, the administrative conservator should use inducements and related incentives in conjunction with persuasion, taking into consideration individual differences as well as prevailing organizational circumstances. Because inducements and in-

insufficient to sustain commitment among the
he administrative conservator should rely on

ive conservator should also seek to minimize
he executive cadre. Dissension within the ex-
oys commitment to larger agency goals and
onservator should be aware of and devise
two sources of dissension: unhealthy compe-
members and loss of faith in the agency's
s function.

at the conservator should constantly work to
ust among members of the executive cadre.
uch purposes include honoring formal and
s with cadre members, fighting for issues
dre members, and supporting decisions and
ers when they have acted appropriately.

le administrative conservator should pay
dre's demographic composition to ensure
preserving the integrity of public bureau-
adre's demographic composition has an
is of cadre members to cooperate. The
demographic composition is influenced
ding the agency's field of action, core
rical development, and level of adminis-

ld and maintain a viable executive cadre
eaucratic leaders are solely driven by
possible that the bureaucratic leader
ty with *fidelity* to the agency and its core
trative executives should expect a de-
ers of the executive cadre. Chester I.
clear when he states that loyalty is an
iization" and without it, "there can be
as a contribution to cooperate" (p. 84).
tic leader (or political executive, for
precedence over or become confused
s values, and its unifying principles.
nds for personal loyalty are dangerous

when such demands serve to undermine the integrity of pul
bureaucracies.

The tension between loyalty to the bureaucratic leader a
fidelity to the agency is visibly manifested in cases invol\
whistle-blowers (see C. Peters & Branch, 1972). Those who dec
to go public with information alleging questionable or ill
activities involving their superiors are often confronted wi
dilemma: Should they remain so-called loyal team players
ignore irregularities, or should they expose questionable ac
superiors to preserve the agency's integrity? On one hand,
answer to this question appears relatively straightforward. Sel
(1992) certainly seems to think so.

> In a (rational-legal) bureaucracy fidelity runs to the institution, n
> to the leader. Indeed it is useful to distinguish "fidelity" fro
> "loyalty." Fidelity suggests a broad context of ideals and respons
> bilities; loyalty is more narrowly focused allegiance. The two ide
> converge when loyalty moves *from mindless to principled partic*
> *larism*, that is, from uncritical support of a group or leader
> appreciation of the moral premises that justify or reinforce al
> giance. . . . The norm of institutional fidelity governs the place
> disobedience in official conduct. Directives from above are pr
> erly resisted if they offend the morality of the institution, and ev
> bureaucratic official has *some* responsibility for interpreting t
> morality. It does not follow, however, that disobedience is justi
> by a personal policy agenda. Fidelity has to do with the prem
> of official conduct, not with parochial interests or individual p
> erences.[4] (pp. 283-284; italics in original)

On the other hand, things are a bit more complex. Because v
blowers publicly report questionable acts of their superio
are vulnerable to acts of retaliation. Examples of retaliate
include denial of promotions and of pay increases, har
through the reassignment to less desirable positions, os
and extensive criticism for being "disloyal." It is safe to
bureaucratic leaders who demand excessive personal lo
more likely than not to resort to retaliation. This possibili
whether one blows the whistle or not.

Bureaucratic leaders who fit the above description
administrative conservators. They bear scrutiny and c

expected or trusted to function as guardians of the broader public interest.

The Interests of a Powerful Few and Tokenism

As pointed out in Chapter 5, the administrative conservator should build and maintain support for the agency's program and activities. This support is essential if public bureaucracies are to accomplish their legally mandated functions. I suggested that the administrative conservator should concentrate on preserving both external and internal support. To sustain external support, the administrative conservator should maintain the agency's favorable public image and sustain strength among key external constituencies. The maintenance of a favorable public image requires that the administrative conservator protect the agency's reputation for consistent compliance with standards used to measure the intrinsic quality of its products or services. It also requires that the administrative conservator ensure that indirect indexes of quality included in official documents remain accurate and meaningful.

I also noted that the administrative conservator should maintain supportive relationships among an alliance of individuals, groups, and organizations who willingly take action on behalf of the agency. To maintain a strong alliance of supporters, the administrative conservator should offer supporters inducements and related rewards in exchange for support. Inducements and rewards available to the administrative conservator include appropriate agency services, benefits, and favors.

The discussion of preserving internal support concentrated on building and maintaining commitment among internal interest groups to core agency values. I suggested that informal co-optation is a useful strategy that can be used by the administrative conservator for such purposes. Informal co-optation involves the incorporation of new elements into the policy-determining structure as a means of "meeting the pressures of specific individuals or interest groups which are in a position to enforce demands" (Selznick, 1948, pp. 34-35). The effectiveness of informal co-optation is contingent, to a large extent, on the successful integration of co-opted groups into the policy-making structure.

The efforts of administrative executives to maintain both external and internal support can go awry. It becomes readily apparent
that bureaucratic leaders may, to ensure external support for their
agency's activities, cater to the interests and desires of a powerful
few while ignoring the broader public interest. Scholars of public
administration and political science have long been concerned
about this problem—for good reasons. The danger is indeed real,
as Nick Kotz (1969) illustrates in his discussion of Congressman
Jamie Whitten and the power he wielded over officials in the U.S.
Department of Agriculture during the administration of President
Lyndon B. Johnson. Kotz describes how both political and career
officials abandoned national public policy initiatives designed to
fight hunger in rural America to maintain Whitten's support.

> From Freeman [the Secretary of Agriculture] on down, every Agri-
> culture Department official knew that hunger spelled "hound dog"
> to Jamie Whitten. (In Southern country jargon, a "hound dog" is
> always hanging around, useless, waiting to be thrown scraps.) Years
> before, the chairman [Whitten] had killed a small pilot project to
> teach Southern Negroes how to drive tractors. "Now that's a hound
> dog project, and I don't want to see any more of them." Whitten's
> opposition to any program resembling social welfare—or aid to
> Negroes—contributed to the failure of War on Poverty programs for
> rural America. When President Johnson signed an executive order,
> giving the Agriculture Department responsibility for coordinating
> the rural war on poverty, Secretary Freeman created a Rural Com-
> munity Development Service (RCDS) to give the Department a focal
> point for helping the poor. . . . Within a year, the Rural Community
> Development Service was dead. "Whitten thought the Service
> smacked of social experimentation and civil rights," a Department
> of Agriculture official said. (p. 124)

Whitten, the so-called permanent secretary of agriculture, chaired
the appropriations subcommittee that funded every item in the
Department of Agriculture's budget. This alone makes it easy to
understand why agriculture officials wanted and, indeed, needed
Whitten's support. But by catering to Congressman Whitten's
personal desires and prejudices in exchange for his support, Department of Agriculture officials ignored and undermined the
broader public interest. I doubt that many public-spirited indi-

viduals would disagree with the assertion that the elimination of hunger among the rural poor, regardless of their race, creed, or color, is the broader public interest.

Strategies intended to build and maintain internal support are also subject to abuse by administrative executives. The strategy of informal co-optation is certainly no exception. As indicated earlier, the effectiveness of informal co-optation is contingent on the extent to which co-opted groups are successfully integrated into the policy-determining structure. Successful integration occurs when co-opted groups perceive that their demands are given serious consideration as evidenced by receiving an equitable share of benefits allocated through the policy-determining structure. When this does *not* happen, integration failures occur. Integration failures may be a result of intended or unintended actions taken by administrative executives. Regardless of the reason, the results are the same: Integration failures undermine the effectiveness of informal co-optation because such failures create a perception of tokenism. Although minorities and women have received the most attention from researchers interested in the question of tokenism, these groups do not hold exclusive rights to the concept. Token status may be bestowed on any group, regardless of its social composition. If co-opted groups perceive that they are merely afforded token status, they are likely to take action to restrict the available modes of administrative action. Co-opted groups are certainly in a position to do so, as Thompson (1967) points out: "Coopting is a more constraining form of cooperation . . . for the extent that co-optation is effective it places an element of the environment in a position to raise questions and perhaps exert influence on other aspects of the organization" (p. 35).

The Leadership of Public Bureaucracies

The abuses discussed above (as well as others not mentioned) are no doubt troublesome. They indicate how bureaucratic leaders, guided by the theory of administrative conservatorship, can resort to behaviors and actions that pose a threat to the public good. But no model of administrative leadership is perfect; it is virtually impossible to ensure that *all* career civil servants will *always* act with the public good in mind. Nevertheless, we Americans should not throw our hands up in despair. Our political system has several built-in safeguards that protect the citizenry from widespread abuses emanating from the actions of administrative agencies. These safeguards, or instruments of administrative accountability, include control by political institutions (legislative, executive, and judicial); normative restraints; pressure group activity; and scrutiny by the press.[5] Although scholars point out the inherent limitations of each method, collectively these instruments of accountability seem to work quite well (B. G. Peters, 1989; see also J. P. Burke, 1986). Administrative agencies in the United States are "more open and responsive than their counterparts in other countries and perhaps more so than other American political institutions" (Cook, 1992, p. 425).

I began this book by arguing that the subject of bureaucratic leadership has not received the scholarly attention it deserves. This lack of interest is somewhat ironic, especially when the skills and professional expertise of career civil servants are needed more than ever. Political leaders cannot and should not be expected to solve alone the complex problems facing our Republic. Indeed, this is too much to ask of any one person or institution: In a free society, the responsibility must be shared by all citizens. Bureaucratic leaders have much to offer, and political leaders can benefit from their assistance, counsel, and advice.

It is time to put leadership back into the administration of public bureaucracies. The theory of administrative conservatorship is a modest step in this direction. I have offered a set of lenses that will enable a better appraisal and prescription for leadership in the administrative state. This set of lenses provides vivid images of leadership based on authority conceived as the "capacity for reasoned elaboration" grounded in the values of our constitutional order, images of bureaucratic leaders faithfully fulfilling their oath to uphold the Constitution, images of bureaucratic leaders leading in the same vein advocated by Aristotle and Plato as they seek to maintain stability of the *polis*, images of bureaucratic leaders who are active participants in governance, and images of bureaucratic leaders who are responsive to the various constitutional masters.

Administrative conservatorship is not a risk-free enterprise because preserving the integrity of public bureaucracies and, in turn, our constitutional processes is filled with risk. Nor is it leadership guided by fear of change and innovation. Rather, administrative conservatorship is statesmanship guided by a moral commitment to preserve the constitutional balance of power in support of individual rights. Bureaucratic leaders are protectors of our Republic and democratic way of life. They are *administrative conservators*, a distinction and vocation worthy of honor and respect.

Notes

1. According to *The Compact Oxford English Dictionary* (1991), Janus is the "name of an ancient Italian deity, regarded as the doorkeeper of heaven and guardian of doors and gates, and as presiding over the entrance upon or beginning of things; represented with a face in the front and another on the back of the head" (p. 890). The term *Janus-faced* often means duplicitous or two-faced.

2. The botched undercover operation was given extensive coverage during 1993 in *The Plain Dealer*, a Cleveland (Ohio) newspaper. A series of articles written by Ulysses Torassa (1993a, 1993b), a staff reporter for the newspaper, outline in detail how the Postal Inspection Service's sting operation backfired. Torassa also provides an account of the congressional hearings chaired by Congressman William Clay (D-Missouri).

3. Marshall and Kuack claimed that they had been misled by their informants, but it was later determined in court that the inspectors had lied to local prosecutors about aspects of the undercover operation. Marshall and Kuack were eventually fired and the chief of the Cleveland Division of the Inspection Service was transferred to another position with significantly reduced managerial and supervisory responsibilities. In addition, the House Post Office Committee, the congressional committee that oversees the U.S. Postal Service operations, widened its probe because of accusations that race played a significant role in the botched sting operation. The charges against the Postal Service employees were dismissed; most employees were reinstated with back pay, were reimbursed for legal expenses, and received a letter of apology. In a public statement on the scandal, Ira T. Carle, inspector in charge of the Cleveland office, said: "We apologize for the pain and indignity that was brought to these employees and their families. . . . We realize that financial compensation alone cannot fully erase the stigma of being falsely accused of these crimes" (Torassa, 1993b, p. A1; see also Torassa, 1993a).

4. From *The Moral Commonwealth: Social Theory and the Promise of Community*, pp. 283-284, by P. Selznick, 1992, Berkeley: University of California Press. Copyright © 1992 by University of California Press. Reprinted by permission granted by the Regents of the University of California and the University of California Press.

5. B. Guy Peters (1989) uses these broad categories to classify the various instruments of control.

References

Adams, B. (1984). The frustrations of government. *Public Administration Review, 44,* 5-13.

Administrative Procedures Act of 1946, 60 Stat. 237 (1946).

Altheide, D., & Johnson, J. (1980). *Bureaucratic propaganda.* Boston: Allyn & Bacon.

American heritage dictionary of the English language. (1982). Boston: Houghton Mifflin.

Appelby, P. (1949). *Policy and administration.* University: University of Alabama Press.

Arsenal's lost-time injury figures vary from industry norm. (1986, March 30). *Roanoke Times and World News,* p. A6.

Aviation Safety Research Act of 1988, 102 Stat. 3011, 49 U.S.C. § 1353 (1988).

Barnard, C. I. (1938). *The functions of the executive.* Cambridge, MA: Harvard University Press.

Barnard, C. I. (1948). *Organization and management.* Cambridge, MA: Harvard University Press.

Bass, B. (1984). Leadership: Good, better, best. *Organization Dynamics, 13,* 26-40.

Bass, B. (1985). *Leadership and performance beyond expectations.* New York: Free Press.

Bayles, M. D. (1987). The justification of administrative authority. In J. R. Pennock & J. W. Chapman (Eds.), *Authority revisited: Nomos XXIX* (pp. 287-301). New York: New York University Press.

Bennis, W. (1989). *Why leaders can't lead: The unconscious conspiracy continues.* San Francisco: Jossey-Bass.

Bennis, W., & Nanus, B. (1985). *Leaders: Strategies for taking charge.* New York: Harper & Row.

Blumenthal, W. M. (1979, January 29). Candid reflections of a businessman in Washington. *Fortune Magazine,* 37-45.

Board of Governors of the Federal Reserve System. (1963). *The Federal Reserve System: Purposes and functions.* Washington, DC: Government Printing Office.

Board of Governors of the Federal Reserve System. (1985). *The Federal Reserve System: Purposes and functions.* Washington, DC: Government Printing Office.

Bob Jones v. United States, 461 U.S. 574 (1983).

Bolton, R. (Ed). (1992). *Culture wars: Documents from the recent controversies in the arts.* New York: New York Press.

Bower, J. (1977). Effective public management. *Harvard Business Review, 55*(2), 131-140.

Bowsher, C. A. (1992). Meeting the new American management challenge in a federal agency: Lessons from the General Accounting Office. *Public Administration Review, 52,* 3-7.

Brest, P. (1980). The misconceived quest for the original understanding. *Boston University Law Review, 60,* 204-238.

Britton, P., & Stallings, J. (1986). *Leadership is empowering people.* Lanham, MD: University Press of America.

Buchanan, J., & Tullock, G. (1962). *The calculus of consent: Logical foundations of constitutional democracy.* Ann Arbor: University of Michigan Press.

Buchwalter, A. (Ed.). (1992). *Culture and democracy: Social and ethical issues in public support for the arts and humanities.* Boulder, CO: Westview.

Budget and Accounting Act of 1921, 42 Stat. 20 (1921).

Bureau of Alcohol, Tobacco and Firearms. (n.d.-a). *ATF facts: Mission and responsibilities* [Pamphlet]. Washington, DC: Author.

Bureau of Alcohol, Tobacco and Firearms. (n.d.-b). *Bureaucratic breakdown* [Pamphlet]. Washington, DC: Author.

Bureau of Alcohol, Tobacco and Firearms, Training Division. (1988). *Long term management change.* Washington, DC: Author.

Burke, E. (1987). *Reflections on the revolution in France* (J. G. A. Pocock, Ed.). Indianapolis: Hackett. (Original work published 1789)

Burke, J. P. (1986). *Bureaucratic responsibility.* Baltimore: Johns Hopkins University Press.

Buzan, B. (1983). *People, states and fear.* Chapel Hill: University of North Carolina Press.

Byner, G. (1987). *Bureaucratic discretion: Law and policy in federal regulatory agencies.* New York: Pergamon.

Carnevale, D. G., & Wechsler, B. (1992). Trust in the public sector: Individual and organizational determinants. *Administration & Society, 23,* 471-494.

Ceaser, J. W. (1993). Reconstructing political science. In S. L. Elkins & K. Soltan (Eds.), *A new constitutionalism: Designing political institutions for a good society* (pp. 41-69). Chicago: University of Chicago Press.

Chase, A. (1987, July). How to save our national parks. *The Atlantic, 260,* 35-44. Used with permission of the publisher.

The compact Oxford English dictionary (2nd ed.). (1991). Oxford, UK: Clarendon.

Congressional Record. 100th Cong., 2d Sess. (1988, Daily ed. September 20 and October 20, 21). Vol. 134.

Congressional Record. 101st Cong., 1st Sess. (1989, Daily ed. July 26). Vol. 135, S. 8806.

Cook, B. J. (1992). The representative function of bureaucracy: Public administration in a constitutive perspective. *Administration & Society, 23,* 403-429.

Cooper, T. L., & Wright, N. D. (Eds.). (1992). *Exemplary public administrators: Character and leadership in government.* San Francisco: Jossey-Bass.

Crenson, M. A., & Rourke, F. E. (1987). By way of conclusion: American bureaucracy since World War II. In L. Galambos (Ed.), *The new American state: Bureaucracies and policies since World War II* (pp. 137-177). Baltimore: Johns Hopkins University Press.

Culbert, S. A., & McDonough, J. J. (1985). *Radical management: Power politics and the pursuit of trust.* New York: Free Press.

Dahl, R. A. (1956). *A preface to democratic theory.* Chicago: University of Chicago Press.

Davis, K. C. (1969). *Discretionary justice.* Urbana: University of Illinois Press.

Defense Appropriations Act, Public Law 98-441, 98 Stat. 1700 (1984).

DeGeorge, R. T. (1976). Authority: A bibliography. In R. B. Harris (Ed.), *Authority: A philosophical analysis* (pp. 141-170). University: University of Alabama Press.

DeGeorge, R. T. (1985). *The nature and limits of authority.* Lawrence: University Press of Kansas.

Department of the Treasury. (1993, September). *Report of the Department of the Treasury on the Bureau of Alcohol, Tobacco, and Firearms: Investigation of Vernon Wayne Howell as known as David Koresh.* Washington, DC: Government Printing Office.

Dimaggio, P., & Powell, W. (1983). The iron cage revisited: Institutional isomorphism and collective rationality in organizational fields. *American Sociological Review, 48,* 147-160.

Doig, J. W., & Hargrove, E. C. (Eds.). (1987). *Leadership and innovation: Entrepreneurs in government.* Baltimore: Johns Hopkins University Press.

Donaldson, L. (1990). The ethereal hand: Organization and management theory. *Academy of Management Review, 15,* 369-381.

Downs, A. (1967). *Inside bureaucracy.* Boston: Little, Brown.

Draper, T. (1991). *A very thin line: The Iran-Contra affairs.* New York: Hill & Wang.

Drucker, P. (1985). *Innovation and entrepreneurship.* New York: Harper & Row.

Dubail, J. (1993, April 11). Childhood lost. *The Plain Dealer,* p. B1.

Dubail, J., & Gillispie, M. (1993a, April 11). Removing children is the last resort. *The Plain Dealer,* p. B3.

Dubail, J., & Gillispie, M. (1993b, August 26). Girl's death starts feud over custody action. *The Plain Dealer,* p. A1.

Dworkin, G. (1988). *The theory and practice of autonomy.* Cambridge, UK: Cambridge University Press.

Dworkin, R. (1982). Law as interpretation. *Texas Law Review, 60,* 527-550.

Easton, D. (1965). *A systems analysis of political life.* New York: John Wiley.

Eskridge, W. N., Jr., & Frickey, P. P. (1990). Statutory interpretation as practical reasoning. *Stanford Law Review, 42,* 321-384.

Fairholm, G. W. (1994). *Leadership and the culture of trust.* Westport, CT: Praeger.

Farazmand, A. (1989). Crisis in the U.S. administrative state. *Administration & Society, 21,* 173-199.

Farm extension programs withering. (1991, August 25). *The Plain Dealer,* p. A12.

Federal Bureau of Prisons. (1985). *Annual report*. Washington, DC: Government Printing Office.

Finer, H. (1941). Administrative responsibility in democratic government. *Public Administration Review, 1*, 335-350.

Ford, J. D. (1980). The occurrence of structural hysteresis in declining organizations. *Academy of Management Review, 5*, 589-598.

Fraley, O. (1993). *The untouchables*. Cutchogue, NY: Buccaneer.

Freedman, J. O. (1978). *Crisis and legitimacy: The administrative process and American government*. New York: Cambridge University Press.

Friedrich, C. J. (1940). Public policy and the nature of administrative responsibility. In C. J. Friedrich & E. Mason (Eds.), *Public policy 1* (pp. 3-24). Cambridge, MA: Harvard University Press.

Friedrich, C. J. (1958a). Authority, reason and discretion. In C. J. Friedrich (Ed.), *Authority: Nomos I* (pp. 28-48). Cambridge, MA: Harvard University Press.

Friedrich, C. J. (Ed.). (1958b). *Authority: Nomos I*. Cambridge, MA: Harvard University Press.

Friedrich, C. J. (1961). Political leadership and the problem of the charismatic power. *The Journal of Politics, 23*, 3-24.

Friedrich, C. J. (1963). *Man and his government*. New York: McGraw-Hill.

Friedrich, C. J. (1972). *Tradition and authority*. New York: Praeger.

Friedrich, D. O. (1980). The legitimacy crisis in the United States: A conceptual analysis. *Social Problems, 17*, 540-555.

Fritschler, A. L. (1989). *Smoking and politics: Policy making and the federal bureaucracy* (4th ed.). Englewood Cliffs, NJ: Prentice Hall.

Gersick, C. (1991). Revolutionary change theories: A multilevel exploration of the punctuated equilibrium paradigm. *Academy of Management Review, 16*, 10-36.

Gillispie, M. (1993, August 25). Toddler died after mother punched her, police say. *The Plain Dealer*, p. A1.

Goodhand, J. (1993, May 27). A county agency just for children. *The Plain Dealer*, p. B7.

Goodnow, F. J. (1900). *Politics and administration*. New York: Macmillan.

Goodsell, C. T. (1993). Reinvent government or rediscover it? *Public Administration Review, 53*, 85-86.

Graber, D. (1976). *Verbal behavior and politics*. Urbana: University of Illinois Press.

Graubard, S. R., & Holton, G. (Eds.). (1962). *Excellence and leadership in a democracy*. New York: Columbia University Press.

Gruber, J. E. (1987). *Controlling bureaucracies: Dilemmas in democratic governance*. Berkeley: University of California Press.

Haber, S. (1964). *Efficiency and uplift*. Chicago: University of Chicago Press.

Hannan, M., & Freeman, J. (1984). Structural inertia and organizational change. *American Sociological Review, 49*, 149-164.

Hargrove, E. C. (1989). Two conceptions of institutional leadership. In B. D. Jones (Ed.), *Leadership and politics* (pp. 57-83). Lawrence: University Press of Kansas.

Hayek, F. A. (1944). *The road to serfdom*. Chicago: University of Chicago Press.

Hays, S. P. (1964). The politics of reform in municipal government in the progressive era. *Pacific Northwest Quarterly, 55*, 157-169.

Heclo, H. (1977). *A government of strangers: Executive politics in Washington*. Washington, DC: Brookings Institution.

Hegel, G. W. F. (1952). *The philosophy of right* (T. M. Knox, Trans.). Oxford, UK: Clarendon.

Henderson, H. (1991). Authoritarianism and the rule of law. *Indiana Law Journal, 66,* 379-456.

Hester, F. E. (1981). [Memorandum to employees]. Washington, DC: U.S. Fish and Wildlife Service.

Hobbes, T. (1957). *Leviathan* (M. Oakeshott, Ed.). Oxford, UK: Basil Blackwell.

H.R. 4686, 100th Cong., 2d Sess. (1988).

H.R. Rep. No. 894, 100th Cong., 2d Sess. (1988).

Huntington, S. P. (1981). *American politics: The promise of disharmony.* Cambridge, MA: Harvard University Press.

Hyneman, C. S. (1950). *Bureaucracy in a democracy.* New York: Harper & Brothers.

Internal Revenue Code of 1954, 68a Stat. 775 (1954), Chapter 64, West (1994).

IRS seizes life savings of 10-year-old girl—$694. (1987, January 17). *The Washington Post,* p. H2.

Is the arsenal safe: Army investigation finds broken rules, lax supervision. (1986, March 29). *Roanoke Times and World News,* p. A1.

Karl, B. D. (1963). *Executive reorganization and reform in the New Deal.* Cambridge, MA: Harvard University Press.

Karl, B. D. (1987). The American bureaucrat: A history of a sheep in wolves clothing. *Public Administration Review, 47,* 26-34.

Kass, H. D. (1990). Stewardship as a fundamental element in images of public administration. In H. D. Kass & B. L. Catron (Eds.), *Images of public administration* (pp. 114-116). Newbury Park, CA: Sage.

Kaufman, H. (1981a). *The administrative behavior of federal bureau chiefs.* Washington, DC: Brookings Institution.

Kaufman, H. (1981b). The fear of bureaucracy: A raging pandemic. *Public Administration Review, 41,* 1-9.

Kaufman, H. (1991). *Time, chance and organization: Natural selection in a perilous environment* (2nd ed.). Chatham, NJ: Chatham House.

Kellerman, B. (1984). *Leadership: A multidisciplinary perspective.* Englewood Cliffs, NJ: Prentice Hall.

Kerwin, C. M. (1994). *Rulemaking: How government agencies write law and make policy.* Washington, DC: Congressional Quarterly Inc.

Kotz, N. (1969). *Let them eat promises: The politics of hunger in America.* Englewood Cliffs, NJ: Prentice Hall.

Kuntz, P. (1989, July 15). HUD scandal prompts panel to halt a key program. *Congressional Quarterly Weekly Report,* 1774-1779.

Lane, L. M., & Wolf, J. F. (1990). *The human resource crisis in the public sector.* New York: Quorum.

Lasch, C. (1991). *The true and only heaven: Progress and its critics.* New York: Norton.

Leiserson, A. (1942). *Administrative regulation: A study of representation of interest.* Chicago: University of Chicago Press.

Levine, C. (Ed.). (1978). Organizational decline and cutback management [Special issue of symposium articles]. *Public Administration Review, 38.*

Lewis, E. (1980). *Public entrepreneurship: Toward a theory of bureaucratic political power.* Bloomington: Indiana University Press.

Long, N. (1949). Power and administration. *Public Administration Review, 9,* 257-264.

Lowi, T. J. (1969). *The end of liberalism.* New York: Norton.

Lowi, T. J. (1979). *The end of liberalism: The second republic of the United States* (2nd ed.). New York: Norton.

Lowi, T. J. (1987). Two roads to serfdom: Liberalism, conservatism, and administrative power. *American University Law Review, 36,* 295-322.

Lowi, T. J. (1993a). Legitimizing public administration: A disturbed dissent. *Public Administration Review, 53,* 261-264.

Lowi, T. J. (1993b). Two roads to serfdom: Liberalism, conservatism, and administrative power. In S. L. Elkins & K. E. Soltan (Eds.), *A new constitutionalism: Designing political institutions for a good society* (pp. 149-173). Chicago: University of Chicago Press.

March, J., & Simon, H. (1958). *Organizations.* New York: John Wiley.

March, J. G., & Olsen, J. P. (1989). *Rediscovering institutions: The organizational basis of politics.* New York: Free Press.

McGowan, C. (1977). Congress, court, and control of delegated power. *Columbia Law Review, 1119,* 1128-1130.

McNeil, K., & Thompson, J. D. (1971). The regeneration of social organization. *American Review of Sociological Review, 36,* 624-637.

Meier, K. J. (1987). *Politics and the bureaucracy: Policymaking in the fourth branch of government* (2nd ed.). Monterey, CA: Brooks/Cole.

Meier, K. J. (1989). Bureaucratic leadership in public organizations. In B. D. Jones (Ed.), *Leadership and politics* (pp. 267-286). Lawrence: University Press of Kansas.

Meindl, J. R., Ehrlich, S. B., & Dukerich, J. (1985). The romance of leadership. *Administrative Science Quarterly, 30,* 78-102.

Merriam Webster's collegiate dictionary (10th ed.). (1993). Springfield, MA: Merriam-Webster.

Metcalf, H. C., & Urwick, L. (Eds.). (1940). *Dynamic administration.* New York: Harper & Brothers.

Miller v. California, 413 U.S. 15 (1973).

Morgan, D. (1990). Administrative phronesis: Discretion and the problem of legitimacy in our constitutional system. In H. D. Kass & B. Catron (Eds.), *Images and identities* (pp. 75-78). Newbury Park, CA: Sage.

Morgan, D. (1994). The public interest. In T. Cooper (Ed.), *Handbook of public administration* (pp. 136-138). New York: Marcel Dekker.

Morgan, D., & Kass, H. (1991). Legitimizing administrative discretion through constitutional stewardship. In J. Bowman (Ed.), *Ethical frontiers in public management* (pp. 286-307). San Francisco: Jossey-Bass.

Mowday, R. S., Steers, R., & Porter, L. (1982). *Employee-organizational linkages: The psychology of commitment, absenteeism and turnover.* New York: Academic Press.

Mulcaly, K. V. (1992). The public interest in public culture. In A. Buchwalter (Ed.), *Culture and democracy: Social and ethical issues in public support for the arts and humanities* (pp. 65-87). Boulder, CO: Westview.

Nachmias, D., & Rosenbloom, D. H. (1980). *Bureaucratic government U.S.A.* New York: St. Martin's.

Nadler, D. A. (1988). Organizational frame bending: Types of change in complex organizations. In R. H. Kilman, T. J. Covin, & Associates (Eds.), *Corporate transformation* (pp. 66-83). San Francisco: Jossey-Bass.

National Endowment for the Arts Appropriation Bill (1990), Public Law 101-121, 103 Stat. 738 (1989).

National Sheriffs' Association Conference. (1988, July 7). *FYI: For Your Information*, 5(4), 1 [Internal agency newsletter of U.S. Marshals Service].

Nelson, W. E. (1982). *The roots of American bureaucracy, 1830-1900*. Cambridge, MA: Harvard University Press.

Oakeshott, M. (1975). *On human conduct*. Oxford, UK: Clarendon.

Office of the Federal Register, National Archives and Record Administration. (1992). *The United States government manual: 1991-1992*. Washington, DC: Government Printing Office.

Officials seize Midland store. (1988, April 13). *The Odessa American*, p. 13A.

Olson, D. H., & Cromwell, R. E. (1975). Power in families. In R. E. Cromwell & D. H. Olson (Eds.), *Power in families* (pp. 3-11). Beverly Hills, CA: Sage.

O'Reilly, J. (1983). *Administrative rulemaking*. Colorado Springs, CO: Shepard's McGraw-Hill.

Osborne, D., & Graebler, T. (1991). *Reinventing government: How the entrepreneurial spirit is transforming the public sector*. Reading, MA: Addison-Wesley.

O'Toole, L. J., Jr. (1984). American public administration and the idea of reform. *Administration & Society, 16*, 141-166.

Pennock, J. R., & Chapman, J. W. (Eds.). (1987). *Authority revisited: Nomos XXIX*. New York: New York University Press.

Perrow, C. (1961). Organizational prestige: Functions and dysfunctions. *American Journal of Sociology, 66*, 335-341.

Perrow, C. (1986). *Complex organizations: A critical essay* (3rd ed.). New York: McGraw-Hill.

Perry, J. L., & Kraemer, K. L. (Eds.). (1983). *Public management*. Palo Alto, CA: Mayfield.

Peters, B. G. (1989). *The politics of bureaucracy* (3rd ed.). New York: Longman.

Peters, C., & Branch, T. (1972). *Blowing the whistle: Dissent in the public interest*. New York: Praeger.

Peters, R. S. (1967). Authority. In A. Quinton (Ed.), *Political philosophy* (pp. 83-96). Oxford, UK: Oxford University Press.

Peters, T. (1981). *In search of excellence*. New York: Harper & Row.

Pfeffer, J. (1981). *Power in organizations*. Marshfield, MA: Pitman.

Pfeffer, J. (1985). Organizational demography: Implications for management. *California Management Review, 28*, 67-81.

Pfeffer, J., & O'Reilly, C. A., III. (1987). Hospital demography and turnover among nurses. *Industrial Relations, 26*, 158-173.

Pfeffer, J., & Salancik, G. (1978). *The external controls of organizations: A resource dependence perspective*. New York: Harper & Row.

Phares, G. C. (1992). The Constitution and public funding of the arts: An uneasy alliance. In A. Buchwalter (Ed.), *Culture and democracy: Social and ethical issues in public support for the arts and humanities* (pp. 115-129). Boulder, CO: Westview.

Police probe death of 1 year old. (1993, August 23). *The Plain Dealer*, p. B6.

Pound, E. T. (1989, September 22). Good connections: How HUD aide used ties to help himself, later PaineWebber. *The Wall Street Journal*, pp. A1, A4.

Prethus, R. (1975). *The organizational society* (Rev. ed.). New York: St. Martin's.

Price, D. K. (1962). Administrative leadership. In S. Graubard & G. Holton (Eds.), *Excellence and leadership in a democracy* (pp. 171-184). New York: Columbia University Press.

Radford Army Ammunition Plant: Facilities, capabilities and products [RAAP informational booklet]. (n.d.). Radford, VA: Radford Army Ammunition Plant.

Raz, J. (1979). *The authority of law.* Oxford, UK: Clarendon.

Reicher, A. (1985). A review and reconceptualization of organizational commitment. *Academy of Management Review, 10,* 465-476.

Rogers, E., & Shoemaker, F. F. (1971). *Communication of innovations: A cross-cultural approach.* New York: Free Press.

Rohr, J. A. (1978). *Ethics for bureaucrats.* New York: Marcel Dekker.

Rohr, J. A. (1986). *To run a constitution: The legitimacy of the administrative state.* Lawrence: University Press of Kansas.

Romzek, B. S., & Dubnick, M. (1987). Accountability in the public sector: Lessons from the Challenger tragedy. *Public Administration Review, 47,* 227-238.

Rosen, B. (1983). Effective continuity of U.S. government operations in jeopardy. *Public Administration Review, 43,* 383-392.

Rosen, B. (1986). Crises in the U.S. Civil Service. *Public Administration Review, 46,* 195-215.

Rost, J. (1991). *Leadership for the twenty-first century.* New York: Praeger.

Rourke, F. E. (1961). *Secrecy and publicity: Dilemmas of democracy.* Baltimore: Johns Hopkins University Press.

Rourke, F. E. (1969). *Bureaucracy, politics and public policy.* Boston: Little, Brown.

Rourke, F. E. (1987). Bureaucracy in the American constitutional order. *Political Science Quarterly, 102,* 217-232.

Rourke, J. T. (1978). The GAO: An evolving role. *Public Administration Review, 38,* 453-457.

Saltzstein, G. H. (1985). Conceptualizing bureaucratic responsiveness. *Administration & Society, 17,* 283-306.

Sarat, A. (1987). In the shadow of originalism: A comment on Perry. In J. R. Pennock & J. W. Chapman (Eds.), *Authority revisited: Nomos XXIX* (pp. 254-266). New York: New York University Press.

Schein, E. (1985). *Organizational culture and leadership.* San Francisco: Jossey-Bass.

Schick, A. (1980). *Congress and money.* Washington, DC: Urban Institute.

Schoenbrod, D. (1993). *Power without responsibility: How Congress abuses the people through delegation.* New Haven, CT: Yale University Press.

Scott, W. G. (1974). Organization theory: A reassessment. *Academy of Management Journal, 17,* 242-254.

Selznick, P. (1948). Foundations of the theory of organization. *American Sociological Review, 13,* 25-35.

Selznick, P. (1949). *TVA and the grass roots.* Berkeley: University of California Press.

Selznick, P. (1952). *The organizational weapon: A study of the Bolshevik strategy and tactics.* New York: McGraw-Hill.

Selznick, P. (1957). *Leadership in administration: A sociological interpretation.* Evanston, IL: Row, Peterson.

Selznick, P. (1987). The idea of a communitarian morality. *California Law Review, 75,* 445-468.

Selznick, P. (1992). *The moral commonwealth: Social theory and the promise of community.* Berkeley: University of California Press.

Shapiro, D. L. (1965). The choice of rulemaking or adjudication in the development of administrative policy. *Harvard Law Review, 78,* 921-972.

Siedman, H. (1980). *Politics, position and power* (3rd ed.). New York: Oxford University Press.

Skowronek, S. (1982). *Building a new American state: The expansion of national administrative capacities, 1877-1920.* Cambridge, UK: Cambridge University Press.

Smith-Lever Act of 1914, 38 Stat. 373 (1914).

Spicer, M. W., & Terry, L. D. (1993). Legitimacy, history and logic: Public administration and the Constitution. *Public Administration Review, 53,* 239-245.

S. Rep. No. 584, 100th Cong., 2d Sess. (1988).

Starbuck, W. H. (1965). Organizational growth and development. In J. G. March (Ed.), *Handbook of organizations* (pp. 451-533). Chicago: Rand McNally.

Stever, J. A. (1988). *The end of public administration: Problems of the profession in the post-progressive era.* Dobbs Ferry, NY: Transactional.

Stever, J. A. (1990). The dual image of the administrator in progressive administrative theory. *Administration & Society, 22,* 39-57.

Swartz, N. L. (1988). *The blue guitar: Political representation and community.* Chicago: University of Chicago Press.

Symposium on administrative law: The uneasy constitutional status of administrative agencies [Special issue of articles from symposium held April 4, 1986]. (1987). *American University Law Review, 36.*

Taylor, F. W. (1911). *The principles of scientific management.* New York: Harper.

Terry, L. D. (1990). Leadership in the administrative state. *Administration & Society, 21,* 395-412.

Thompson, J. D. (1967). *Organizations in action.* New York: McGraw-Hill.

Tichy, N., & Devanna, M. A. (1986). *The transformational leader.* New York: Warner.

Tichy, N., & Ulrich, D. (1984). The leadership challenge: A call for the transformational leader. *Sloan Management Review, 26,* 58-67.

Torassa, U. (1993a, June 19). Probe of postal sting widening. *The Plain Dealer,* p. B1.

Torassa, U. (1993b, December 1). Postal workers say sting ruined lives. *The Plain Dealer,* p. A1.

Truman, D. (1951). *The governmental process.* New York: Knopf.

Tulis, J. K. (1987). *The rhetorical presidency.* Princeton, NJ: Princeton University Press.

Tushman, M. L., Newman, W. H., & Nadler, D. A. (1988). Executive leadership and organizational evolution: Managing incremental and discontinuous change. In R. H. Kilman, T. J. Covin, & Associates (Eds.), *Corporate transformation* (pp. 102-130). San Francisco: Jossey-Bass.

U.S. Congress House Committee on Agriculture. (1913). *Cooperative agricultural extension work* (Report No. 110), 63rd Cong., 2d Sess. Washington, DC: Government Printing Office.

U.S. General Accounting Office. (1987). *Reports issued in June 1987.* Washington, DC: Government Printing Office.

U.S. General Accounting Office. (1988a, June). *Defense procurement fraud: Justice's overall management can be enhanced.* Washington, DC: Government Printing Office.

U.S. General Accounting Office. (1988b, September 22). *Whistleblowers: Management of the program to protect trucking company employees against reprisal.* Washington, DC: Government Printing Office.

U.S. General Accounting Office. (1991a, June 18). *FAA information resources: Agency need to correct widespread deficiencies.* Washington, DC: Government Printing Office.

U.S. General Accounting Office. (1991b). *Reports and testimony: December 1991.* Washington, DC: Government Printing Office.

U.S. General Accounting Office. (1991c). Tax system modernization: Attention to critical issues can bring success [Testimony by Howard G. Rhile, Director of General Government Information Systems, before the Senate Committee on Governmental Affairs, June 25, 1991]. Washington, DC: Government Printing Office.

U.S. Marshals preserve role in hunting fugitives. (1988, June 8). *Drug enforcement report, 4,* 1.

U.S. Marshals Service. (n.d.). *Outline of U.S. Marshals activities.* Washington, DC: Author.

U.S. Senate Subcommittee of the Committee on Appropriations. (1982). *Proposed dissolution of Bureau of Alcohol, Tobacco, and Firearms.* Washington, DC: Government Printing Office.

Vance, C. S. (1992). Misunderstanding obscenity, art in America. In R. Bolton (Ed.), *Culture wars: Documents from the recent controversies in the arts* (pp. 220-226). New York: New York Press.

Virginia Joint Legislative and Audit Review Commission. (1979). *Virginia Polytechnic Institute and State University Extension Division.* Richmond, VA: Author.

Waldo, D. (1948). *The administrative state.* New York: Ronald.

Walker, W. E. (1986). *Changing organizational culture: Structure, strategy and professionalism in the General Accounting Office.* Knoxville: University of Tennessee Press.

Wamsley, G. L. (1990). The agency perspective: Public administration as agential leaders. In G. L. Wamsley, R. N. Bacher, C. T. Goodsell, P. Kronenberg, J. Rohr, C. Stivers, O. White, & J. Wolf (Eds.), *Refounding public administration* (pp. 114-162). Newbury Park, CA: Sage.

Wamsley, G. L., & Zald, M. M. (1976). *The political economy of public organizations.* Bloomington: Indiana University Press.

Webster's tenth new collegiate dictionary. (1993). Springfield, MA: Merriam-Webster.

Wheldon, T. D. (1953). *The vocabulary of politics.* New York: Pelican.

When an accident isn't. (1986, March 30). *Roanoke Times and World News,* p. A1.

Whetten, D. A. (1980). Organizational decline: A neglected topic in organizational science. *Academy of Management Review, 5,* 577-588.

White, J. B. (1982). Law as language: Reading law and reading literature. *Texas Law Review, 60,* 415-445.

White, L. D. (1939). *The study of public administration.* New York: Macmillan.

Wildavsky, A. (1988). Ubiquitous anomie: Public service in an era of ideological dissensus. *Public Administration Review, 48,* 753-755.

Wildavsky, A. (1990). *The new politics of the budgetary process.* New York: Harper-Collins.

Wilkins, A. L. (1989). *Developing corporate character.* San Francisco: Jossey-Bass.

Will, G. (1983). *Statecraft as soulcraft: What government does.* New York: Simon & Schuster.

Williams, R. M., Jr. (1969). The concept of values. In D. L. Sills (Ed.), *International encyclopedia of social sciences.* New York: Macmillan/Free Press.

Wilson, H. (1975). Complexity as a theoretical problem: Wider perspectives in political theory. In T. LaPorte (Ed.), *Organized social complexities* (pp. 281-331). Princeton, NJ: Princeton University Press.

Wilson, J. Q. (1975). The rise of the bureaucratic state. *The Public Interest, 41*, 77-103.

Wilson, J. Q. (1978). *The investigators: Managing FBI and narcotic agents.* New York: Basic Books.

Wilson, J. Q. (1989). *Bureaucracy: What government agencies do and why they do it.* New York: Basic Books.

Wilson, W. (1978). The study of administration. In J. M. Shafritz & A. C. Hyde (Eds.), *Classics of public administration* (pp. 1-17). Oak Park, IL: Moore. (Original work published 1887)

Wisconsin Senate Bill No. 2746, 100th Cong., 2d Sess. (1988).

Wolf, J. F. (1987). Disinvesting in the administrative capacity for public action. *International Journal of Public Administration, 10*, 209-234.

Wolin, S. S. (1960). *Politics and vision: Continuity and innovation in western political thought.* Boston: Little, Brown.

Wood, B. D. (1988). Principals, bureaucrats, and responsiveness in clean air enforcement. *American Political Science Review, 82*, 213-234.

Yates, D. (1982). *Bureaucratic democracy: The search for democracy and efficiency in American government.* Cambridge, MA: Harvard University Press.

Zaleznick, A. (1989). *The managerial mystique: Restoring leadership in business.* New York: Harper & Row.

Zimmerman, J. (1994). *Curbing unethical behavior in government.* Westport, CN: Greenwood Press.

Index

Adams, B., 5
Adams, P. A., 110
Administration, leadership in, 15-25.
    See also Public administration;
    Leadership, bureaucratic
Administrative conservator, 183
    administrative executive as, 29
    compliance of with letter of the
        law, 86-89
    compliance of with spirit of the
        law, 82-86
    conserving mission, 65-66, 71-112
    conserving support, 66-67, 145-170
    conserving values, 66, 116-142
    defining mission, 65
    leadership roles of, 61
    preservation of institutional
        integrity by, 44-60
    strategies for binding parochial
        group egotism, 163-168
    strategies for building/maintaining
        executive cadre commitment,
        118-136, 176-177

strategies for building/sustaining
    commitment among internal
    interest groups, 164-168, 179
strategies for maintaining external
    alliances, 155-163, 168, 179-181
strategies for maintaining favorable
    public image, 148-155, 168
strategies for preserving authority
    of public bureaucracies, 81,
    89-100, 112
Administrative conservatorship, xi,
    xx, xxi, xxiii, 25-30, 172, 183
    administrative elites and, 26
    as framework for measuring
        administrative leadership
        effectiveness, 30
    as statesmanship, 29-30
    authority and, 76
    autonomy and, 53
    functions of, 64-67
    needs of organizational members
        and, 26
    preservation of institutional
        integrity and, 26, 44-60

About the Author

Larry D. Terry is Associate Professor of Public Administration in the Maxine Goodman Levin College of Urban Affairs at Cleveland State University. His research interests include public administration theory, the role of bureaucratic leaders in governance, the works of Carl J. Friedrich, and statutory interpretation from the perspective of public administrators.

In addition to his academic career, he has held a variety of administrative positions at the federal, state, and local levels. He has also served as a consultant to diverse organizations including the U.S. Department of the Army, U.S. Forest Service, U.S. Department of Veterans Affairs, the Ohio Department of Mental Health, and the Communication Workers of America (international headquarters).